Macintosh *WordPerfect* Guide

Donald Richard Read

Library of Congress Cataloging-in Publication Data

Read, Donald Richard.
Macintosh wordperfect guide.

Includes index.
1. WordPerfect (Computer program) 2. Macintosh (Computer)—Programming. 3. Word processing.
I. Title.
Z52.5.W65R4 1988 652'.5 88–25661
ISBN 0–87455–150–1

Editor: Robert Bixby

Printed in the United States of America

10 9 8 7 6 5 4 3 2 1

COMPUTE! Books, Post Office Box 5406, Greensboro, North Carolina 27403, (919) 275-9809, is a Capital Cities/ABC, Inc. company and is not associated with any manufacturer of personal computers. Macintosh is a trademark and Apple is a registered trademark of Apple Computers. *WordPerfect* is a registered trademark of WordPerfect Corporation. Rolodex is a registered trademark of Rolodex Corporation.

Contents

Foreword

Macintosh WordPerfect Guide is your guide and reference to *WordPerfect,* the best-selling word processor for the Apple Macintosh. In this book, you'll explore *WordPerfect*'s power features, like using the search-and-replace operation and how to generate mountains of form letters, each with a personal touch.

WordPerfect brings together all the necessary tools found in the best word processors, and the most powerful features found in desktop publishing software. And *Macintosh WordPerfect Guide* helps you exploit all these important features quickly and easily. Before long you'll find yourself using professional formatting features, the spelling checker, the electronic thesaurus, and the many other power features that have won *WordPerfect* its place at the top of the heap of productivity software.

Written in plain English, this book will have you up to speed with *WordPerfect* in no time at all. And once you've mastered this powerful word processor you'll find *Macintosh WordPerfect Guide* is the perfect guide and reference—earning its place next to your Mac again and again.

Chapter 1

How to Use This Book to Make Your Work Easier

Chapter 1

How to Use This Book to Make Your Work Easier

When you walk into the kitchen, chances are you're not there to study the theory of food preparation. You're there to fix dinner. If you don't have your recipes memorized (and you're not one of those natural culinary geniuses who can whip up magical dishes without consulting recipes), you probably use a cookbook or some sort of recipe collection.

The recipes tell you, step by step, what to do. They tell you the quantities to measure, mixing techniques, when to add what, and how long to bake, fry, broil, poach, roast, steam, boil, or grill.

When you're finished, you don't necessarily have a theoretical understanding of the chemistry of culinary combinations. What you have is dinner. This book was written for those computer users who want to learn how to do a task in the least amount of time.

If you need to do a number of jobs with a word processor, and you want to learn as quickly as possible how to do those jobs with *WordPerfect*, this is the book for you.

WordPerfect is the new Macintosh version of the powerful word processing software that already dominates the market for PC-type computers. Released in the spring of 1988, the Macintosh version should come to play a similarly commanding role among Macintosh-based word processors. Its long list of features make the program a powerful, versatile tool for writers of all kinds—and now that that power has been teamed up with the easy-to-learn, easy-to-use, graphics-based Macintosh computer, *WordPerfect* should be more prominent than ever.

This long list of features, however, has presented an obstacle to some users who felt that *WordPerfect* looked like too much to learn. The printed documentation for the program can also be intimidating, because software documentation must be encyclopedic: It must explain every feature, define every term, prepare the user for every contingency. That is the responsibility of the software publisher.

For this reason, the documentation for *WordPerfect,* like the documentation for any powerful software package, takes up a very fat book. The heart of this book is the Reference section. It is, in fact, an encyclopedia that presents *WordPerfect's* features in alphabetical order and great detail. (The *WordPerfect* Corporation meets their responsibility especially well: Their manuals are attractively designed and easy to read, and as a rule, the people who write their documentation resist the temptation to lapse into the sort of convoluted computer-speak that infects so much software and hardware documentation.) This book doesn't attempt to duplicate that reference encyclopedia. Instead it takes you, step by step, through a number of jobs you're likely to encounter in your day-to-day work.

You may want, from time to time, to look back at *WordPerfect's* Reference section or to look at the documentation that came with your Macintosh. You will have no trouble doing that; this book is compatible with the original hardware and software documentation, and I have tried to stay with the Macintosh terminology as it is used in the Apple and *WordPerfect* documentation. You should find, however, that this book minimizes your need to go to other sources.

Chapter 2 provides a refresher course on the Macintosh itself. It runs through its basic commands, maneuvers, and mouse manipulations. Chapter 3 gets you up and running with *WordPerfect,* and reminds you that one of the beautiful things about the Mac is its interface: the screen, menus, prompts, icons, and so on. The interface makes any new Macintosh program much easier to learn.

This is a how-to-do-it book—how to format, write, and print a business letter with *WordPerfect;* how to turn the addressing and printing of envelopes into an automatic job with a few keystrokes; how to increase your productivity by using the *WordPerfect* shortcuts that let you turn out memos, newsletters, financial reports, press releases, and mass mailings with the kind of speed that until now you only dreamed of. You will also learn how to automate your address book or Rolodex. Perhaps most importantly, you'll learn how to tap the power of macros, which are miniature computer programs that remember your keystrokes and repeat them at your command.

As you work through the recipes in this book, you'll discover that most of the *WordPerfect* features are explained along the way. To find out how to use a specific feature or command, check the index. It will send you to a page where you'll learn not only the procedures for using a *WordPerfect* feature, but you will see how the feature is used in the context of a larger job.

The procedures will be most useful if you follow them step by step, just as if you were a cook trying a recipe for the first time. You may want to use the sample text, addresses, and other included data the first time through to be sure you are carrying out each step correctly. Then, when you feel confident about a routine, go through it again using your own text, addresses, and salutations, so when you finish you can save the formats, macros, and boilerplate paragraphs to be used over and over again.

You will almost certainly discover that you want to make your own modifications to these recipes. That's what any chef does. An extra pinch here, a special little macro there, and before long, you'll make *WordPerfect* your own tool. Able to assist with your own tasks, it is a custom word and information processor that meets all your needs.

Chapter 2

Getting Started with a Macintosh

Chapter 2

Getting Started with a Macintosh

If you are already well acquainted with the Macintosh and how it operates, you probably won't need this chapter. But if you're new to the machine or could use a brief review, this chapter will walk you through the basic operations and procedures that make the Mac perform.

This chapter should be particularly useful for users familiar only with the PC version of *WordPerfect* who are now adding the Mac to their repertoire of computer skills.

The Mac represents a world entirely different from the traditional keyboard-based machine exemplified by the IBM. You are going to be using a *mouse, icons, pull-down menus,* and other features that have made the Mac so popular.

Starting up the Macintosh

When you turn on the power, Macintosh first shows you an icon representing a disk (Figure 2-1).

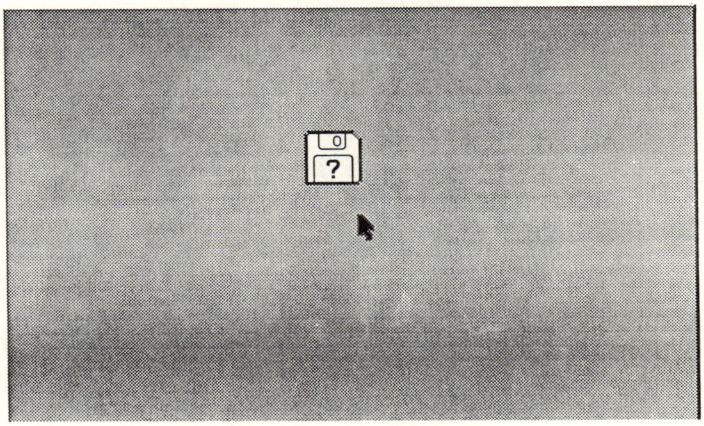

Figure 2-1. The icon that first appears when the Mac is turned on without any application programs present.

An *icon* is a picture that represents an object or action. In this case, the picture of a floppy disk with a flashing question mark is prompting you to insert the System disk in the main disk drive (the drive in the body of the Mac). Insert the System disk into the slot under the monitor screen and push it in until it locks into place. (If you're unfamiliar with the $3\frac{1}{2}$-inch disk, the metallic shield on the disk should go in first, and the label should be on top.) The disk icon will turn into a Macintosh icon with a smiling face, and the Mac will start loading the program.

Next, you'll see the *Desktop*. The Desktop is like a desk blotter on which you will perform your work. The Desktop contains icons representing the disks currently available (and their directories, if you have a disk open), and a menu from which you can make choices by clicking and dragging with the mouse.

If you have your *WordPerfect* System disk in the drive, you should see two icons at this point: the icon for the *WordPerfect* System disk labeled *System*, and the Trash icon which represents the wastebasket. When you delete a file, you will do so by dragging it from within its directory to the wastebasket.

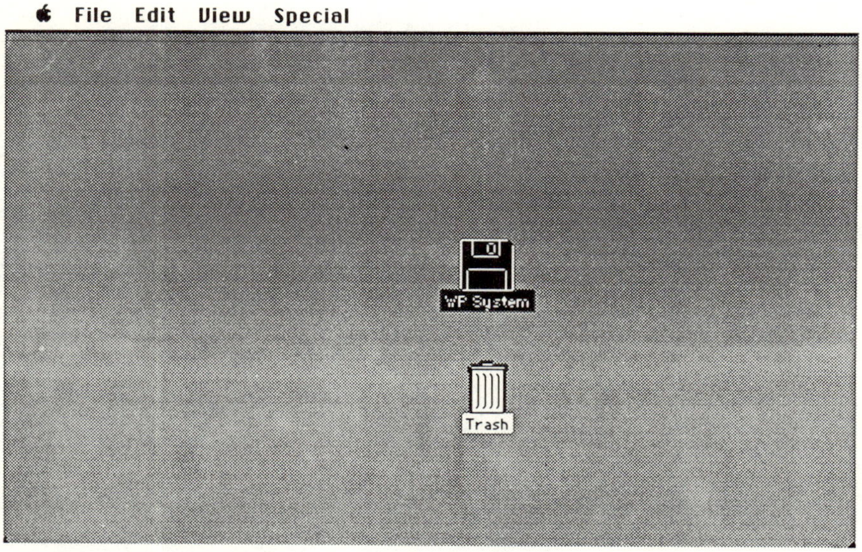

Figure 2-2. The Desktop with the *WordPerfect* System disk inserted.

The next step (assuming you have two floppy disk drives) is to insert the *WordPerfect* System disk into your external disk drive. Soon you'll see either a black icon representing the *WordPerfect* program disk (Figure 2-3) or a picture of the *WordPerfect folder* (Figure 2-4).

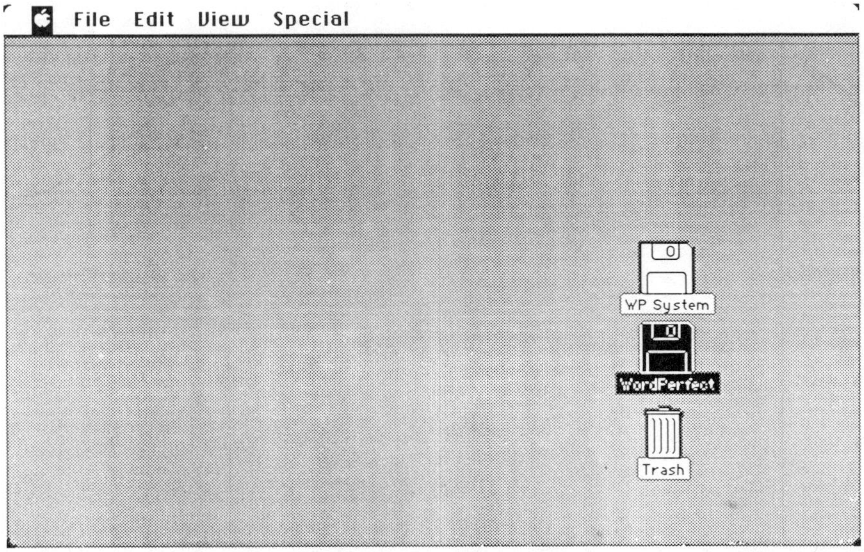

Figure 2-3. The Desktop after you insert the *WordPerfect* program disk. The disk icon is *highlighted* in black, meaning that it is ready to be opened.

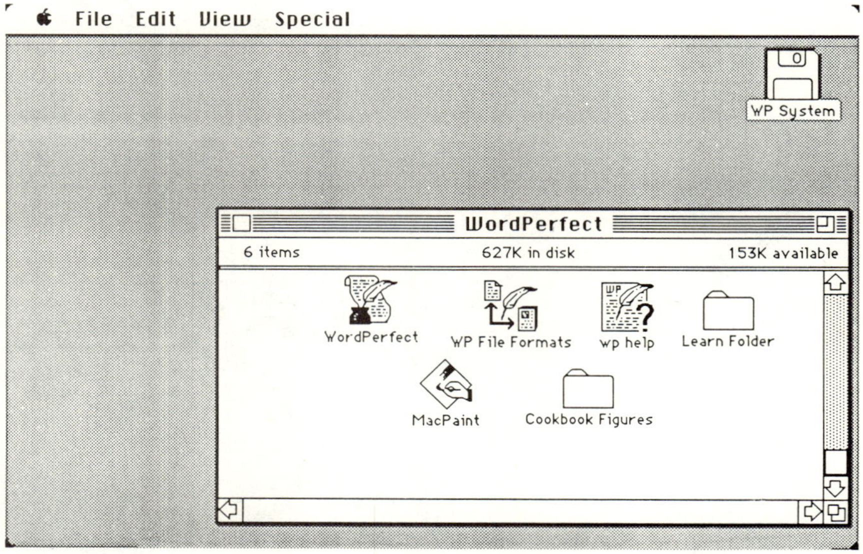

Figure 2-4. The opened *WordPerfect* program disk or folder.

The folder includes icons representing the *WordPerfect* program, *WordPerfect* formats, *WordPerfect* defaults, and so on. The *WordPerfect* icon is an ink bottle and a quill pen superimposed upon a sheet of text. All files subsequently created with *WordPerfect* will be identifiable by a quill pen. Icons can also be thought of as files or programs. In fact, if you prefer DOS file listings to a screen full of icons, you can pull down the menu titled View and elect to have the files listed by name, date, size, or kind (*MacPaint* and Cookbook Figures don't come with *WordPerfect*).

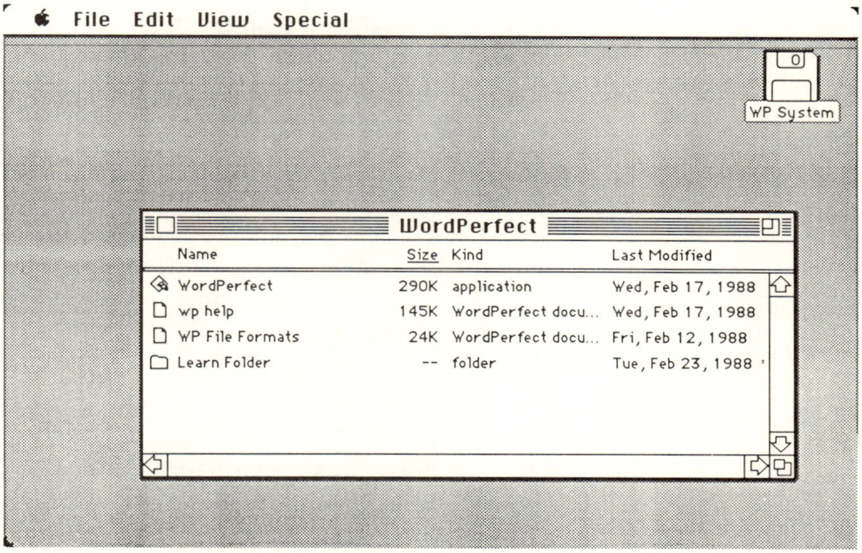

Figure 2-5. *WordPerfect* files viewed in order of descending size. This listing may be obtained by selecting by Size on the View menu.

If, instead of an open folder, you see the black icon for the *WordPerfect* program disk, open the disk by moving the *pointer* (the pointer is the arrow that moves in response to the movements of the mouse) to the icon and clicking twice on the mouse button. An alternate way of opening the disk is by pointing to the File menu heading, pressing the Mouse button, dragging the pointer to Open, and releasing the button. Another way to open a disk is to hold down the Command key and press *O*.

After you have taken a look at the open *WordPerfect* folder, close it again by clicking on the *close box*. You'll find the close box in the upper left-hand corner of the folder. You may also close files by selecting Close from the File menu, or press Command-K.

You are now ready to load *WordPerfect*. But first a word about the use of the mouse, the keyboard, the pull-down menus, and other Mac utilities.

How You Talk to the Macintosh

Giving commands to a Mac is very easy. You communicate with the computer via an interpreter known as a *user interface.* The Mac interface is famous for its ease of use, and discussions about the newest computers are full of references to Mac-type interfaces. In the case of the Mac, the interpreter consists of the screen, icons, pull-down menus, mouse, and keyboard. In other words, you use some combination of these items or tools to give commands to the computer and to respond to questions or requests the computer gives back.

The mouse is the primary tool for pointing and selecting. It's an input device about the size of a deck of cards connected to the computer by a long wire. As you move the mouse on your desk, you'll see a black arrow (the *pointer*) moving around your screen. You may point to an icon, or you may point to a pull-down menu heading.

The menu headings, shown along the top of each of the figures in this chapter, show

- An apple
- File
- View
- Special

Selecting with the Mouse

To select something, move the mouse on your desk until the pointer touches something you wish to select. You then do one of three things with the mouse button:

- Press the button and hold it down.
- Click the button once (press and release quickly, like hitting a typewriter key).
- Quickly click the button twice.

Holding down the mouse button with the pointer on the menu bar pulls down a menu. Clicking the button confirms a selection, and clicking it twice opens a file or starts a program.

Be careful: In spite of efforts to maintain strict standardization of interaction with the Macintosh, there may be exceptions.

The Pull-Down Menus

Let's take a look at those pull-down menus for a moment to see how they work and what they mean.

The File menu. Roll the mouse until the pointer is touching the word *File.* Hold down the mouse button. The File menu will open and you will see a list of several options shown in Figure 2-6.

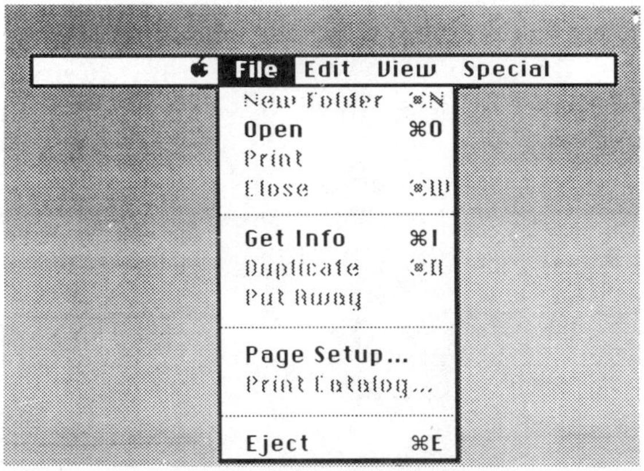

Figure 2-6. The pull-down File menu. Words in bold type tell which options or actions you may choose right now. Shaded options are not immediately available.

Each of these options will be explained later in the book as used.

You'll notice that some of the words on the menu list—Open, Get Info, Page Setup, and Eject—are in bold type, while the rest of the words are barely visible. The words in bold type represent actions you can take at this time; the others are not available to you right now. In other words, you may open a file, get information about a file, specify the page setup you want, or eject the disk. You may not create a New Folder or take any other actions indicated by the light gray type on the menu.

Release the button and the File menu disappears. Push it again, and the File menu is back (as long as the pointer is on

File). While you hold the button down, slide the mouse toward you (this maneuver is referred to as *Click and Drag*) so the pointer moves down the menu, highlighting one item at a time. Stop when the pointer reaches Eject, then release the mouse button. You have just ejected the *WordPerfect* program disk.

Push the disk back in, and the *WordPerfect* program disk icon will reappear on your screen.

The black *WordPerfect* icon tells you that the *WordPerfect* folder or disk has been *selected*. If you now tell the Mac to open a folder or eject a disk, it will understand that you are referring to the black icon and that's the one it will act on.

The Edit menu. Now pull down the Edit menu. The choices here are shown in Figure 2-7.

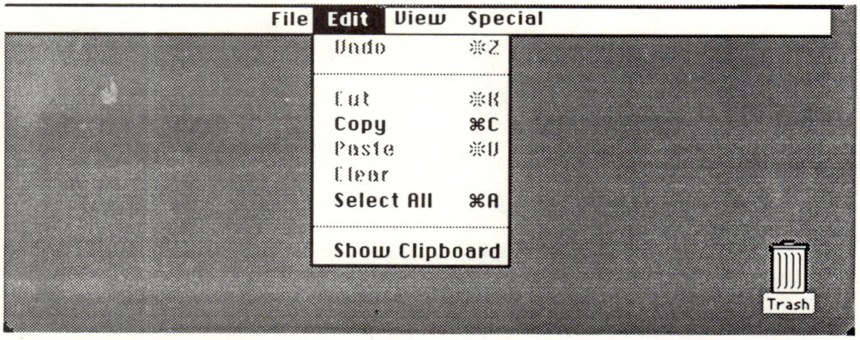

Figure 2-7. The Edit menu.

At the moment, the available options refer to disk names and disk actions. For example, if you pull down the Edit menu and drag the pointer to Select All, and then release the mouse button, you'll see that all three icons—*WordPerfect* System, *WordPerfect*, and Trash—have turned black. This means they are all ready for action, and the action you select will apply to all three disks or folders.

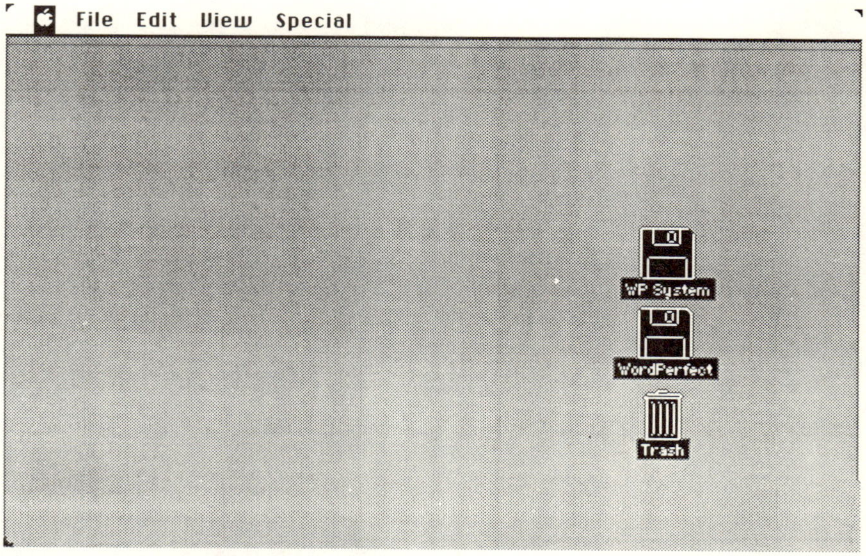

Figure 2-8. The Desktop after you have chosen Select All from the Edit menu. All three icons are black, meaning that any action you choose will apply to all three files or disks.

To unselect the icons, simply click the mouse button when the pointer is not touching one of the icons.

The View menu. The View menu lets you look at the contents of a disk or folder either by icon or by list, according to your own preference. The default option (a *default option* is a choice that is made for you if you make no choice yourself) is to display the contents of a folder as an array of icons. You have five other options:

- You may view the contents with each file or folder represented by a Small Icon as shown in Figure 2-9. This method can be convenient when a folder gets very full and there isn't room for many large icons on the screen. The drawback is that the icons are so small that it's hard to make sense of them as pictures.
- You may view the contents listed alphabetically by Name. If you are an old PC DOS user, you might be more comfortable

with this type of file listing. You also get more information about the files in the listing: size, kind, and date and time of creation or last modification (Figure 2-10).

- If you select by Date, you will see the same listing with the files rearranged by date, with the most recent files at the top of the list (Figure 2-11).
- If you elect to have the files listed by Size, the same list will be reorganized. The largest files will be on the top, and folders will be at the bottom of the list (Figure 2-12).
- Your final option is to choose to view files by Kind. The list will group the various kinds of files: documents at the top, applications next, and folders at the bottom (Figure 2-13).

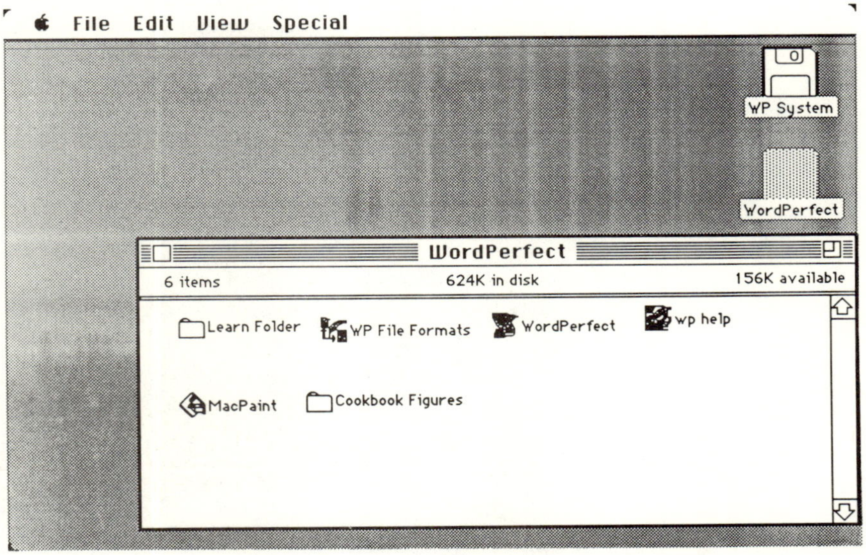

Figure 2-9. This is the way a folder looks when View by Small Icon is selected.

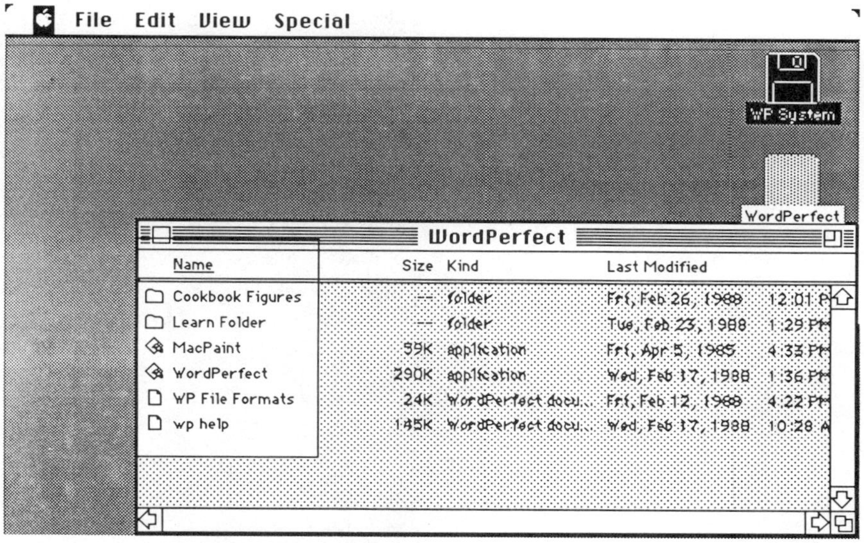

Figure 2-10. The contents of a folder when View by Name is selected. Files are listed alphabetically by filename.

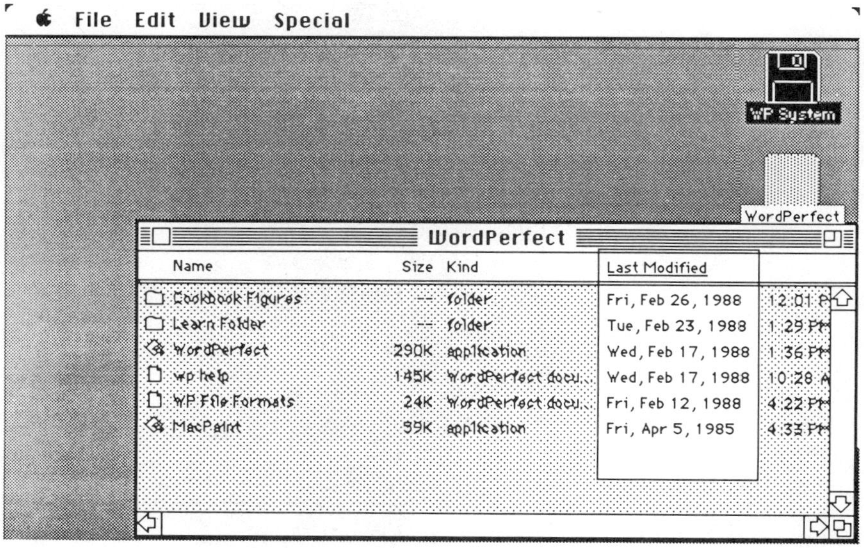

Figure 2-11. When View by Date is selected, the files with the most recent dates are listed first.

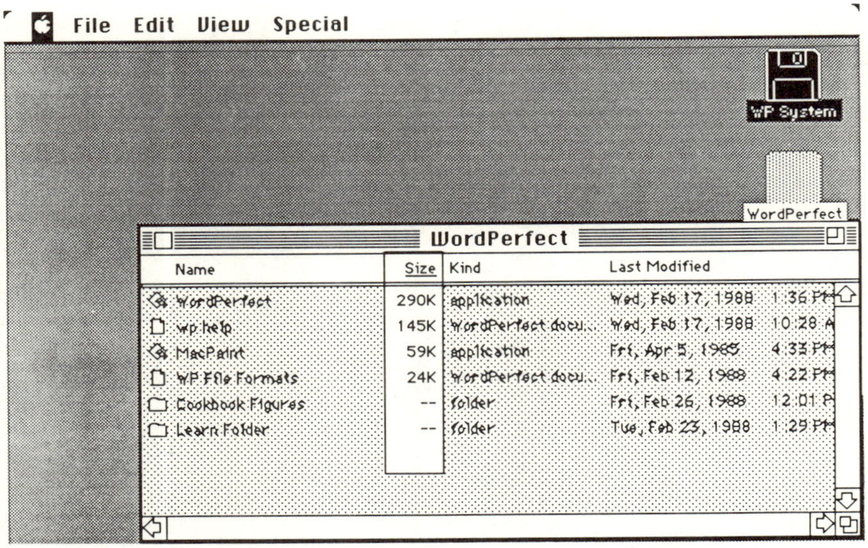

Figure 2-12. When View by Size is selected, files are listed in order of descending size, with the largest file first.

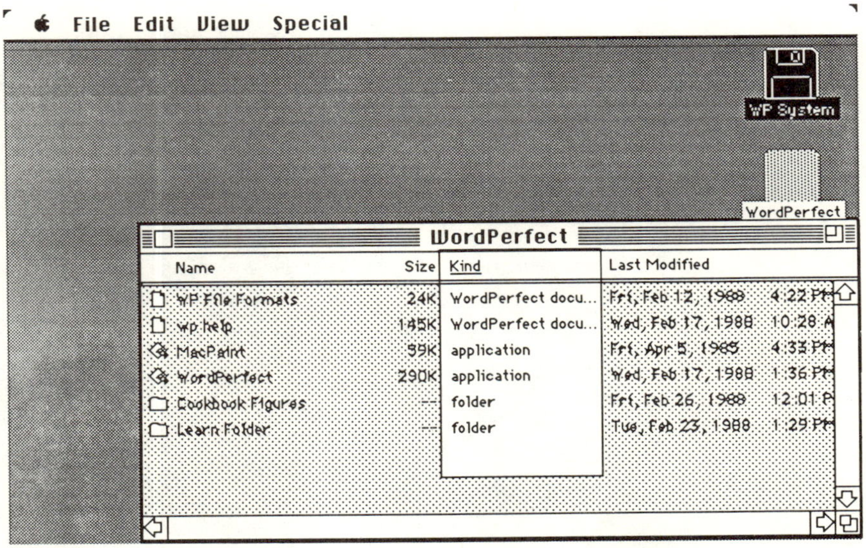

Figure 2-13. When View by Kind is selected, files are grouped according to type, with documents first, applications next, and folders at the bottom.

The Special menu. The pull-down menu headed Special (Figure 2-14) performs a number of odd jobs.

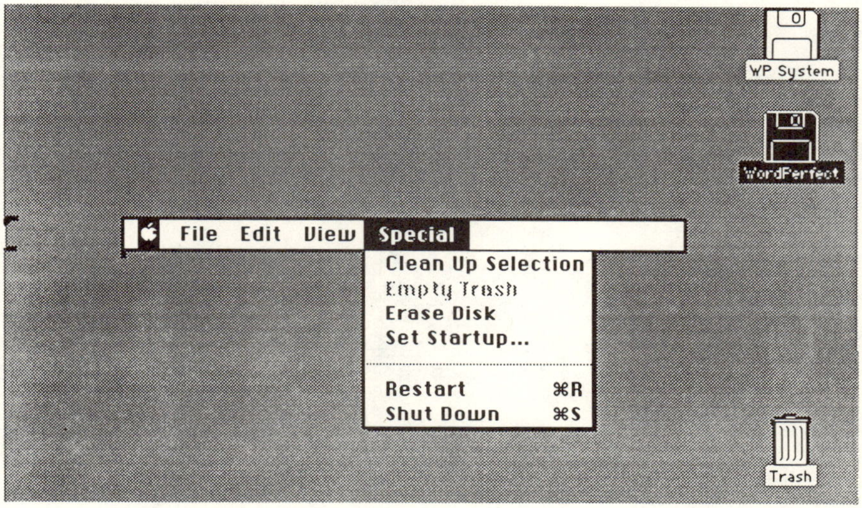

Figure 2-14. The Special menu. When there is no trash in the trash can, the Empty Trash option is shaded and cannot be used.

Despite its name, there is nothing special here. These are simple housekeeping chores. The item names are self-explanatory.

There is one trick involving the Special menu for which you might have special use. If you have collected too many files on one disk, and their icons are hanging over each other in your *window* (a window is a rectangular area containing your files or text), making them difficult to read or select, here is a way to line them up.

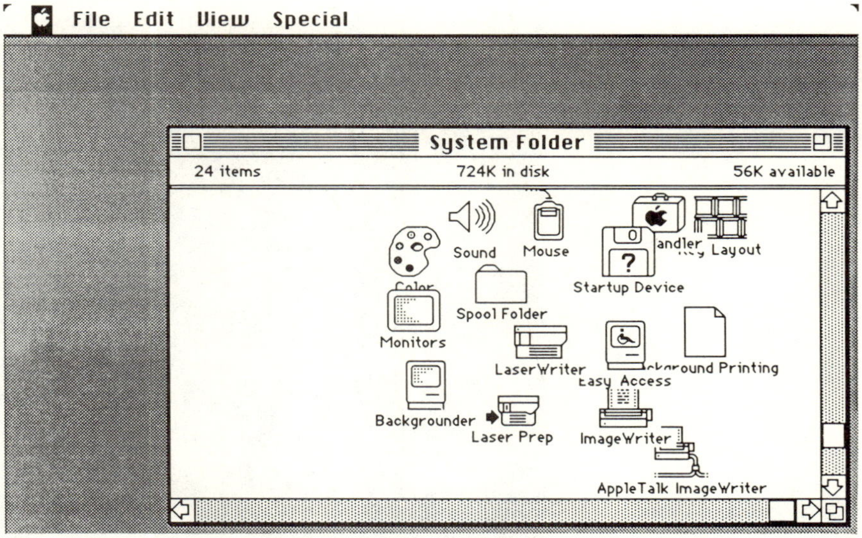

Figure 2-15 A messy window, with file icons in a state of anarchy.

In Figure 2-15 the utility files in the System Folder on the System disk have been deliberately jumbled. Here's how to straighten them out: While pressing the Option key at the left-hand side of your keyboard, pull down the Special menu and select Clean Up Window by releasing the mouse button. You can see the results in Figure 2-16.

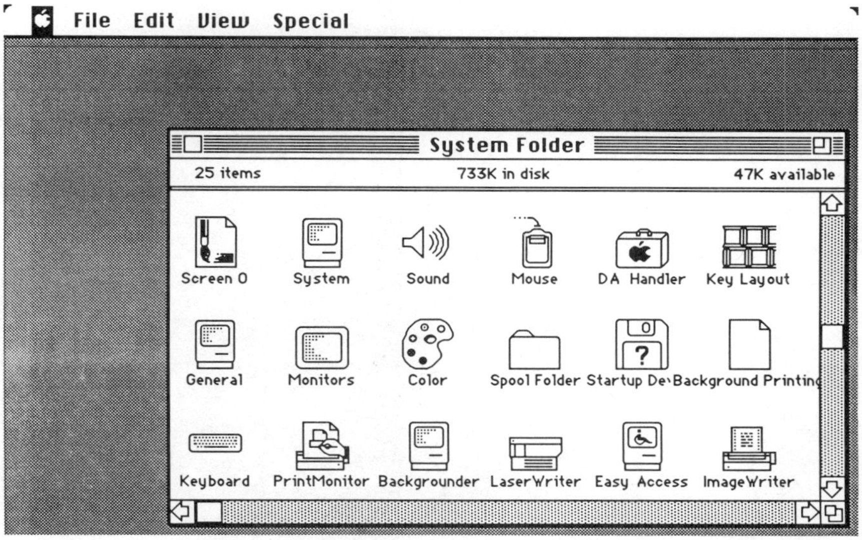

Figure 2-16. The system file icons neatly arrayed after the Clean Up Window maneuver.

The Trash

We've talked about almost everything on the screen except the Trash. The garbage can icon at the lower right of your screen is, like most other icons or items on your screen, a folder. You can open the trash just like any other folder, take a look at the files in it, and decide whether you want to resurrect them. Just as you can empty the trash, you can also save the contents of the trash, open the lid and recycle it by bringing it back to useful life. In fact, it might be more appropriate to call it deep storage rather than trash. As long as your files are in the trash, they aren't lost forever. You can retrieve material from the trash just as you can from any other folder.

If you want to retrieve a file from the Trash, however, you should act quickly. Files in the Trash can be permanently discarded or lost in at least three ways:

- By selecting Empty Trash on the Special menu
- By opening a new application

• By turning off or restarting the Mac

Let's toss something into the trash and see what happens. First, to demonstrate that Trash truly is a folder, highlight or blacken the trash icon by clicking on it once.

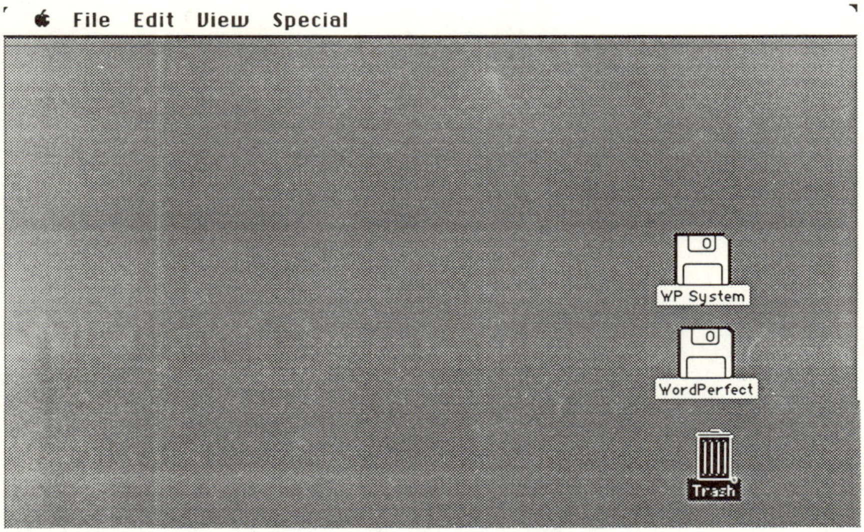

Figure 2-17. The Trash icon highlighted and ready for action.

Now open the trash in the usual manner: Pull down the File menu, highlight Open, and release the mouse button. The open Trash folder looks like any other open folder, with zero items present.

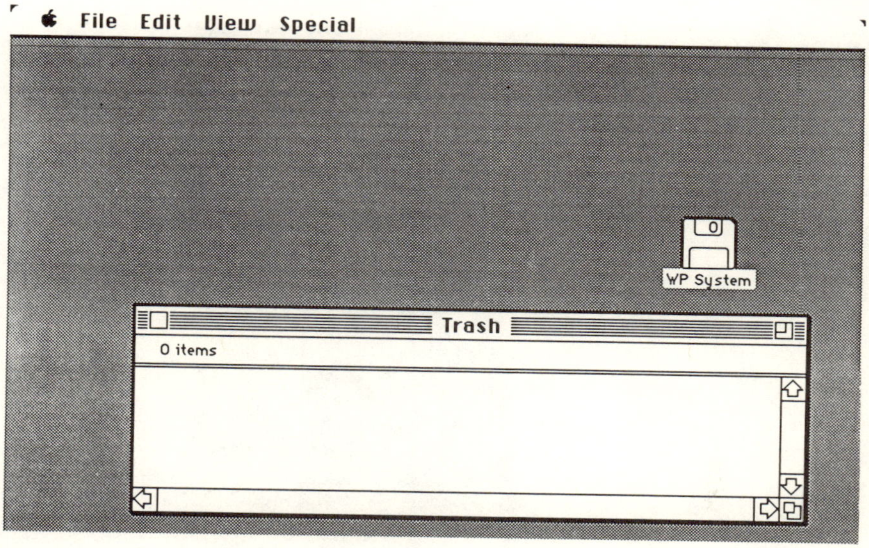

Figure 2-18. The opened trash file, with nothing in it.

What happens to that file if we dump some garbage? Close the trash file by clicking on the close box in the upper left corner of the trash folder.

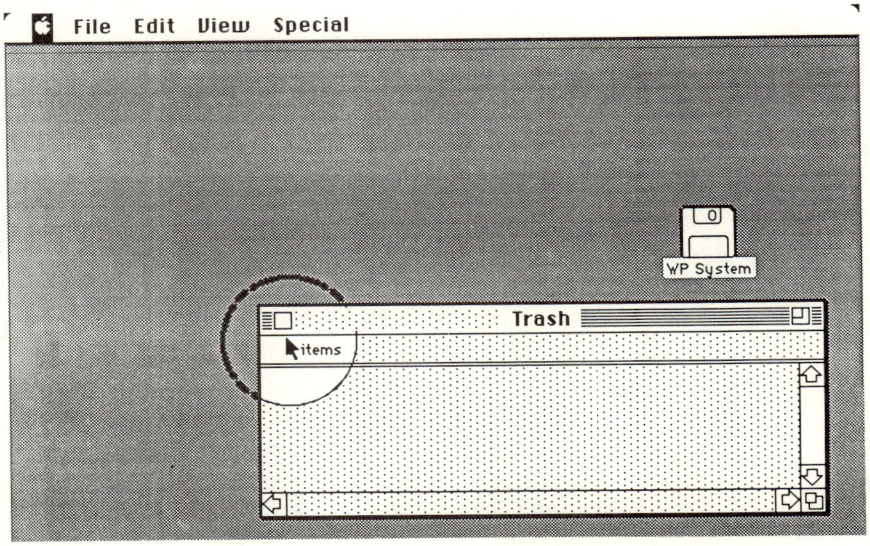

Figure 2-19. The close box circled on the Trash folder. You may close the Trash folder, or any other file or folder, by moving the pointer to the close box and clicking once.

If you highlight an icon in another folder and drag it to the trash can, the file will be transferred from its original folder to the Trash. The Trash icon will appear to bulge if anything is in it.

A Few More Mac Maneuvers

Before we move along to *WordPerfect*, we should review a few more basic Mac moves.

Copying a disk. Before doing anything else with your *WordPerfect* disks, you must copy them and store the originals in a safe place. Work only with copies of the originals.

You should store your original disks in a dry, dark place, at a distance from your computer. If you use your Mac at home, storing your disks in a desk drawer at work would make sense. Put them on a high shelf in a closet at home if your Mac is at work. The storage should be a constant temperature that would be comfortable for you. Don't store them in the glove box of your car, for instance, or in the deep freeze. The disks should be far from sources of magnetism like telephones, motors, or televisions.

Nearly everyone is negligent to some extent when it comes to making backup copies of disks. Yet that neglect can be costly. If your work disk goes bad, you may never be able to resurrect your files. All your work will vanish without a trace. On the Mac, copying disks is very easy. Make backup copies of disks frequently (perhaps weekly) and back up your often changed files even more frequently (daily).

Let's make a copy of the *WordPerfect* System disk. Begin by ejecting the *WordPerfect* program disk from your external drive. That can be done in two ways:

- Highlight or select the *WordPerfect* program disk and drag it to the Trash. In a few seconds, the disk will be ejected.
- Highlight the *WordPerfect* program disk, then pull down the File menu and select Eject.

Many users prefer the second method because there is no ambiguity about the requested action: You are ejecting, not trashing.

Insert a new, blank disk into the external drive. You may use an old disk with worthless data on it, but this is risky; the disk has a reduced lifespan because it has already been used for a period of time.

If the disk is new, you must Initialize it. If it is a used disk, simply click on the disk you want to copy and drag its icon across the screen until it covers the disk that will receive the copy. Both icons will be highlighted briefly until you release the mouse button.

As soon as you release the mouse button, you will see a cautionary dialog box. It reminds you of the names of the two disks, and tells you which disk is in which drive.

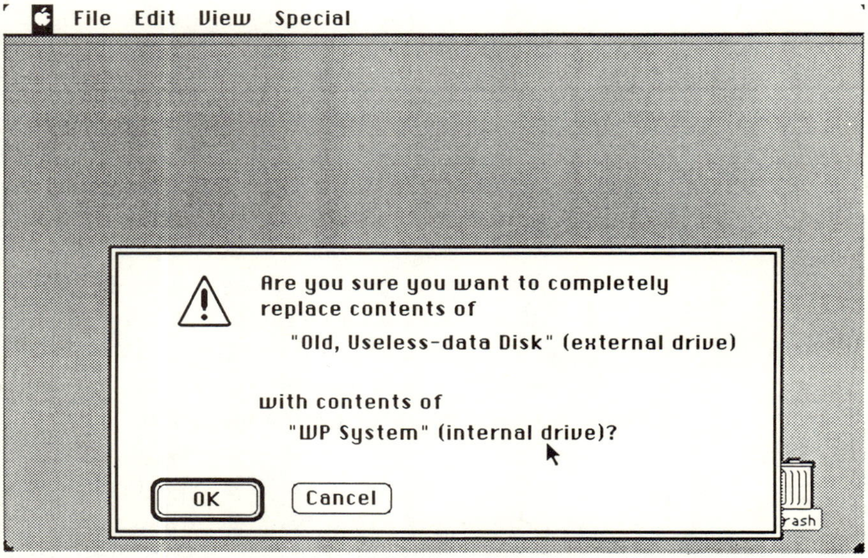

Figure 2-20. The Mac checks to be sure you have your disks straight.

If you have mixed up the two disks, it isn't too late to avoid an error. Just click on Cancel, and the operation will cease. If everything is all right, however, click on OK and the copying process will proceed. The Mac will show you a dialog box at the top of the screen, giving you a play-by-play account as all the files are read from the original and written to the new copy. When the copy is complete, the two disk icons will appear on the monitor again with the new copy highlighted.

Below, in the subsection "Selecting multiple files, folders, or disks" you will see how to confirm that the two disks contain the same files.

Naming and renaming disks, folders, and files. Now that you have made the copies, let's assume that you want to rename the backup disks to distinguish them from the originals. It's a snap: Select the disk you want to rename by clicking once on its icon.

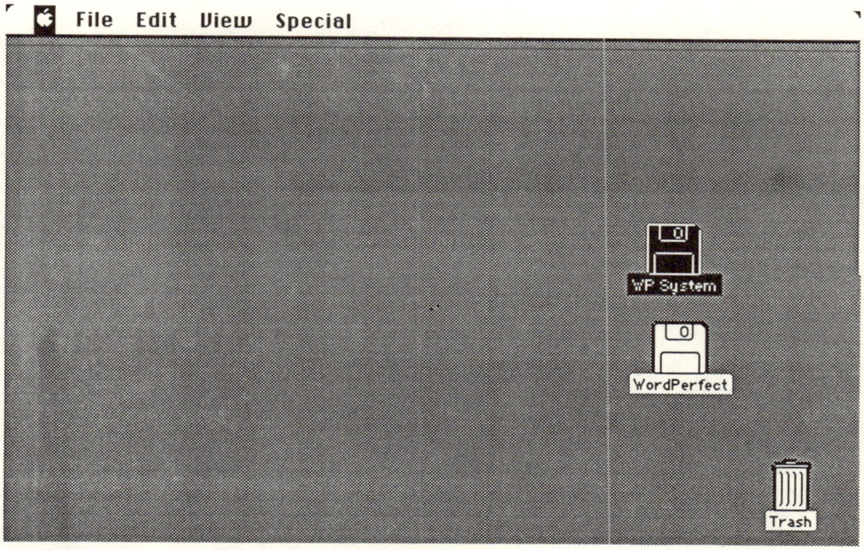

Figure 2-21. The *WordPerfect* System disk icon has been selected, and we are ready to change its name.

Simply type the new name. The *WordPerfect* System disk has been selected, and you're going to rename it *System Backup*. As you type the first letter, the original name disappears and the first letter of the new name appears in white under the icon. Finish typing the new name, press Return or click the mouse button with the pointer outside the disk icon, and you're finished.

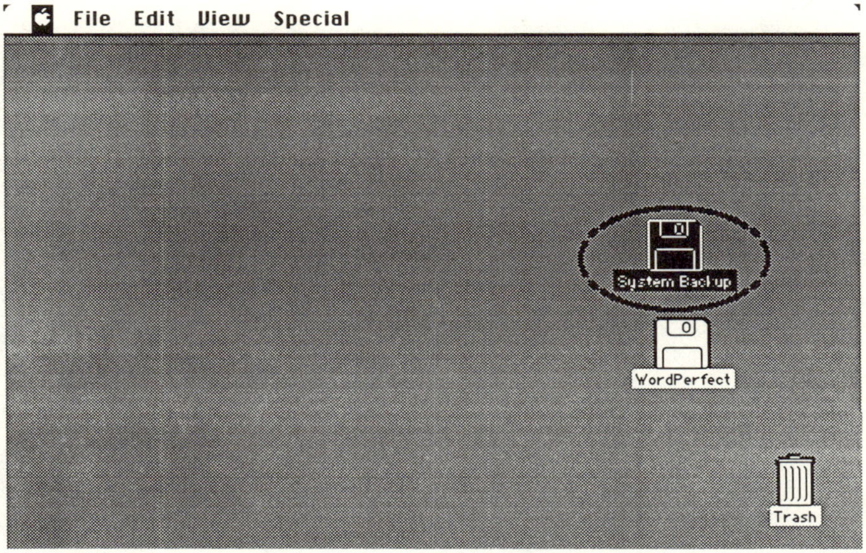

Figure 2-22. The *WordPerfect* System disk icon with its new name: System Backup.

Folders and individual files are named, or have their names changed, in just the same way you changed the name of the *WordPerfect* System disk: Click on the icon for the file or folder, and then start typing its new name.

Selecting multiple files, folders, or disks. The Mac makes it easy to select several disks or files and act on them simultaneously. As we discussed you can select or highlight everything on the screen by choosing Select All from the Edit menu. If you want to select two or three items, and not every one, draw a rectangle around the items with which you want to work. This will select everything inside the rectangle as a unit.

Suppose you want to get information simultaneously on eight different files in the system folder at once. The files are labeled General, Background Printing, Startup Device, mouse, Backgrounder, LaserWriter, Easy Access, and ImageWriter. Picture a rectangle enclosing those eight files, and move the pointer to one of the rectangle's corners.

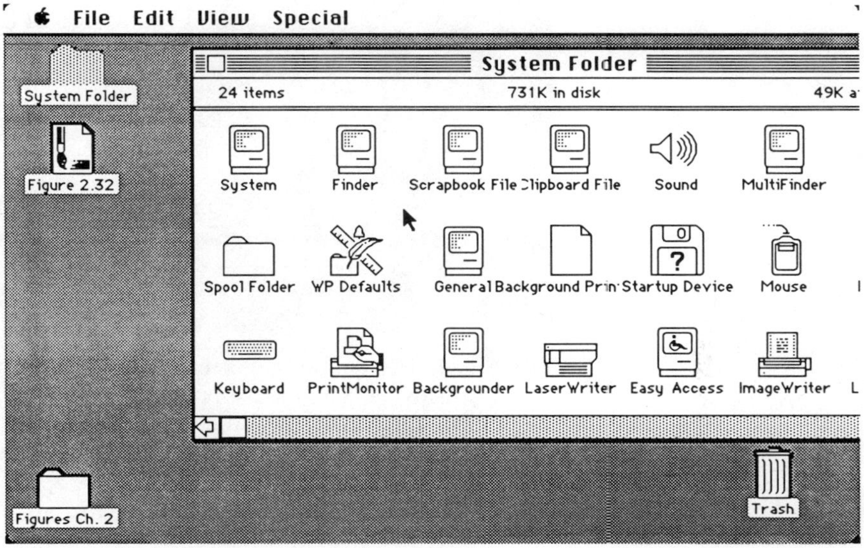

Figure. 2-23. The pointer ready to begin outlining the eight selected files.

Now press and hold the mouse button while dragging the mouse diagonally to the opposite corner. A rectangle will emerge from the tip of the pointer as you go.

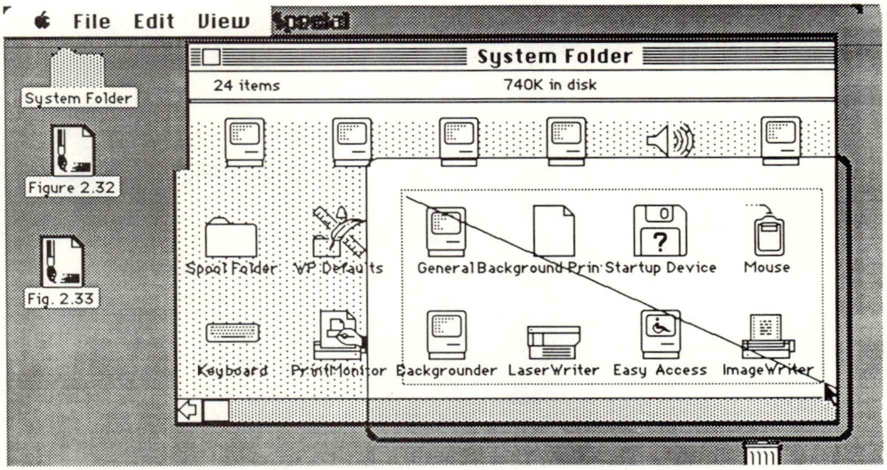

Figure 2-24. The pointer-generated rectangle surrounding the files you want to select or activate. The mouse pointer was dragged along the diagonal line. At this point, you are still holding down the mouse button.

When you release the mouse button, every file or icon inside the rectangle will be selected.

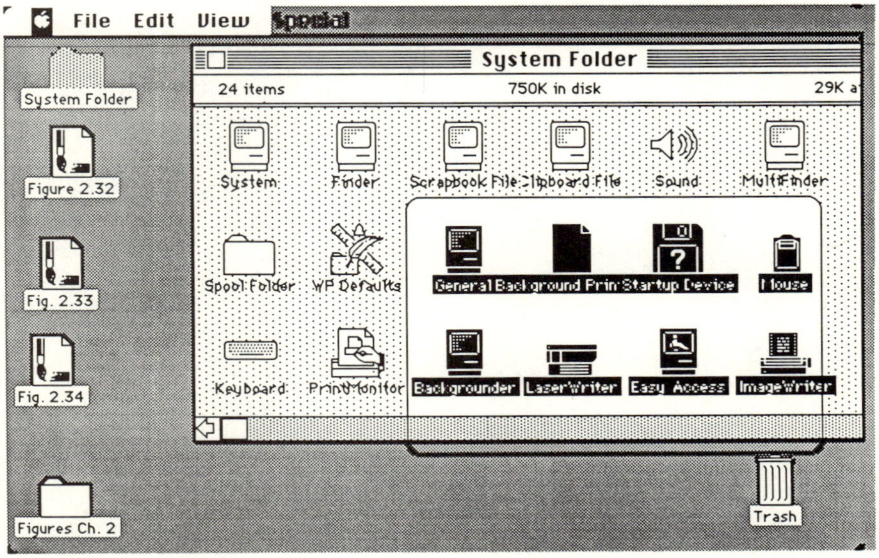

Figure 2-25. The selected files after you release the mouse button.

You may now Get Info on all eight files by pulling down the File menu and selecting Get Info.

When you release the button, eight information cards will appear on the screen, and you can learn about the eight system files at the same time.

You could also delete a number of files at one time. This is probably a more practical use of the multiple-file maneuver. Select all the files to be sent to the Trash in the same manner detailed above. Then drag all the files to the Trash by moving the pointer to any one of them, pressing and holding the mouse button, and dragging the whole lot to the Trash until the pointer highlights the Trash can. When the mouse button is released, all the files highlighted will be trashed.

Checking the WordPerfect System disk copy. Now you might want to Get Info for the *WordPerfect* System disk and the copy you made. Highlight both disks either by drawing a rectangle around them or highlight the first icon by clicking on it, and then hold down the Shift key and click the second icon. You can click on as many files as you like with the Shift key depressed. They will all be highlighted. This Shift-Click trick is convenient for selecting a series of things that can't be contained in a rectangle.

If you now select Get Info from the File menu, both information cards will appear on the screen (Figure 2-26).

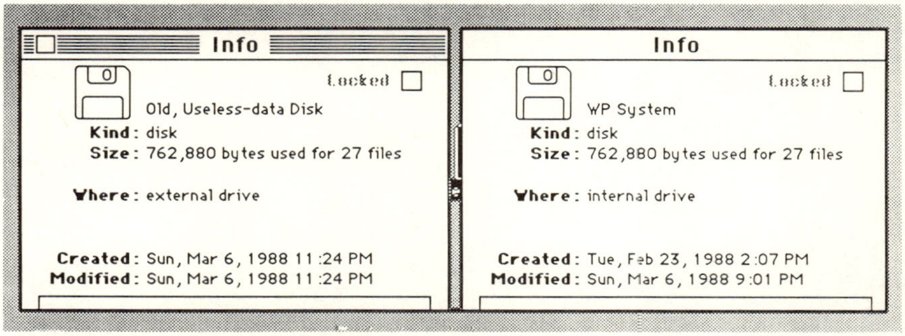

Figure 2-26. The information cards for the original and the copy disk, showing identical numbers of bytes and files.

Erasing a disk. Do you need a blank disk for storing *WordPerfect* documents? You might want to erase another disk that contains data you don't need.

To erase a disk, insert it into one of your disk drives. Click on its icon and pull down the Special menu. Finally highlight Erase Disk (Figure 2-27).

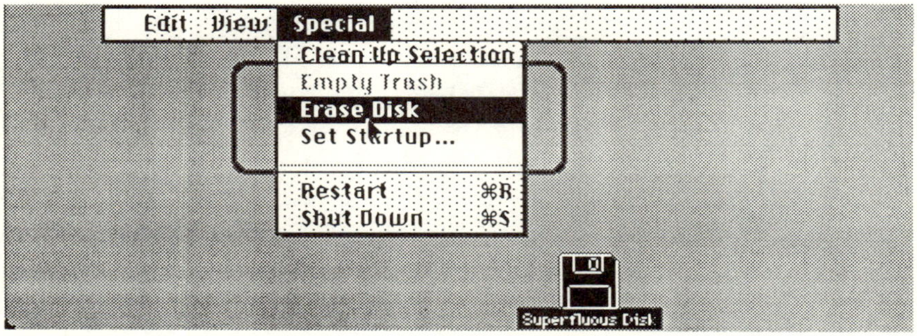

Figure 2-27 The Special menu with Erase Disk highlighted.

When you release the mouse button, you will see a dialog box (Figure 2-28). It checks to be sure you want to erase the disk, telling you the name and drive of the disk (so you'll be sure to erase the right one), and offering you the choice of three actions: Cancel, One-Sided, and Two-Sided.

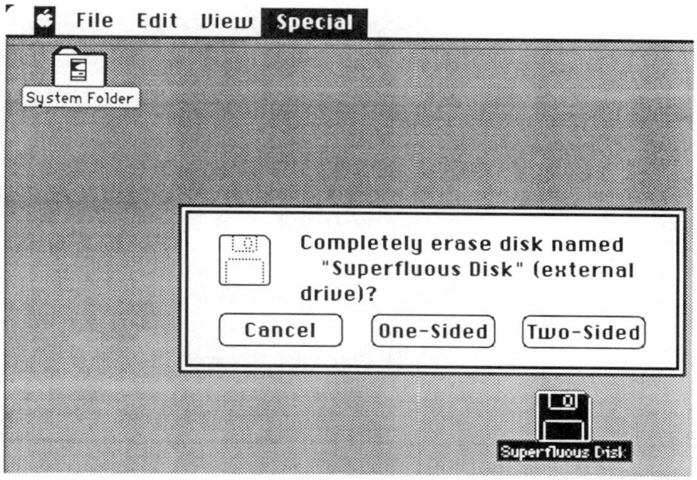

Figure 2-28. The dialog box, checking to be sure the command you entered wasn't given by mistake.

Look at the screen carefully. If, for some reason, you have instructed the Mac to erase the wrong disk, you can avoid disaster by simply clicking on Cancel at this point. If you're on the right track, however, you should click on One-Sided or Two-Sided, depending on what kind of disk you have and whether you want it formatted on one or both sides. As a rule you will want to click on Two-Sided.

The Mac will then erase the disk. The dialog box will read *Initializing disk . . .*, and the pointer will turn into a wristwatch, meaning it's momentarily busy. When the process is complete, you can confirm that the superfluous disk is now empty by highlighting it and selecting Open from the File menu. The opened disk reveals that there are 0 items present on the disk and you have 779,000 bytes of space available to fill.

Changing the size and position of windows. To make it more convenient to see what's on your screen, and to work with and between different documents and applications, the Mac makes it possible for you to manipulate windows or open files in various ways. A quick review might be helpful:

Changing size. You can resize your window larger or smaller by clicking on the *size box* (the box in the lower right-hand corner of the window) and dragging the window to the dimensions you want. You can also switch between the window's normal size and a window that fills the entire screen by clicking on the *zoom box* (the zoom box is located in the upper right corner of the window).

Moving a window. To move the entire window, position the pointer on the *title bar* at the top of the window, hold down the mouse button, and drag the window where you want it to be. The title bar extends across the top of the window, and you may touch it at any point except the close box (upper left) or the zoom box (upper right).

Scrolling. When a file or folder contains more files or icons than can be displayed in a window at one time, the Mac makes it possible to change the view by scrolling up and down or right and left. This is accomplished by using the *scroll bars* at the bottom and right edges of the folder or window as shown in Figure 2-29.

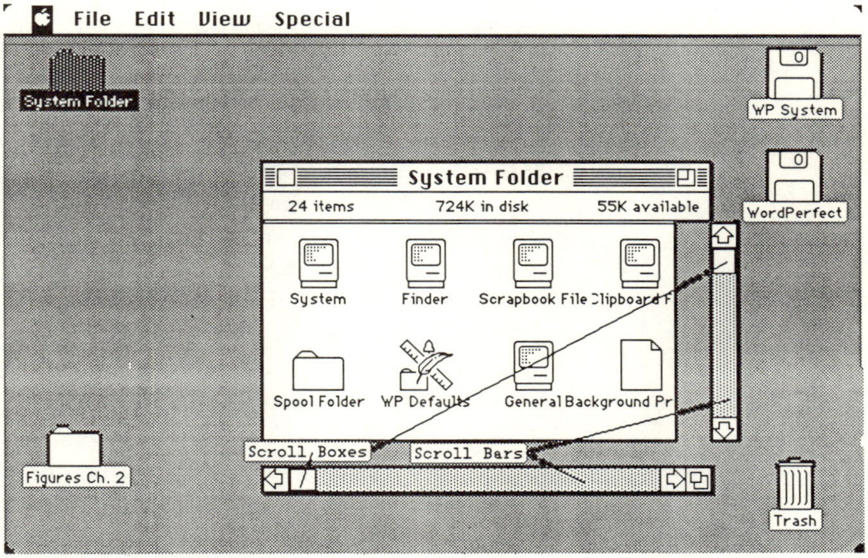

Figure 2-29. The scroll bars on the system folder.

The scroll bars have three parts: a *scroll box,* which indicates your position in the file or document, two arrows, and a gray area. By clicking and dragging the scroll box, you can position yourself within the folder. The position of the scroll box tells you the position of the window. If it's halfway up the gray area, you are halfway through the document. Clicking on an arrow drags the scroll box in the direction of the arrow. This is good for scrolling line-by-line. By clicking in the gray area, you can move through the file by *pages* (a page is defined as the area visible in the window).

Making disks or windows active or inactive. If you have several windows on your screen, how do you know which are active and which are inactive? An active window has the title bar "turned on." That is, the title bar has a visible close box, zoom box, and *stripes* or *ribs.* Also, the active folder is always the folder that appears to be lying on top of the other folders.

On an inactive window, the title bar is blank except for the title of the file or folder or disk. To change the active window, simply move the mouse pointer to the window you want to make active and click the button. Immediately, the window on which you clicked will spring to the foreground, with close and zoom boxes visible and with stripes on the title bar.

Conclusion

Those are the basics of the Macintosh. If you're like most users, you'll learn how to use the Macintosh in virtually no time, and over a longer period, you may even pick up the perception that it understands what you want it to do. Some people are spoiled by working with a Mac. They never want to change computers again.

But, if you think the user interface is merely a fast and friendly way of working with files, wait until you see it working with a powerful application like *WordPerfect.* You'll discover a whole new world of power. While many other computers running word processing software are like interactive typewriters, the Macintosh running *WordPerfect* is more like an eager assistant.

Chapter 3
Introduction to *WordPerfect*

Chapter 3

Introduction to *WordPerfect*

You're ready to load up *WordPerfect.* By now, you should have made backup copies of your original disks and put them carefully away. With the System Backup disk inserted into the internal drive, and the *WordPerfect* Backup disk inserted into the external drive, you see the two icons and the Trash on your screen (see Figure 3-1).

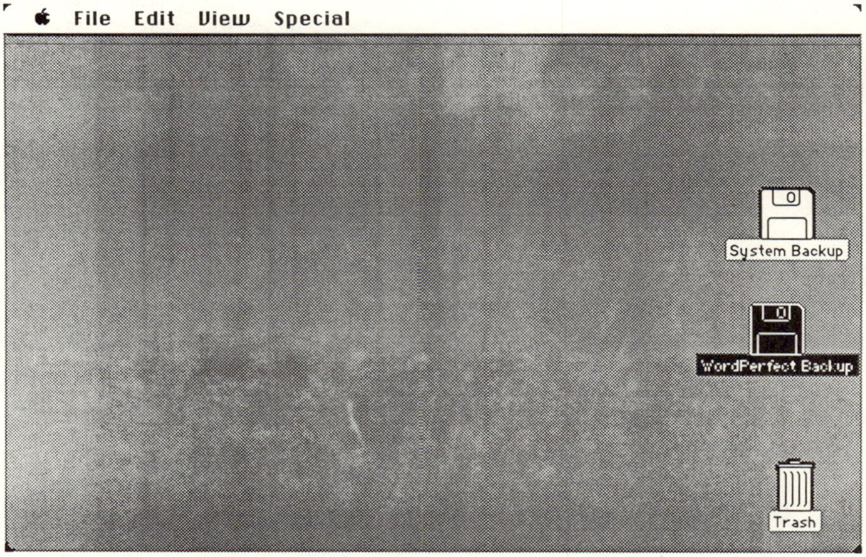

Figure 3-1. The opening screen as you load *WordPerfect,* using backups of both your System and *WordPerfect* disks.

The *WordPerfect* Disk

When you open the *WordPerfect* disk, you see icons for four files as shown in Figure 3-2.

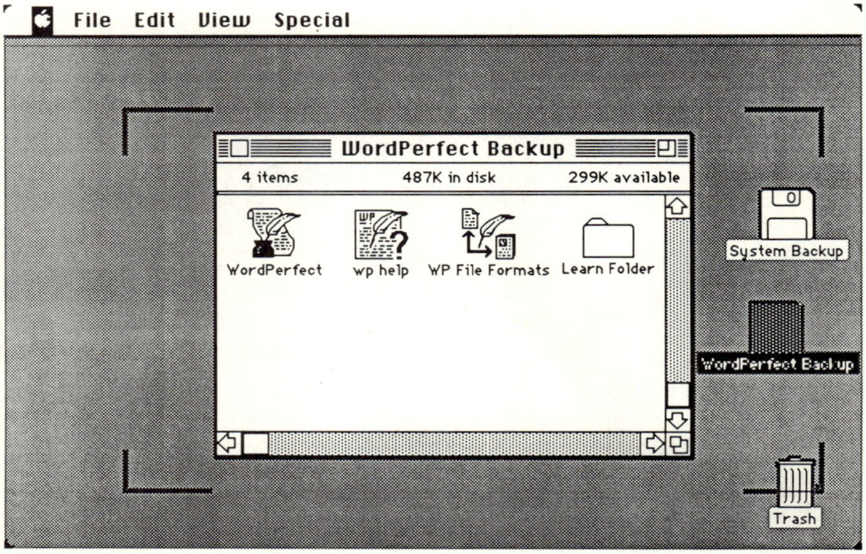

Figure 3-2. The opened *WordPerfect* folder.

The *WordPerfect* program. The *WordPerfect* program icon (far left in Figure 3-2) shows a quill pen, an ink bottle, and a sheet of manuscript. (The quill pen is the *WordPerfect* logo, appearing on all *WordPerfect* programs, documents, files, and so on.)

The wp help file. The wp help file icon (second from left in Figure 3-2) is identified by its question mark. It represents the file you access when you are stumped or when you need to have some function explained or clarified. (More about the Help function shortly.)

The WP File Formats file. The WP File Formats file icon (second from right in Figure 3-2) is identified by two arrows at right angles. You'll see its function discussed later.

The Learn Folder. If you click the Learn Folder open, you'll see that it contains 13 *WordPerfect* documents with names such as Trees Learn, New Cabin, and so on. These files (shown in Figure

3-3) are all part of a self-tutorial you might want to work through. For details, see the Learning section of your *WordPerfect* manual.

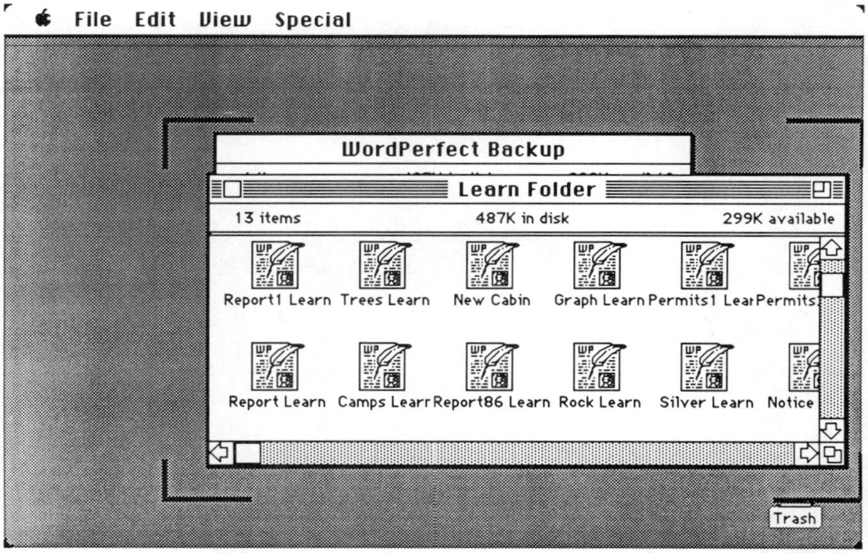

Figure 3-3. The opened Learn Folder.

If you've already worked through the tutorial, or if you feel you don't need it or want it on your *WordPerfect* Backup disk, you can Trash the folder and create some more room on your disk.

Running *WordPerfect*

To open *WordPerfect*, use one of the following procedures:

- Highlight the *WordPerfect* program icon and select Open from the File menu.
- Click twice on the *WordPerfect* program icon.
- Highlight the *WordPerfect* icon, and enter Command-O from the keyboard.

As discussed earlier, these keyboard options are available for many *WordPerfect* maneuvers, but they won't be pointed out every time. The shortcuts are noted on the pull-down menus and listed alphabetically on the Quick Reference pamphlet that came with your software.

The *WordPerfect* Opening Screen

The clean, uncluttered screen has always been the essence of the *WordPerfect* word-processing concept. When you start to work on a new document, you are presented with a blank screen, as if you are dealing with a blank sheet of paper.

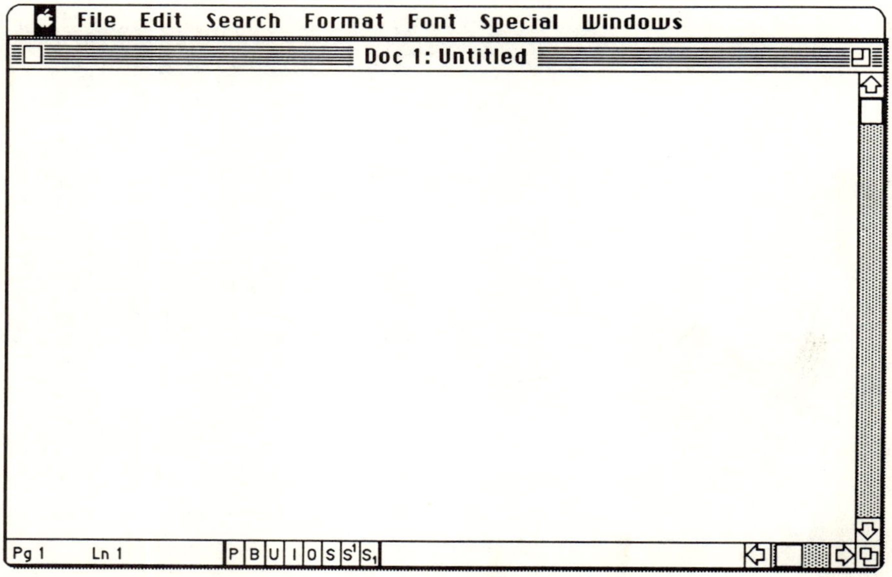

Figure 3-4. The opening *WordPerfect* screen.

The opening screen on the Mac isn't quite as blank as the opening screen of *WordPerfect* for the PC. You'll see a number of familiar items from the opening Mac screen: pull-down files, title bar, scroll bars at the right and bottom, close box, zoom box, the size box, and so on. The combination of these features is known as the standard Macintosh interface. That's one of the most attractive features of the Mac: Once you know how to interact with the computer through the interface, any Macintosh program will have a familiar look. You will be able to move around in the program and perform many operations even if you've never seen the program before.

This isn't generally true of PC programs. Programs written for the PC tend to differ radically from each other. Often when you load a new program you will have absolutely no idea what to do first unless you consult the program documentation. This situation may change when the extended version of the OS/2 operating system becomes available, however. The Presentation Manager will provide PC users with a standard interface similar to the one available on the Macintosh since 1984.

New Features

Although most of the items on the screen are familiar, you have probably noticed some new features. These include:

New pull-down menus. These new menus include Search, Format, Font, and Windows.

New menu items. You will find new items on every other pull-down menu: On the File menu, for example, only the Open, Close, and Print options look the same. A list of new choices has been added: New, Retrieve, Save, Save As, Save Copy As, File Management, Print Options, WP Defaults, Transfer, and Quit.

Submenus. Get to a submenu by selecting an item on the main menu, then dragging the pointer to any of the menu items that includes a black triangle. For example, if you select the Special menu, you see that every item on the menu except Thesaurus . . . and Merge . . . has a black triangle to its right (Figure 3-5).

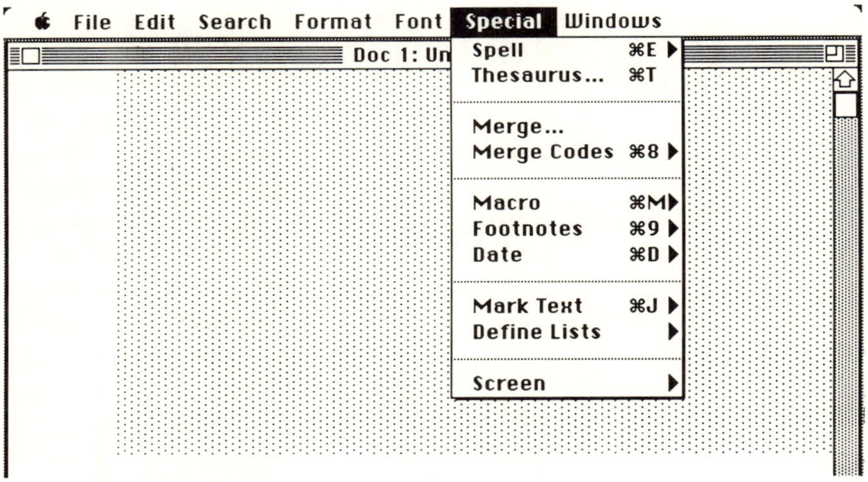

Figure 3-5. The Special Menu. Note the black triangles or arrows that indicate submenus.

You may select any submenu by releasing the mouse button on that item. For example, if you drag the pointer to Screen, the Screen submenu will pop out to the right of the Special menu (Figure 3-6).

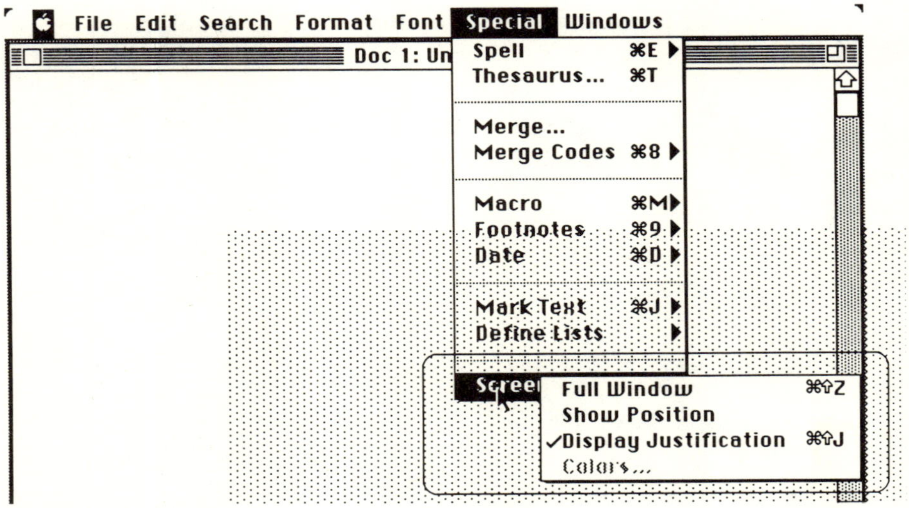

Figure 3-6. The Screen submenu of the Special menu. At this point, you are still holding down the mouse button.

Once the Screen submenu appears, you have two choices of action:

- You may simply release the mouse button, which will leave the Screen submenu on the monitor screen for your consideration.
- You may drag the pointer to the right and select any of the items on the submenu just as you would select a main menu item.

If you select the Full Window option when you release the mouse button, the screen will be almost totally blank except for the status line at the bottom and the flashing black square that indicates the position of the Apple or Desk Accessory menu. This is the Great White Page that the *WordPerfect* developers endlessly pursue (they call it Moby Screen in Orem, Utah). It allows you to work without the distraction of menus, formatting codes, or scroll bars.

All of these items are quickly available, however. To get to any pull-down menu, just move the pointer to the top of the screen and the menu bar reappears. And if you really don't mind having the menu headings and the scroll bar on the screen while you work, just select Full Window again from the Special menu (it's a toggle switch) and all the screen gadgetry comes back.

A new status line at the bottom of the screen. This status line tells you what's happening on the page.

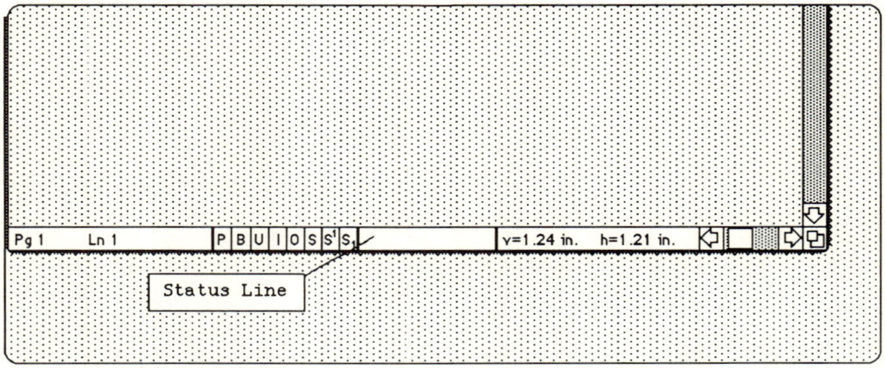

Figure 3-7. The status line, showing (from left to right) page number, line number, typeface, vertical and horizontal coordinates, scroll bar, and size box.

On the status line, proceeding from left to right, you see

- The current cursor location
- The style of typeface you are using at the moment
- The vertical and horizontal coordinates of the cursor
- The horizontal scroll bar

The current cursor location. The current cursor location is shown by page and line number. The cursor is the vertical line flashing in the upper left-hand corner of the screen.

The style of typeface you are using at the moment. The letters stand for Plain, Bold, Underline, Italics, Outline, Shadow, Superscript and Subscript. The Superscript and Subscript letters have numbers to indicate where their baseline will be in relationship to the text line. These typeface indicators not only tell you what type style is active at any moment or location on the page, but they are also toggle switches for turning on and off the functions they represent. Activate the indicators by touching them with the pointer and clicking.

If you want to shift to bold type, simply touch the pointer to the B in the status line and click. The *B* then appears in boldface and everything you type will be in boldface until you give a new instruction. To return to plain type, either toggle back by clicking *B* again, or click on *P*, which stands for Plain. You can turn on any combination of type styles. To turn off type style indicators, simply click on *P*.

The vertical and horizontal coordinates of the cursor. If you can't see this information, pull down the Special menu, go to the Screen submenu, and select Show Position. The vertical and horizontal positions or coordinates of the cursor will appear at the right end of the status line. Vertical distances are measured from the top of the page and horizontal distances from the left edge of the page. To remove this information, pull down the Special menu, drag down to the Screen submenu, and select Hide Position.

Scroll bar. At the right end of the status line is a small scroll bar. It works just like any other scroll bar. This is the horizontal or lateral scroll bar. It lets you move from side to side on the page.

The ruler. One of the handy features of *WordPerfect* is the ruler. You will use the ruler in various ways from time to time, but for the moment let's see what it can tell you about the dimensions of the page and the screen.

Once these dimensions are entered into the ruler, you can select Copy Ruler from the Format menu and place a copy of the current ruler in the Clipboard to use the same format later in the document or in another document. Simply use the Paste command from the Edit menu to insert it.

Go to the Format menu and select Show Ruler.

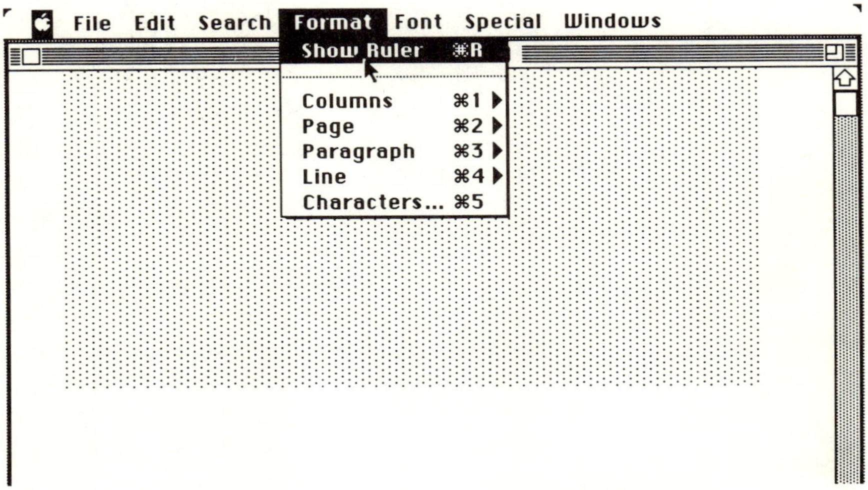

Figure 3-8. Selecting Show Ruler from the Format menu.

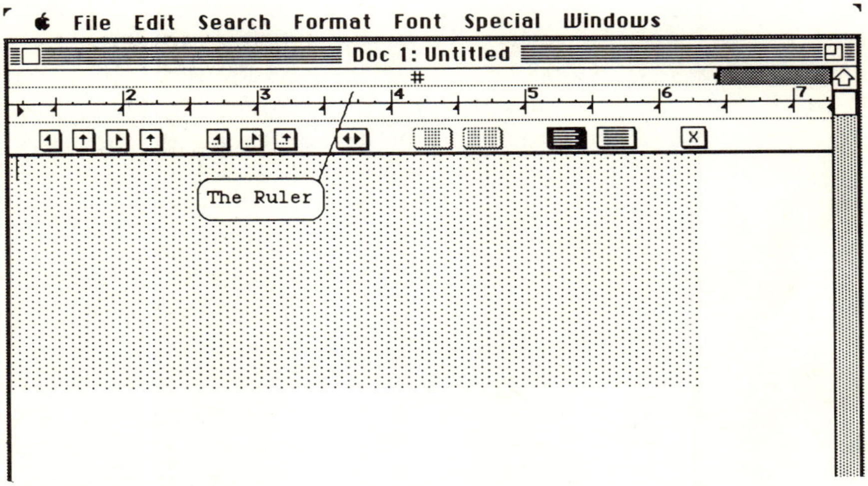

Figure 3-9. The ruler.

When you release the mouse button, you see a ruler along with a number of flags and icons at the top of your screen, just under the title bar. The ruler is marked off in inches, and the visible part of the ruler extends from about 1.25 inches to about 7.25 inches—or roughly six inches. So at any position on the screen, you are looking at a six-inch wide section of the page.

Move the pointer to the scroll box in the horizontal scroll bar, press the mouse button, and drag the scroll box to the left as far as it will go. If you look at the ruler now, you see that the zero-point of the ruler is at the left edge of the screen, and that the right edge of the screen is just past the six-inch mark. You also notice the cursor flashing at approximately the 1.25-inch mark. If the position data is visible at the right end of the status line, you can see that the horizontal location of the cursor is 1.21 inches.

Drag the horizontal scroll box as far to the right as it will go (or put the pointer on the right-pointing arrow and press the mouse button until the scroll box has moved all the way to the right end of the gray area). If you look at the ruler now, you see that the right edge of the screen is just past the 14.5-inch mark on the ruler. You will also notice that the flashing cursor is no longer visible. The reason for this is that the cursor is well to the left of the portion of the page you can see in the *window.*

The screen is a window on a portion of a page that is about six inches wide. By the position of the scroll box in the horizontal scroll bar you can tell whether you are looking at the left side, the right side, or the center of a page.

Since there is no vertical ruler, you can't visualize the vertical dimension of the window in quite the same way. But there's another way to gain this perspective.

Begin by making the ruler disappear. Go to the Format menu and select Hide Ruler. Note that to the right of the words *Hide Ruler* (or *Show Ruler,* when the ruler is hidden), you can see a clover shape and the letter *R.* This means that an alternate way of toggling the ruler on and off is to press Command-R. To do this, hold down the Command key (the key with the clover shape on it) and press *R.* Each option that had a Command-Key-press combination to its right can be invoked in a similar manner.

Notice that when the cursor is on Line 1, its vertical position is about 1.25 inches (v = 1.24 in.) from the top of the "paper." Tap the Return key to move the cursor down the screen until it rests on top of the status line. At that point you are on Line 18, and the vertical position is 5.01 inches from the top of the page (v = 5.01 in.). This tells you that the vertical height of the screen or window is about 5.01 in. − 1.24 in. = 3.77 in. plus one line. So under normal circumstances, you can see in the window an area of the page that measures about four inches high by six inches wide.

If you divide 17 lines by 3.77 inches, you get 4.5 lines per inch. In other words, if you use the default selections of type style and size, you should be getting about 4.5 lines per inch. (Default settings are settings the Mac uses if you don't instruct it to use anything different.)

If you keep hitting the Return key until the cursor is at the bottom of the page, you'll notice that the last line is line 40. If you check the position coordinates, you see that the vertical distance from the top of the page is 9.9 inches. Now, to double check, subtract 1.24 inches (distance of Line 1 from top of page) from 9.9 inches (distance of Line 40 from top of page). That's 8.66 inches. Divide 39 lines by 8.66 inches; that gives you almost exactly 4.5 lines per inch.

The default top and bottom margins are set at 1.0 inch. If the last line of text is line 40, 9.9 inches from the top of the page, and you add the 1-inch bottom margin, you have a page 10.9 inches long. That rounds off to 11 inches—the standard length of a piece of business stationery.

You can see now that (according to *WordPerfect* running on a Mac) a page is 14 inches wide by 11 inches long, and you're looking at that page through a window that measures six inches wide by four inches long. The area of the window is 24 square inches; the area of the total page is 154 square inches. So at any one time you can see only 16 percent of the total page.

That's not as bad as it sounds, unless you are actually working with a 11 × 14 sheet of paper. If you're working with standard 8.5 × 11 sheets, the screen allows you to see 26 percent of the page. And if you consider the actual default text area, approximately 6 inches wide by 9 inches long, the screen allows you to see 44 percent of the working area.

Using the keyboard. Another improvement of the *WordPerfect* interface over the Desktop is that it offers more possibilities for use of the keyboard. In the early days of Macintosh, you could have divided the world into two kinds of people: keyboard people (PC users) and mouse people (Mac users). But evolution is bringing the two worlds together, and before long there may be a single standard keyboard/mouse interface that everyone will use. *WordPerfect* has gone a long way for the keyboard people: As mentioned above, nearly every function that can be carried out or accessed by the mouse can also be accomplished via keyboard commands.

All the main menu items that have keyboard options are accessed via a Command-Keypress command. All of the submenu items with keyboard options, however, are accessed via a command that has one more element: the Shift key, symbolized by an upward-pointing arrow. Consequently, after selecting the Date function from the main Special menu by typing Command-D, select Insert Function from the Date submenu by typing Command—D. In other words, while holding down the Command and Shift keys (either Shift key will do), tap *D*. Therefore, submenu keyboard commands always take the form Command—Keypress.

There are many more maneuvers you can perform via the keyboard. For a listing of most of them, see the Quick Reference pamphlet that came with your software. You should also check the *Getting Started* section of your *WordPerfect* manual for some more keyboard hints and shortcuts.

You'll come to use some combination of mouse commands and keyboard commands as your proficiency grows. It all depends on what you find most convenient.

Changing pointer functions. You discover something different about the pointer as you look at the opening *WordPerfect* screen. The pointer has now been overtaken by relativity: What it is depends upon where it is.

Around the top, right, and bottom edges of the screen, the pointer is still a pointer, used to select menus, drag scroll boxes, select font styles, and so on.

In the central area of the screen (the working area) the pointer becomes an I-beam (Figure 3-10), that helps you position the cursor a document. You'll see how that works as soon as you begin your first document.

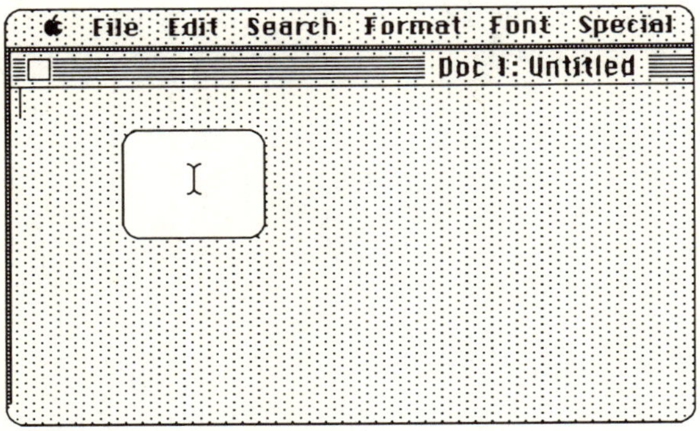

Figure 3-10. The pointer as an I-beam.

In the lower left-hand corner of your screen the pointer is changed into the word *GO*. (See Figure 3-11.)

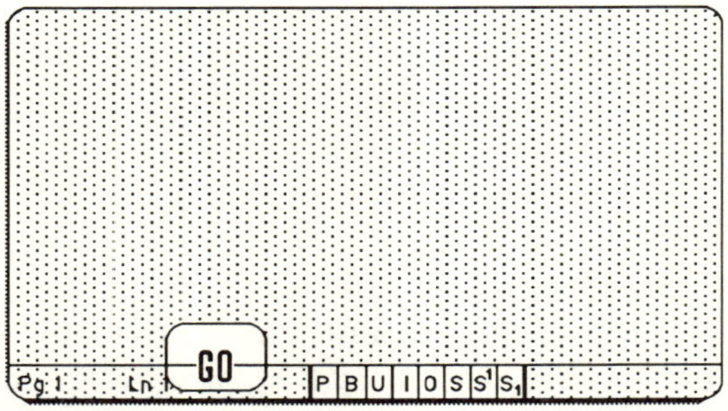

Figure 3-11. The pointer as the word GO. In this mode, it lets you move quickly to another specified page.

This is a quick search or relocation function that lets you move to another specified page. Click the mouse button when the pointer is in the GO mode. A dialog box will appear on your screen asking to what page you want to go, and giving you three choices:

- Type a page number and click the pointer on OK to confirm your selection.

- Click on Previous to move to the previous page.
- Click on Cancel, which tells the Mac that you're happy where you are and you don't want to go anywhere.

That just about covers the elements of *WordPerfect* that make its opening screen different from the opening Macintosh Desktop screen. You're about ready to get into your first *WordPerfect* document. But first, a brief digression about dialog boxes, which were mentioned in the previous paragraph.

The Dialog Box

On many occasions when you instruct the Mac to perform some function, it answers with a dialog box on the screen, full of questions and choices. It's a little like a conversation. You say *Do this,* and the Mac says, in effect, *Be more specific. How do you want me to do it? Here are your options.* The Mac also says, *Are you sure that's what you wanted to do? If you're not, click cancel, and nothing will be affected.*

Dialog boxes are very helpful and versatile, allowing you to do a great deal of work with a minimum of fuss. Let's take a look at one of the more involved dialog boxes, the File Management dialog box (Figure 3-12).

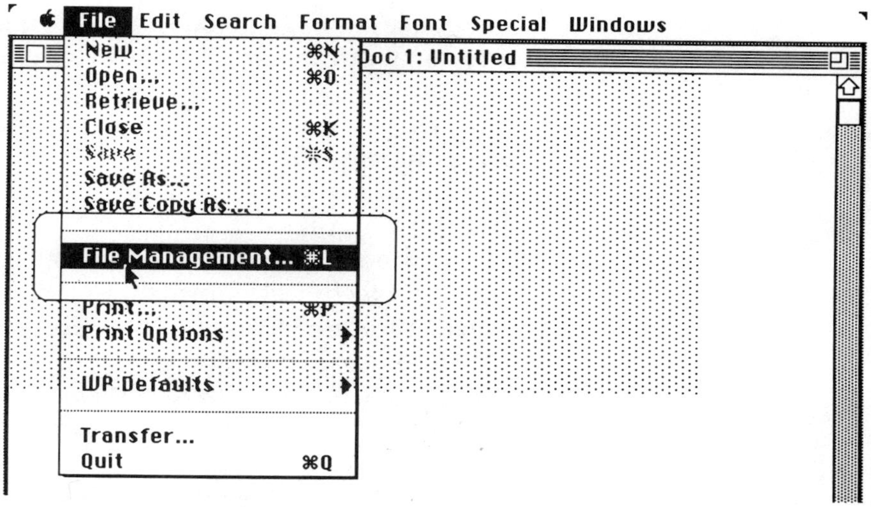

Figure 3-12. Selecting File Management . . . from the File menu.

Select File Management . . . from the File menu. (As you see, you can make the selection either by dragging down to File Management on the File menu, or by entering Command-L from the keyboard.)

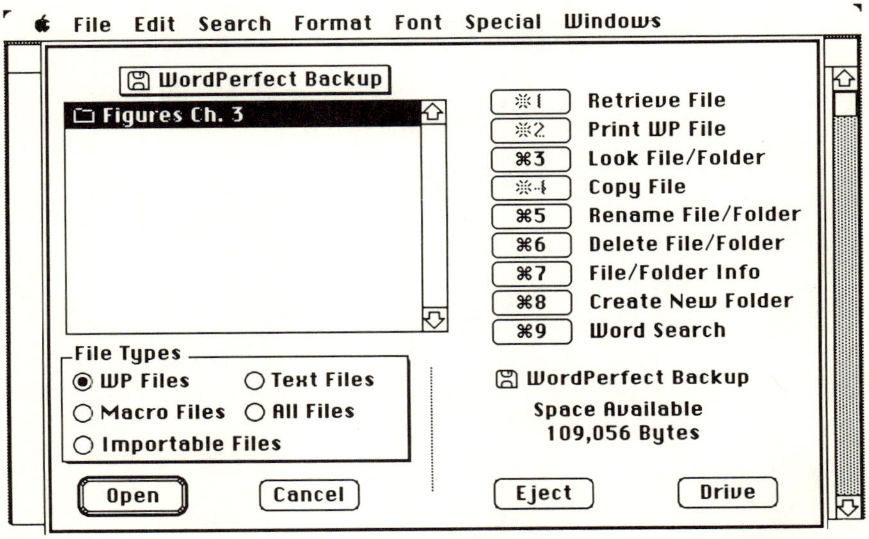

Figure 3-13. The File Management dialog box.

The File Management dialog box fills your screen. It allows you to carry out many different file management jobs:

- Deletes files
- Copies files
- Renames files
- Looks through files
- Tells you how much space is available on each disk
- Gives you technical information about each file
- Switches from one drive to another
- Ejects a disk
- Looks selectively at different types of files
- Prints a document

Since file management is such an important function and information resource, it deserves special attention.

File Management

As you look at the File Management dialog box on your screen or in Figure 3-13, you may not see very many files on the *WordPerfect* Backup disk. You simply may not have many files on this disk so far. The files on the disk are not *WordPerfect* files and for that reason are still hidden. Most of your files may be in folders, and all you can see in the file box right now are folder names.

Look at the lower left-hand corner of the File Management dialog box. You'll see a small box called File Types. In that box five file types are listed:

- WP Files
- Text Files
- Macro files
- Importable Files
- All Files

WP Files—WP files are *WordPerfect* documents or files which may be opened as *WordPerfect* documents. This is the default selection.

Text File—These are files that contain only ASCII characters, and none of the special characters used as formatting codes in word processing programs. This group might include files that were transmitted to you via a modem, or files created with another word processor and then stripped of the special, non-ASCII characters.

Macro Files—Macro files are the *WordPerfect* Macros or shortcuts that you create to make your work easier. You'll see more about Macros later in this book.

Importable Files—Importable files include all files that you can open or load in *WordPerfect.*

All Files—This means exactly what it says. It is a count of all files on the disk, no matter what kind.

What you see depends upon what you ask for. If you look at Figure 3-13 you can see that WP Files is indicated by the darkened circle. For this example, say the only item listed under *WordPerfect* Backup is a folder (full of *MacPaint* files) named Figures Ch. 3. When WP Files is specified, all folders are listed whether they contain *WordPerfect* document files or not. The Mac is telling you simply that there are some folders on the disk. You'll have to open them to see whether they contain *WordPerfect* documents.

Open the Figures Ch. 3 Folder by selecting Figures Ch. 3. Click anywhere on the folder icon or on the text itself. Click on the Open box in the lower left-hand corner of the dialog box.

The file box goes blank. Is the Figures Ch. 3 Folder empty? No. It simply has no *WordPerfect* files. Click on the circle next to Macro Files. Nothing happens. Nothing happens when you click on Importable Files and Text Files. Now click on the circle next to All Files. Suddenly the box is full of filenames. Since they are a special type of file, they show up only when you ask to see All Files.

Move the pointer to the Figures Ch. 3 title box and press the mouse button. It becomes a menu as shown in Figure 3-14. In effect, this menu is a toggle switch that lets you move back and forth between a Folder listing (what you see when the heading is Figures Ch. 3) and a disk listing (when the heading is *WordPerfect* Backup).

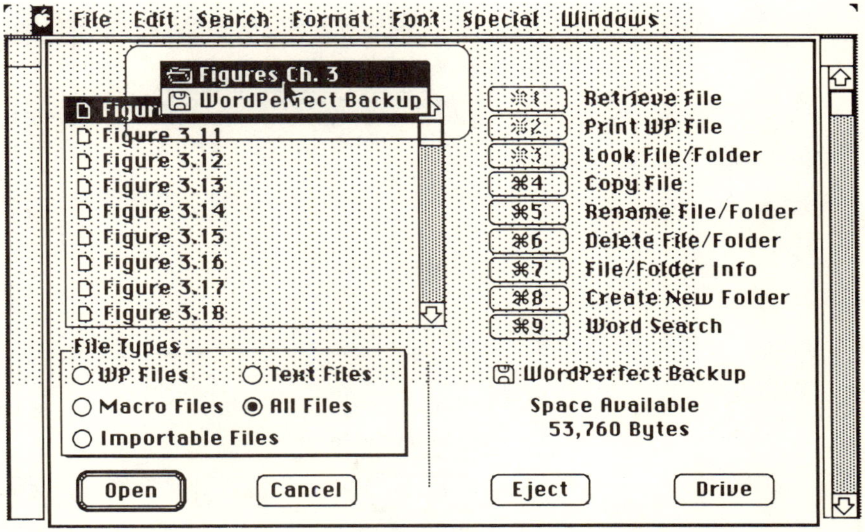

Figure 3-14. The menu that allows you to toggle between a Folder listing and a disk listing.

If you drag the pointer down to select *WordPerfect* Backup and release, you return to the disk listing. This time, however, the box is full of filenames, since All Files is still selected under File Types.

If you look at the right side of the File Management dialog box, you see a list of *action options.* By selecting an action option, you cause a change in the file.

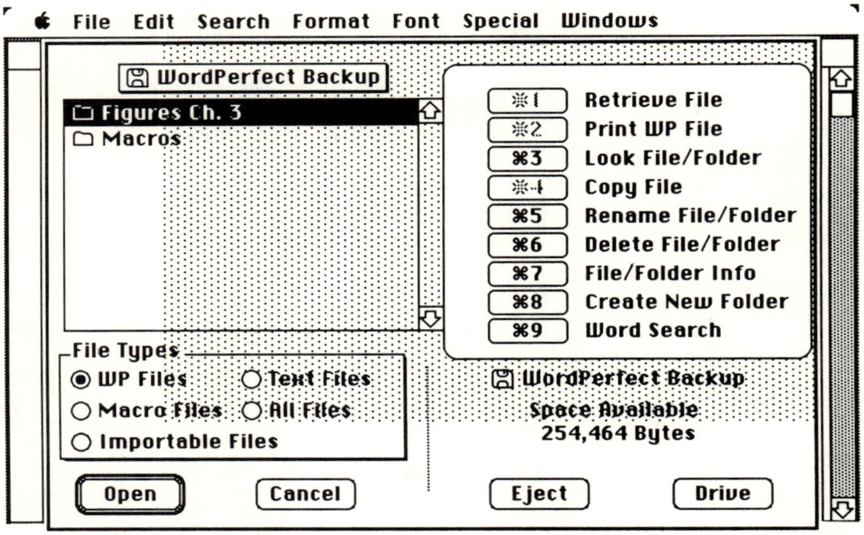

Figure 3-15. The action list in the File Management dialog box.

Notice that some of the choices are in dark type and some are shaded. Only the choices in dark type are available for any selected file.

For example, in Figure 3-16 you will notice that the Desktop file is selected and choices 1–3 are all in gray type. That means that your only action options are choices 4–9.

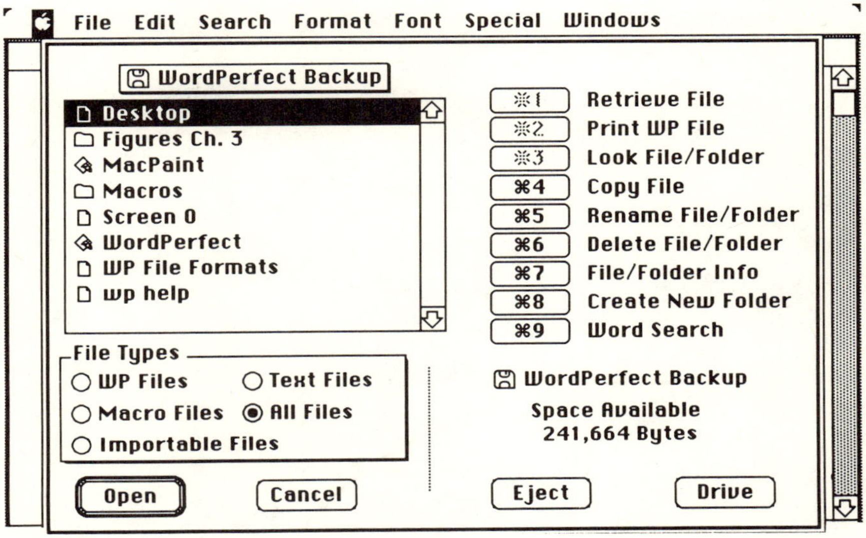

Figure 3-16. With the Desktop file selected, choices 1–3 are in shaded type and are therefore unavailable for this selection.

On the other hand, if you select another folder, you may see an entirely different selection of available options. The type of file determines what you may do with it.

To illustrate how these action options work, let's select the file titled Screen 0 and rename it. Screen 0 happens to be a *screen dump* (a picture of what the screen looks like at a given moment). To rename it so it's called Figure 3-13, click on the option that reads Rename File/Folder (or you may enter Command-5 on the keyboard).

Another dialog box will appear, asking what new name to give to the file now called Screen 0. It also provides you with the opportunity to Cancel if you make a mistake or change your mind. Type in *Figure 3-13* and click on OK. When you return to the file listing, you see there no longer is a file named Screen 0. It has been renamed to Figure 3-13.

The other choices or action options work in similar fashion. You'll see them in use as they become necessary.

In the next chapter you'll start getting some work done. Click on Cancel to return to the text screen.

Chapter 4

Writing with *WordPerfect:* The Business Letter

Chapter 4

Writing with *WordPerfect:* The Business Letter

After completing Chapter 3, you know your way around the main menus and screen maneuvers of *WordPerfect*. Since this book intends to help you get to work as quickly as possible, no more time is going to be spent learning features. Instead, let's jump ahead to the most common word processing job in the workplace: the business letter.

The features you need will be covered as you go along. By the time you get to the end of this chapter, you'll know how to use a surprising number of *WordPerfect* features. In addition, you may pick up a few tips on good business communications as a special bonus.

Getting Started

Here is a review of the steps necessary to get *WordPerfect* rolling on the Macintosh:

Step 1. Turn on the Macintosh.
Step 2. Insert the System Backup disk into the internal disk drive.
Step 3. Insert the backup *WordPerfect* program disk into the external disk drive.
Step 4. Click on the *WordPerfect* icon to select it, then open *WordPerfect* by selecting Open from the File menu.

For the moment, don't worry about details like formatting, placement of the date, the address block, the size of your letterhead, and so on. Let's just start typing to get a feel of how this program puts text on the page.

So you'll have something to work with, you're going to write a letter to Frank Lupo, chief executive officer of Worldwide Wigwams. The text follows. Just copy this right onto your Mac:

Dear Mr. Lupo:

As corporate travel manager for Wanton Widgets, Inc., I am responsible for the booking overseeing of travel arrangements and expenses for all employees at our seven locastions in the U.S. and Puerto Rico.

I recently watched a program on the nationally syndicated TV show, "Now Cut That Out!" which focused on the hotels owned by Worldwide Wigwams, Inc. and some allegations made by chambermaids, bellhops and other people in or close to the hotel industry to the effect that in order to cut expenditures and improve your profit margi, WWI has been skimping on service and amenities. As a result, guests are being shortsheeted, the genuine English muffins are being replaced with chaep imitations from the Pacific Rim, and at least some of the people interviewed on the show feel that Worldwide Wigwams is courting financial disaster.

Your response to these allegations was that WWI does not take shortcuts to save dollars or to increase the occupancy rate, and that the people making the allegations were a bunch of union agitatoors
or other distyruntled eimployees with personal axes to grint.

Now Frank, I hopw you're telling the truth, and that the comfort of your guests is Worldwide Wigwams' number one priority. There is another matter, however, that I wish to discuss with you that I am very concerned about, and it is a matter that few people have spoken about. I refer to the your evening turndown and after-dinner mint program.

There has been a fair amount of publicity lately about the English muffin substitutions and the mounting liability your chain is icurring as guests injure themselves jumping into short-sheeted beds. There has been alomost no publicity, however, about what the turndown-and-after-dinner-mint (TDADM) practice is custing American Ccompanies—and that cost is substantial.

At our company, for example, we estimate that the TDADM practice has aded 17% to our corporate travel bill. This added cost comes from a number of factors:

. Reduced efficiency of our traveling employees who lose sleep because of the caffeine in the after-dinner mints;

. Loss of key clients because our employees show up for crucial meetings with chocolate in their ears (they didn't notice it on their pillows).

We have tried to institute controls, stipulating, for example, that employees take the most economical travel options and that they turn all dinner mints over to the company. The program is so addictive, however, that none of our ppolicies have proven easy to enforce. While this may seem the result of clever marketing to you, I can assure you that Worldwide Wigwams and the other major hotel chains are building up quite an acocount of ill will and resentment, and that this pent-up resentment will boil over at a time when you most need our support.

I suggest that you take one of two actions: eigher stop the protgrams before they do further damage to your industry and to the Ame5rican economy, or switch to carob or decaffeinated chocolate.

Like you, we support the idea of free markets and open competition. But we cannot endure a situation where you are permitted to gouge your captive clientele with impunity, while driving competition out of the market with anti-competitive practices that they cannot afford. If you and your industry colleagues can't bring yourselves to find a just remedy for the TDADM problem, we will be compelled to join the rising cry for chocolate regulation and warning labels on all dinner mints. We would rather not do that.

Sincerely,
Odysseus Voyageur
Corporate Travel Manager

That's a truly horrible letter. It's prolix and full of mistakes, but that's perfectly all right. The great thing about writing with a word processor is that you can put words down at will, without concerning yourself about whether they are spelled right or whether they make your point effectively. You don't have to struggle to attain perfection (or near perfection) on the first or second draft. With a good word processing program it's easy to correct mistakes and move text around.

Saving Your Work

Saving a File

Let's jump into that mess and straighten it out. But first, save a copy of the original so later on, if you want to return to its virgin form you can do so. Let's call the file *Lupo Draft.* Here's how to save the file:

Step 1. Pull down the File menu and select Save As . . .

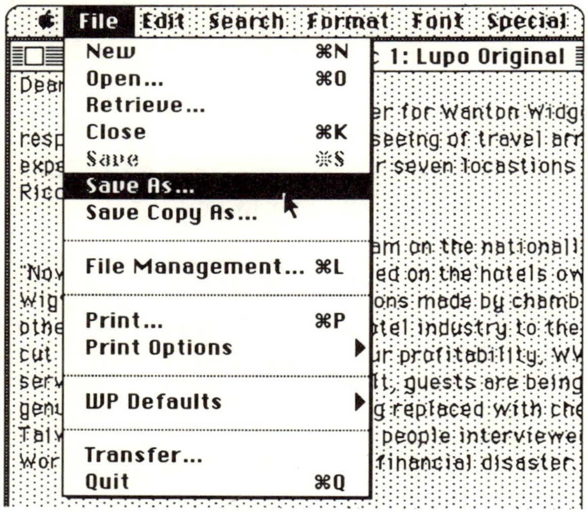

Figure 4-1. The File menu with Save As . . . selected.

Step 2. When the Save As . . . Dialog Box appears on your monitor, you will see that the box under *Save Document As:* has been selected.

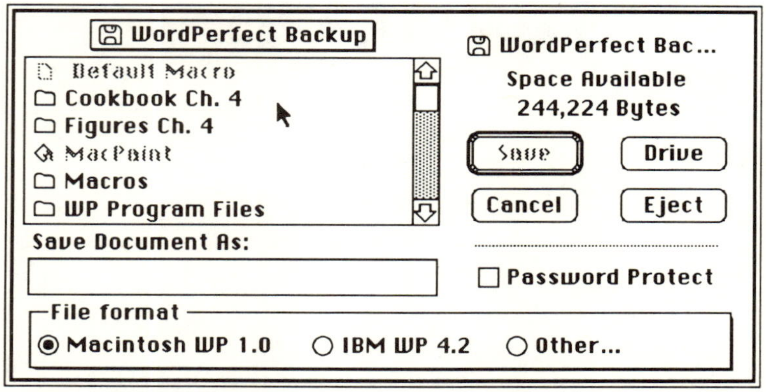

Figure 4-2. The Save As . . . Dialog Box, ready for the name of this file.

Type in *Lupo Draft.*

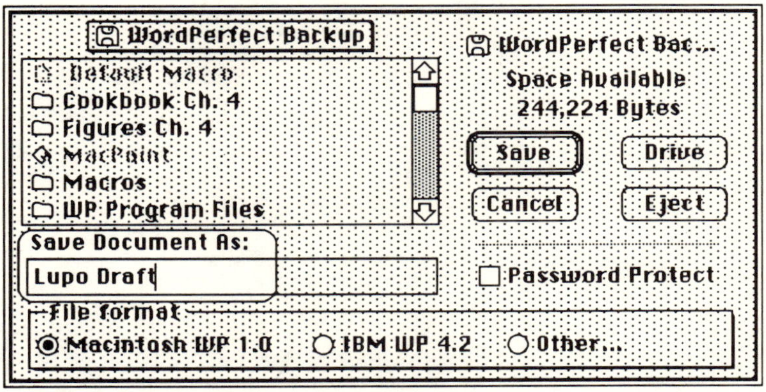

Figure 4-3. The Save As . . . Dialog Box after you type in the title Lupo Draft.

Step 3. Click on Save in the Dialog Box. You will be returned to the document, which will now be titled *Doc 1: Lupo Draft*.

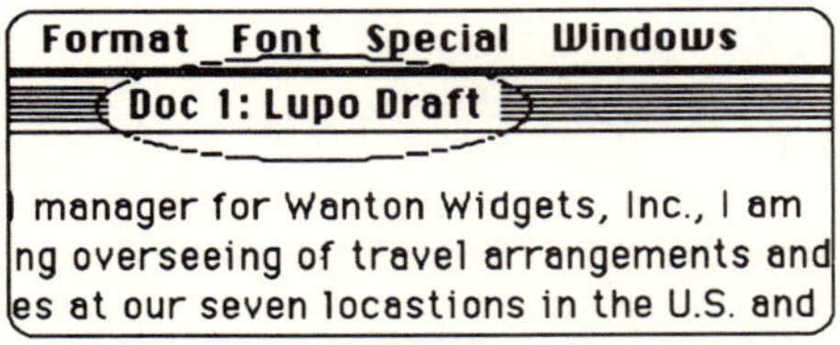

Figure 4-4. The first draft of your letter with its new name: Doc 1: Lupo Draft.

Introduction to Simple Editing

Now that a draft is saved to disk, it's time to eliminate all those misspellings and typos. (Later on you'll see how to use the Speller utility to check and correct spelling; for now, however, let's just do it manually.)

Deleting Text

How to delete. The first typo is in the word *locastions*. You'll want to delete the first *s*. With the mouse, move the pointer to the point between the *s* and the *t* and click the mouse button. This places the blinking cursor at that position.

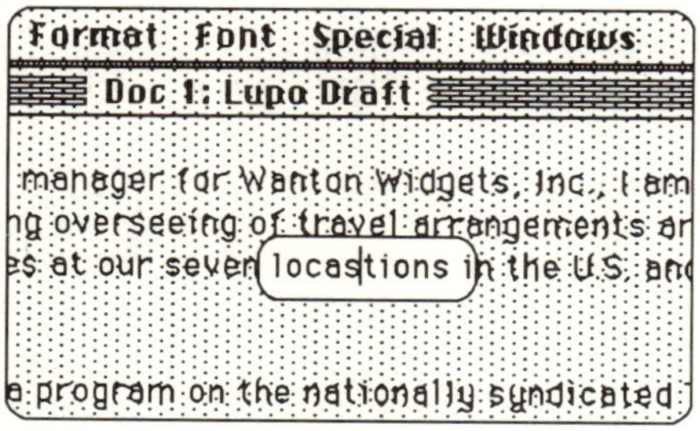

Figure 4-5. The cursor placed after the offending letter in *locastions.* When you hit the Delete (or Backspace) key, it will be deleted.

Now simply hit the Delete (or Backspace) key and the letter is deleted and the word closes up.

Inserting Text

How to insert. Next, correct the word *margi* by placing the cursor after the *i* and typing in the letter *n*. The text should shift to accommodate the inserted letter. You have the choice of whether to use insert mode (which shifts text to accommodate additional writing) or typeover mode (which allows you to type over existing text). These modes are toggled by selecting Typeover on the Edit menu. When a check mark appears beside the Typeover selection, you are in typeover mode. Otherwise, you are in insert mode.

Replacing Text

How to replace a selected block. The next typo is in the word *chaep.* A simple insertion or deletion won't do here. You have to reverse the order of the letters *ae. WordPerfect* makes it easy to replace one block of text with another. Select or highlight the block you want to replace. Selecting a block is as simple as everything else on the Macintosh. Simply click the mouse button with the pointer ahead of the first character in the block and hold the button down as you drag the pointer to the space just beyond the last letter in the block.

When the block is selected, just start typing the new block without doing anything else. The program deletes the old block and substitutes whatever you type.

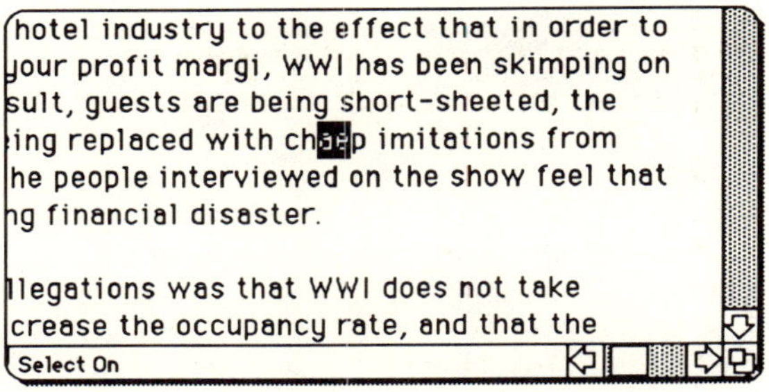

Figure 4-6. The word *chaep* with the *ae* selected for deletion and replacement.

Type *ea.* That's all there is to it. Typing deletes the selected block and replaces it with *ea.*

When you run into larger blocks to delete and replace, you'll see just how convenient this feature can be.

Correct the spelling of *agitatoors* by positioning the cursor after either of the *o's* and hitting the Delete (or Backspace) key.

Correct the typo in *distyruntled,* using the same procedure you used to correct *chaep.* Select the letters *ty* by the click-and-drag method. Type a *g.*

Go through the rest of the letter and correct the other misspellings. For now, only correct misspellings. You'll come back to the other errors when you're finished.

You have now finished making all those corrections. Let's go back now and make some additional small corrections before you get into the big stuff.

How to Use Show Codes

In the fourth paragraph, there is that curious space after *Worldwide Wigwams'*. A break like this usually means that you inadvertently hit the Return key and inserted a carriage return or *hard return* into the text. To find out for sure, look at the coded instructions inserted into the text.

Showing Formatting Codes

To look at the codes, select Show Codes from the Edit menu.

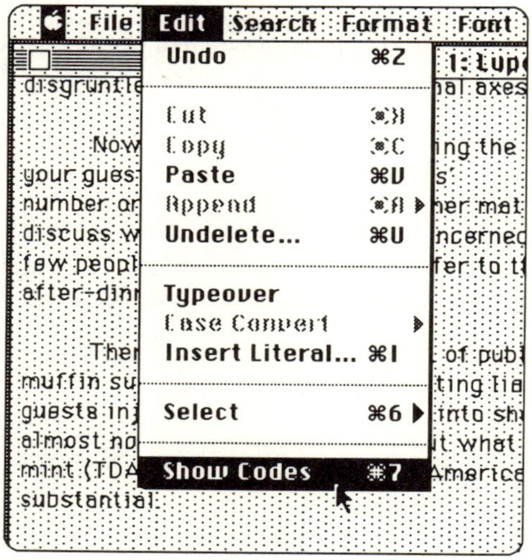

Figure 4-7. Selecting Show Codes from the Edit menu.

If you look at the portion of your monitor screen under the status line, you will see the first few lines of your letter. You will also see a number of unfamiliar symbols. These symbols are icons for the codes inserted into your document invisibly to tell the computer what to do. The code icons (from now on they'll be called *codes* instead of code icons) include the cursor (represented by a black rectangle), a space (the small diamond), and a hard return or carriage return.

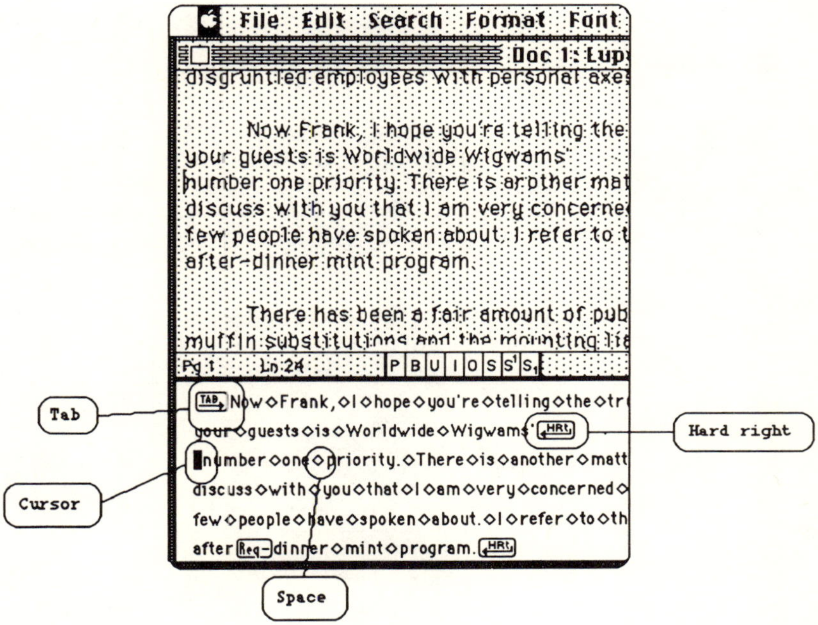

Figure 4-8. The screen with codes revealed. Note the codes for the cursor, a space, and a hard right.

To find out what's going on in the Worldwide Wigwams' line, scroll down to it and position the cursor immediately after *Worldwide Wigwams'*. Where the codes are shown, you see the hard right (or hard return) code (HRt) next to the cursor symbol. As suspected, that's the problem.

Figure 4-9. The cursor symbol and the hard return code following *Wigwams'*.

The solution is simple: Move the cursor one space to the right (or whatever you have to do to position the cursor to the right of the HRt code), then hit the Delete (or Backspace) key and add a space.

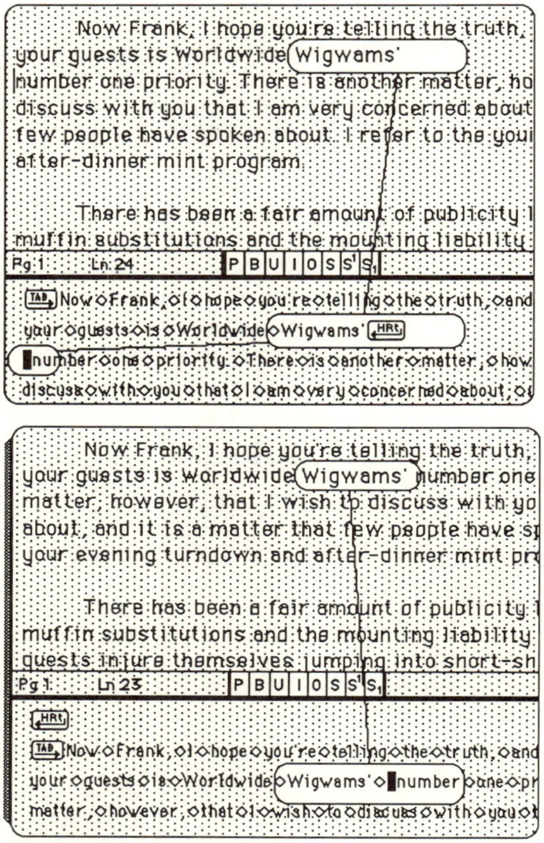

Figures 4-10 and 4-11. The text and the codes before and after the extra hard return is deleted.

As you see, that solves the problem.

Troubleshooting and error-correcting by working through the revealed codes is one of the handiest procedures you can master. Frequently things happen on the screen that seem to make no sense. If you can't imagine how they got that way, or how to straighten them out, call up the codes and you will see exactly what and where the problem is.

You'll see much more about the codes as you go along.

To make the codes go away, select Hide Codes from the Edit menu.

More Simple Editing

Continuing through the letter, find the sentence that reads *I refer to the your evening turndown and after-dinner-mint program.* Most people will read that sentence and completely miss the error. It's the kind of error easily skipped over in a quick proofreading job, and an error against which the Speller utility is powerless. The error is the word *the.*

Select and delete. Here's how to remove any character, word or phrase, no matter how long:

Step 1. Select the item or passage you want to delete. Since you have already seen how to select an item through the click-and-drag method, you'll use a different gimmick this time. Position the cursor immediately in front of the *t* in *the.*

Step 2. Choose Select On from the Select submenu of the Edit menu or press Command-Shift-N.

Step 3. With the cursor movement keys, move the cursor to the right three spaces until all of the word and the space following it are selected.

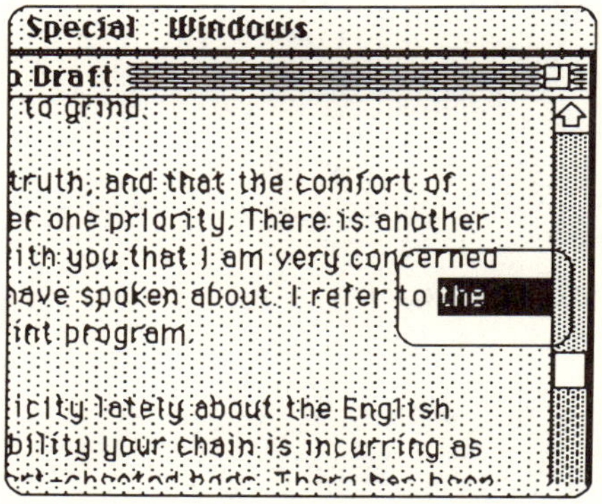

Figure 4-12. The extra word selected for deletion.

Step 4. Press the Delete (or Backspace) key.

Major Editing

That takes care of the smaller editing problems. But what about the larger maneuvers required to accomplish the kind of editing that will make the letter sound better?

This letter needs major work. Let's mark the problem passages, starting from the beginning. But how do you get to the beginning? Return to the "top" of the document in at least four ways:

Moving to the Top of Text

- Use the Go to . . . function.
- Use the status line.
- Use the keyboard, press Enter, Enter, Up Arrow (this shortcut doesn't work on some Macintoshes).
- Use the scroll box on the right-hand side of the screen.

Use the Go to . . . function.

Step 1. Select Go to . . . from the Search menu (or type Command-G).

Figure 4-13. Selecting Go to . . . from the Search menu.

Step 2. Type *1* (the number of the page to which you want to go) into the Go to . . . dialog box.

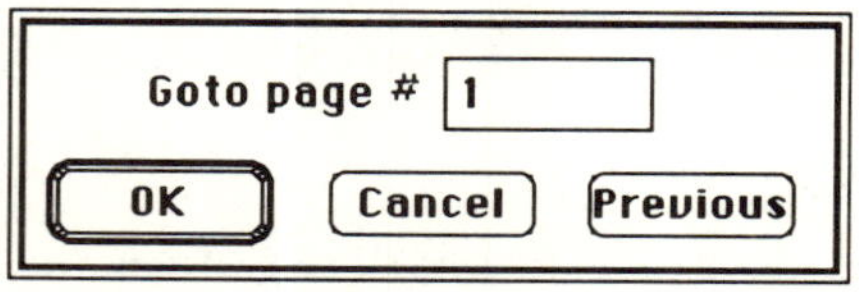

Figure 4-14. The Go to . . . dialog box with page number 1 entered.

Step 3. Click on OK in the Go to . . . dialog box or hit the Return key.

Using the status line. Move the pointer into the status line in the lower left-hand corner of the screen and click the mouse button when the pointer turns into the word GO. Then proceed as in Steps 2 and 3.

Using the keyboard. Press Enter, Enter, Up Arrow. (This may not work on some Macintoshes.)

Use the scroll box on the right-hand side of the screen. Move the pointer to the scroll box on the right-hand side of the screen. Hold the mouse button down and pull the scroll box all the way to the top of the scroll bar.

The Macintosh and most successful programs written for it are so friendly that you will often find many procedures can be accomplished in several different ways, and almost all procedures can be accomplished using either the keyboard or the mouse. There is no best way. The best way for you is usually what you find most convenient at the moment.

Now you are back at the beginning of the document. Let's turn from proofreading to editing and walk through this letter quickly to see how you might improve it, and how *WordPerfect* makes editing easier.

First, identify and mark the problems before you attempt to correct them.

As editor, you are going to want to make some cuts and additions, and move some things around. Use *Strikout* where you think words, phrases, or passages should be deleted or changed. Where you think additions should be made, indicate that they are tentative by using *Redline.* Let's see what that means:

How to use Redline. First, the letter takes too long to get to the point. It's important to get your message right up front. So let's Redline a new first paragraph.

Using Redlines

Step 1. Position the cursor at the beginning of the first paragraph.

Step 2. Select Characters . . . from the pull-down Format menu.

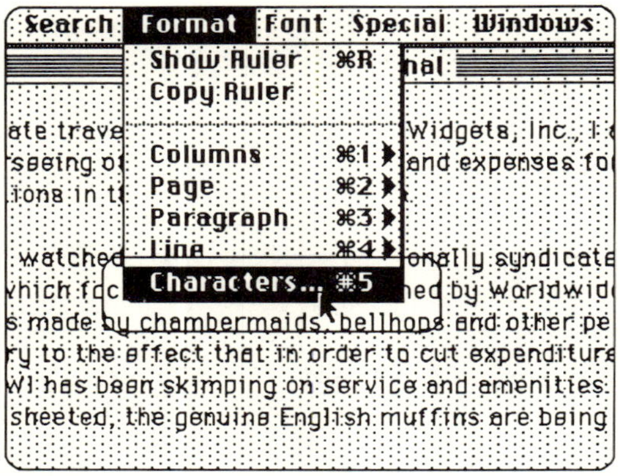

Figure 4-15. Selecting Characters . . . from the Format menu.

Step 3. Click on Redline in the Characters . . . dialog box.

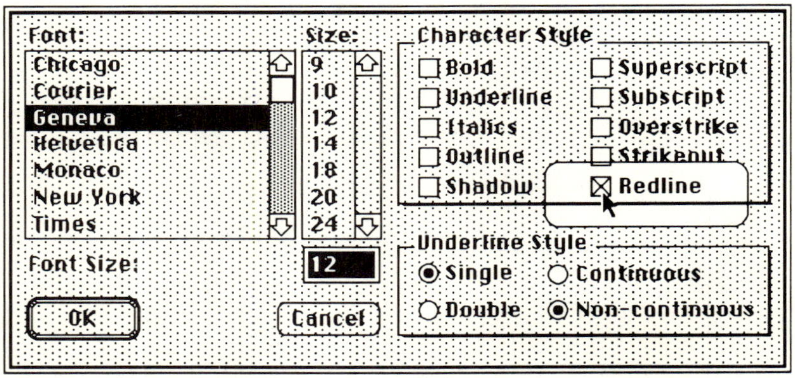

Figure 4-16. Choosing Redline in the Characters . . . dialog box.

Step 4. Click on OK in the Characters . . . dialog box to return to the letter.

Step 5. Start typing the text with which you want to replace the first paragraph. You will now see a dark vertical line at the left-hand margin of each line of new text you add.
Here's the text to type:

> As far as the business community is concerned, your evening turndown and after-dinner-mint program is a Trojan horse. It looks like a gift, but it's costing us a bundle. We want you to do something about it.

Then hit a Right Arrow (to get you out of the Redline mode) and two Returns.

You see that the Redline mark extends along the left-hand margin of that whole paragraph.

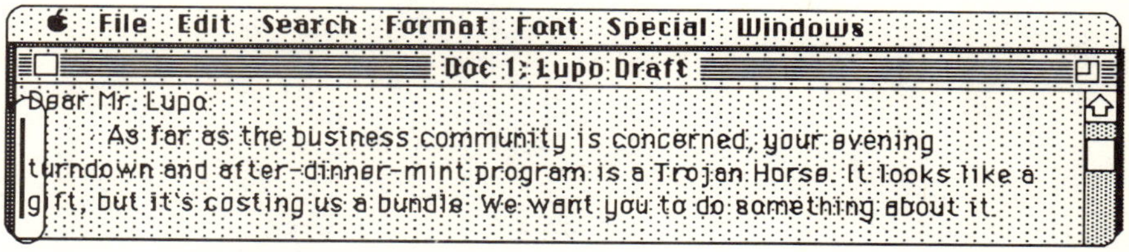

Figure 4-17. The dark vertical line indicating that the text in the line it marks is proposed and tentative.

How to use Strikeout. In the first paragraph of the original letter, the clause beginning *I am responsible . . .* is a mess. You should strike it out for later revision. Here are the steps:

Using Strikeout

Step 1. Select the clause by positioning the cursor in front of the *I*, pressing the mouse button, dragging the cursor to the end of the paragraph, and releasing the button.

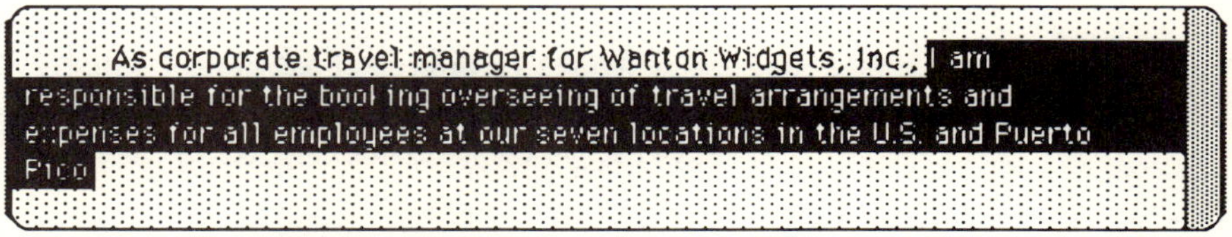

Figure 4-18. The problem clause selected for Strikeout.

Step 2. Select Characters . . . from the Format menu.

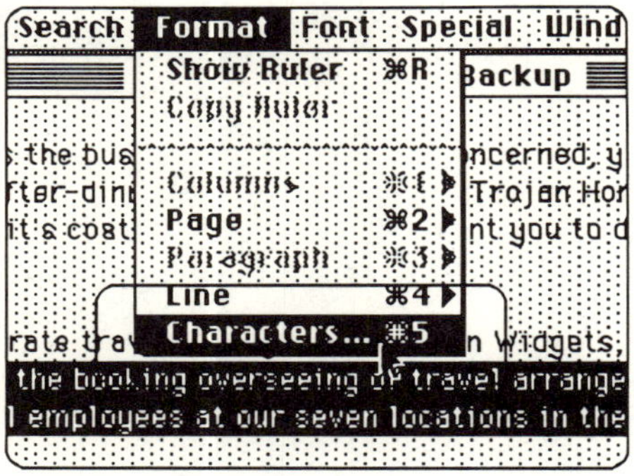

Figure 4-19. Selecting Characters . . . from the Format menu.

Step 3. Click on Strikeout in the Characters . . . dialog box.

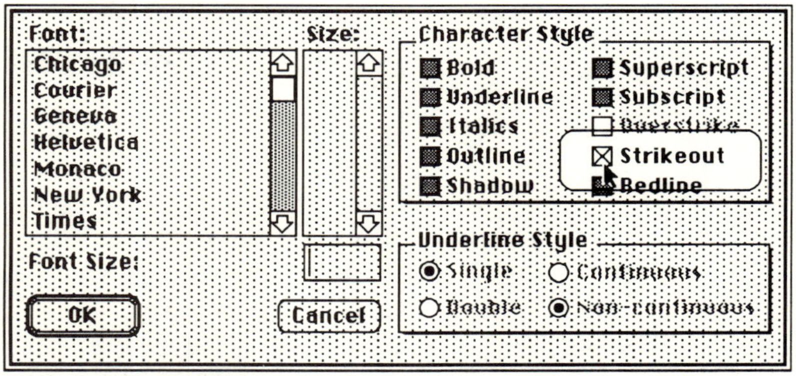

Figure 4-20. The Characters . . . dialog box with Strikeout selected.

Step 4. Click OK in the dialog box. When you're returned to the letter, the selected passage will have a line through it.

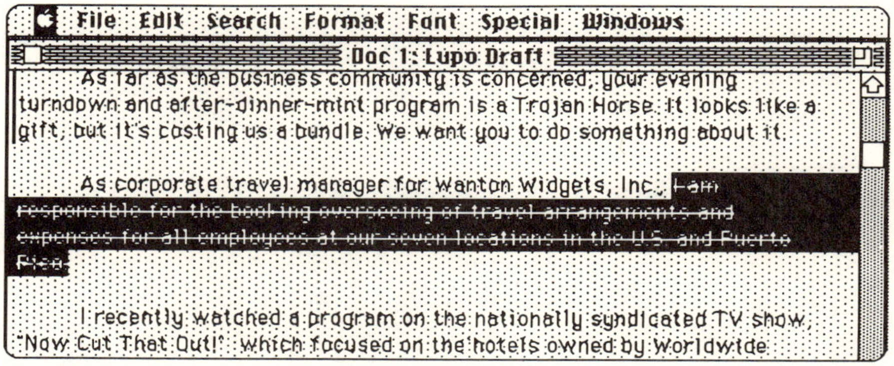

Figure 4-21. The selected passage marked for Strikeout.

In the next paragraph, Strikeout the first sentence, beginning, *I recently watched . . ..* The steps are just the same as above: (1) Select the sentence by the click-and-drag method; (2) Select Characters . . . from the Format menu; (3) Click on Strikeout in the Characters . . . dialog box; (4) Click on OK to return to the text.

In the paragraph beginning *you have tried to institute . . .,* strike out the word *stipulating.* It just doesn't sound right, and you'll have to check on its exact meaning.

Finally, strike out the second sentence of the final paragraph: *But you cannot endure . . ..* What you cannot endure is purple prose about abusing your clientele with impunity.

Now return to the beginning of the letter and straighten out a few things. The Redlined paragraph is a much better opening; it's what the letter is really about. Keep it. Later you'll make it a permanent addition.

In the next paragraph, redline a new clause:

Step 1. Position the cursor in front of the *I* in *I am responsible . . ..*
Step 2. From the Format menu, select Characters . . . and click on Redline.
Step 3. Type *I book travel and oversee T&E expenses for all employees at our seven locations in the U.S. and Puerto Rico.*

In the next paragraph, let's tighten up that first sentence that you've struck out. Activate Redline as above, position the cursor at the beginning of the paragraph, and type:

> In a recent edition of the nationally syndicated TV show, "Now Cut That Out!," that focused on the hotels owned by Worldwide Wigwams, Inc., chambermaids, bellhops, and other people in or close to the hotel industry alleged that WWI has been skimping on service and amenities in order to cut expenditures and improve your profit margin.

The next paragraph isn't bad. Just delete the word *other* in front of *disgruntled employees,* since the *union agitators* may not necessarily be employees.

In the paragraph beginning *Now Frank,* you can give the first sentence a bit more bite by cutting some of it. Strike out the following: *you're telling the truth, and that.* Simply Select the passage, and activate Strikeout as above.

How to italicize. Now you'll make a new move. Let's give the sentence emphasis by putting the word *is* in italics. Since the word is already on the screen, simply select it and turn on italics:

Changing Type Style

Step 1. Select *is* by clicking twice on the word.

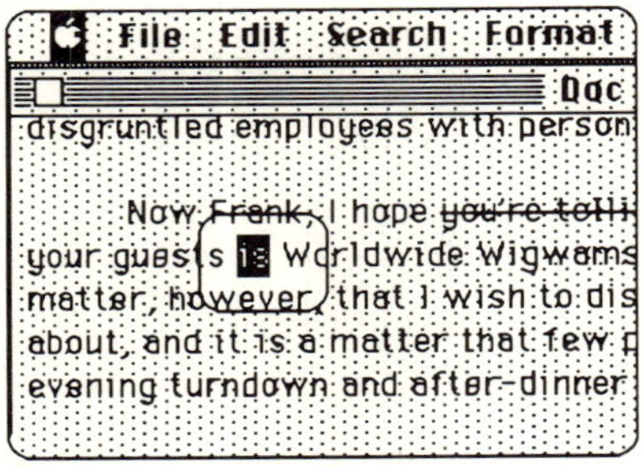

Figure 4-22. The word *is* selected for italicizing.

Step 2. Click on the letter *I* in the status line at the bottom of the screen.

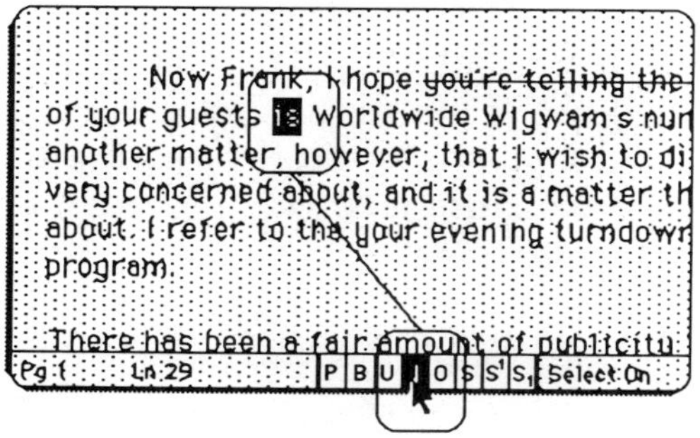

Figure 4-23. Selecting *I* (for *Italics*) on the status line.

The word *is* (still Selected) appears in italics. So does the *I* in the status line.

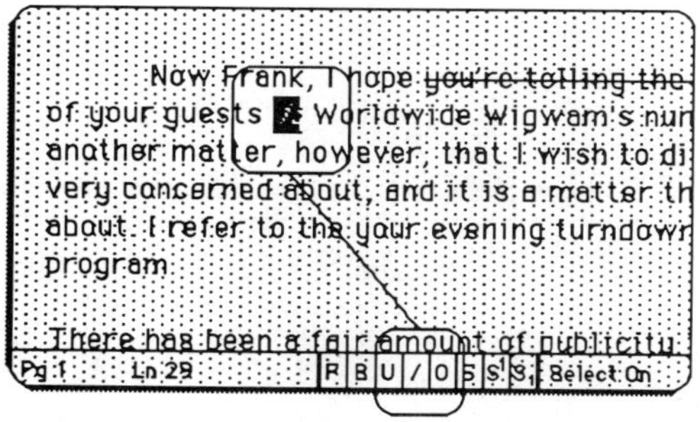

Figure 4-24. The word *is* after selecting italics in the status line.

Step 3. Click the mouse button to "deselect" the word *is*.

Select and replace. To reduce wordiness in the next paragraph, you can replace the first part of the first sentence with a shorter phrase. Use the Select-and-Replace technique.

Step 1. Select the clause *There has been a fair amount of publicity lately about*. Use a different selecting technique this time:

- Position the cursor before the first word of the clause.
- Turn on Select by typing Command-Shift-N. Notice the highlighted Select On that appears in the status line (Figure 4-25).
- Move the cursor to the right, using the Right-Arrow key until the entire clause is selected or highlighted (Figure 4-26).

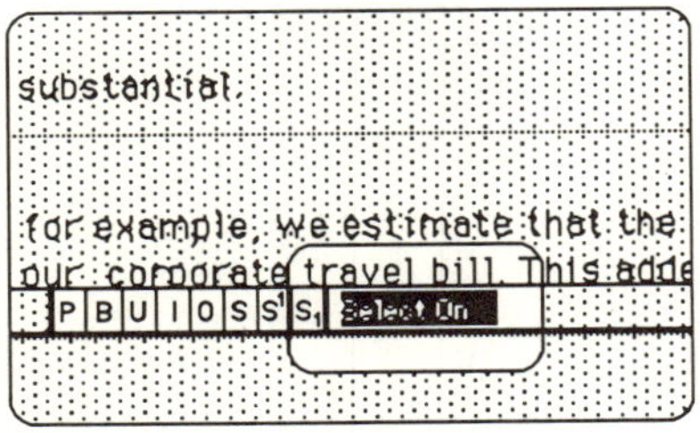

Figure 4-25. After pressing Command-Shift-N, Select On appears in the status line.

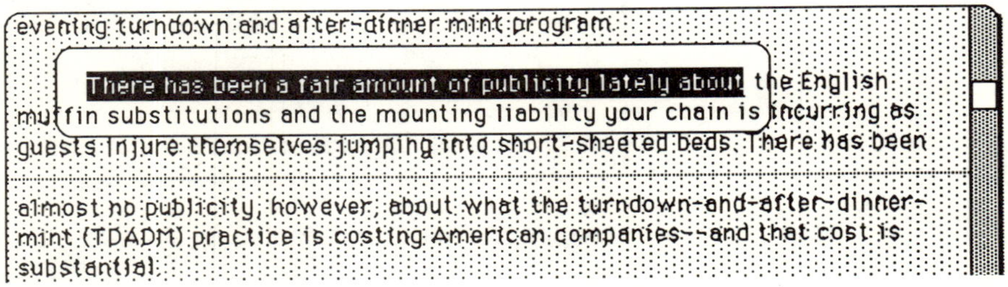

Figure 4-26. The clause you want to replace has been selected.

Step 2. Type the phrase *Recent news stories focus on*. That will replace the clause. Note that as soon as you start typing, the selected clause disappears and the words you are typing take its place.

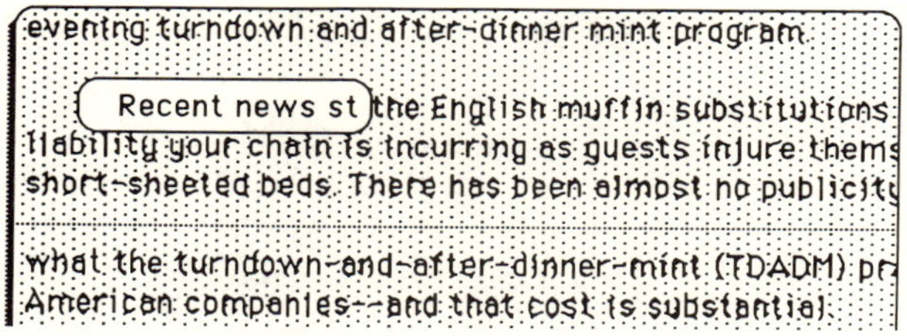

Figure 4-27. As you begin typing, the selected clause is deleted and the characters you are typing appear in its place.

Now it is an intelligent, forceful paragraph.

Cut and Paste. You should move some things around. The original lead paragraph (the paragraph that begins, *As corporate travel manager . . .*) should go between the fifth and sixth paragraphs. The simplest way to move a paragraph is with Cut and Paste:

Step 1. Select that paragraph beginning *As corporate travel manager . . .*. Be sure you have included all codes. You can do that by positioning the cursor in the first line of the paragraph, then pressing Enter, Enter, Enter, Left Arrow (if this doesn't work on your Macintosh, press Left Arrow repeatedly). This puts the cursor at the extreme left end of the line, before any codes. Pull down the Edit menu and release the mouse button on Paragraph in the Select submenu.

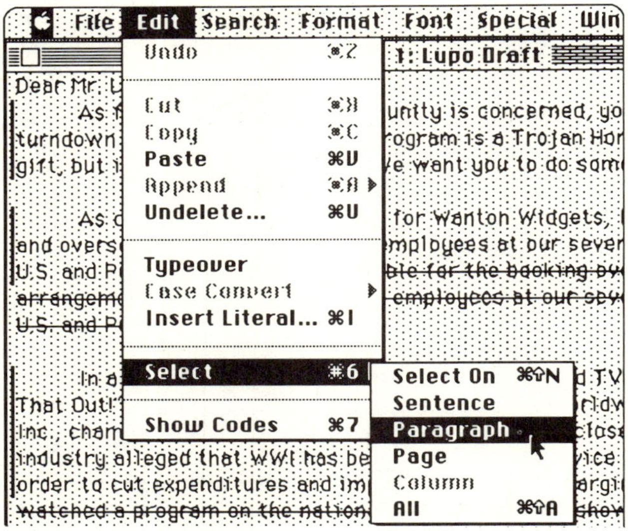

Figure 4-28. Choosing Paragraph from the Select submenu of the Edit menu.

This selects the entire paragraph you want to move.

Step 2. Select Cut from the Edit menu.

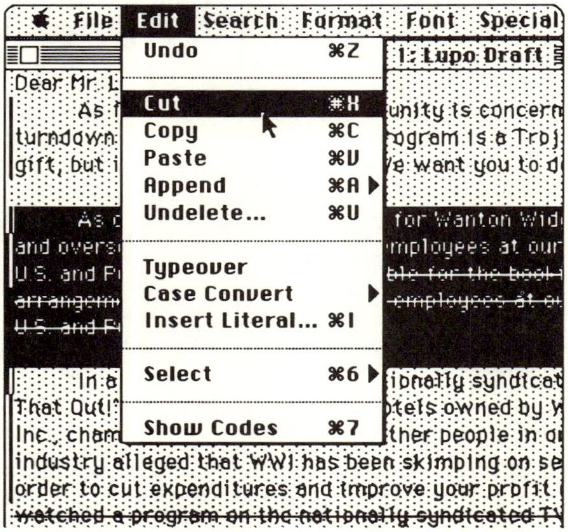

Figure 4-29. Selecting Cut from the Edit menu.

When the pull-down menu disappears, the paragraph is gone. But the Mac doesn't forget it. That paragraph, along with the two previous cuts you made, will be held in the Mac's Clipboard, and can be restored with the Undelete function.

Examining Contents of Clipboard

Looking at the Clipboard. To confirm that our paragraph hasn't disappeared, pull down the Windows menu and select Show Clipboard.

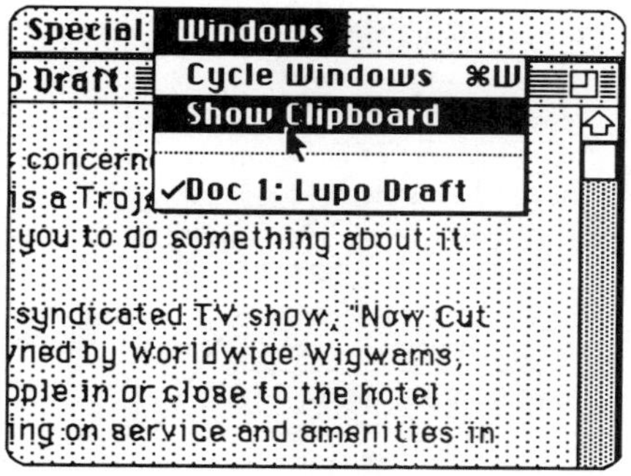

Figure 4-30. Selecting Show Clipboard from the Windows menu.

When you release the mouse button, the Clipboard window appears at the bottom of the screen with the text of the deleted paragraph displayed in code form.

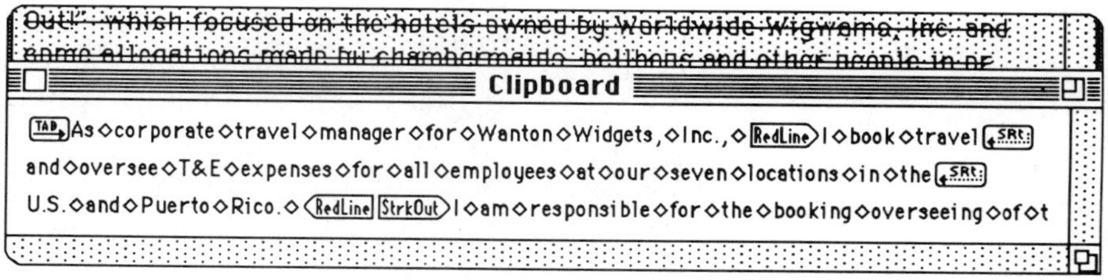

Figure 4-31. The Clipboard window with the text from the deleted paragraph.

It's time to paste the text in place. Close the Clipboard window by clicking in the Close Box. Now let's paste that paragraph in front of the one that begins *At our company, . . .*:

Step 1. Position the cursor at the beginning of the paragraph that begins *At our company, ...*
Step 2. Select Paste from the Edit menu.

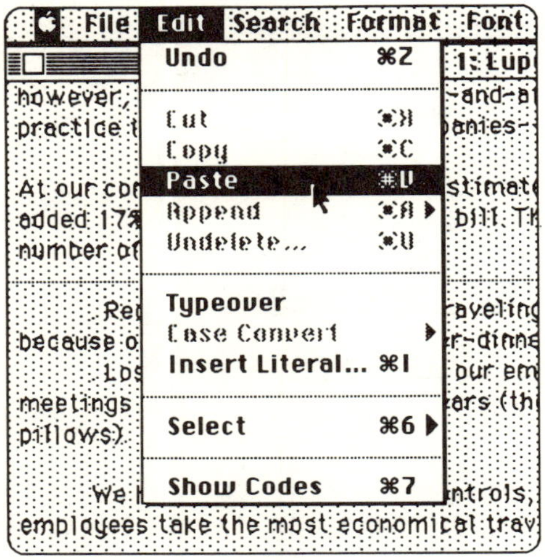

Figure 4-32. Selecting Paste from the Edit menu.

When you release the mouse button, the paragraph will be where you want it.

You should now attach the next paragraph. Try deleting the space between the sentence marked for strikeout *(I am responsible for . . .)* and the first sentence of the following paragraph.

Step 1. Position the cursor in the last line of the Struckout sentence after *Puerto Rico.* Then press Enter, Enter, Right Arrow. (If this doesn't work on your Macintosh, simply press the Right-Arrow key repeatedly.)
Step 2. Press Command-Shift-N to turn on Select.
Step 3. Using the Arrow keys, extend the selected area up to the beginning of the next sentence.

As corporate travel manager for Wanton Widgets, Inc., I book travel and oversee T&E expenses for all employees at our seven locations in the U.S. and Puerto Rico. ~~I am responsible for the booking overseeing of travel arrangements and expenses for all employees at our seven locations in the U.S. and Puerto Rico.~~

At our company, for example, we estimate that the TDADM practice has added 17% to our corporate travel bill. This added cost comes from a number of factors:

Figure 4-33. The space between the two sentences selected for deletion.

Step 4. Choose Cut from the Edit menu. When the text returns, the space has been removed.

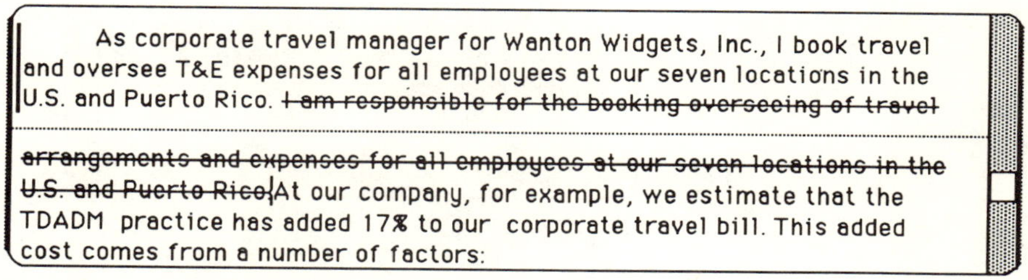
As corporate travel manager for Wanton Widgets, Inc., I book travel and oversee T&E expenses for all employees at our seven locations in the U.S. and Puerto Rico. ~~I am responsible for the booking overseeing of travel arrangements and expenses for all employees at our seven locations in the U.S. and Puerto Rico.~~At our company, for example, we estimate that the TDADM practice has added 17% to our corporate travel bill. This added cost comes from a number of factors:

Figure 4-34. The sentence beginning *At our company . . .* has now become part of the previous paragraph, and when the strikeout section is removed, it should be the second sentence in the paragraph.

How to Use the Thesaurus

Let's deal with the word *stipulating*. Is that really the word you want to use? Well, *WordPerfect* doesn't really have a defining dictionary built in (the Speller dictionary simply checks spelling), but it does have a thesaurus, which is a dictionary of synonyms. Can you get some help there? Let's find out.

If you're using a Mac with a hard disk drive, and you installed the files correctly from the disks you received, simply move the cursor to the word *stipulating* and select Thesaurus from the Special menu.

If your Mac has two floppy disk drives, you can follow this sequence:

Using the Thesaurus

Step 1. Position the cursor anywhere in the word *stipulating*.
Step 2. Choose Thesaurus . . . from the Special menu.

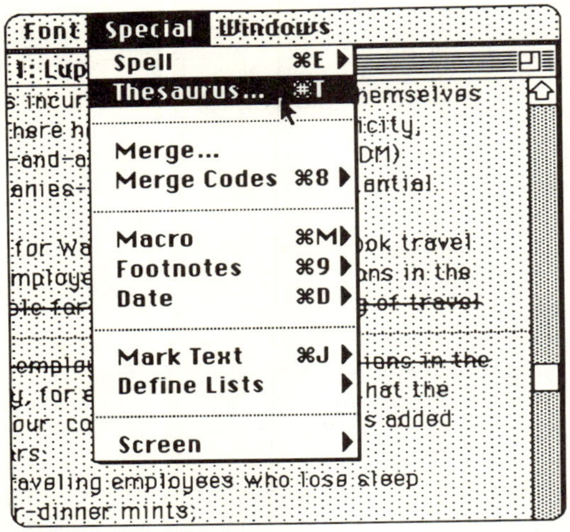

Figure 4-35. Choosing Thesaurus . . . from the Special menu.

Step 3. You'll see a dialog box for the current disk.

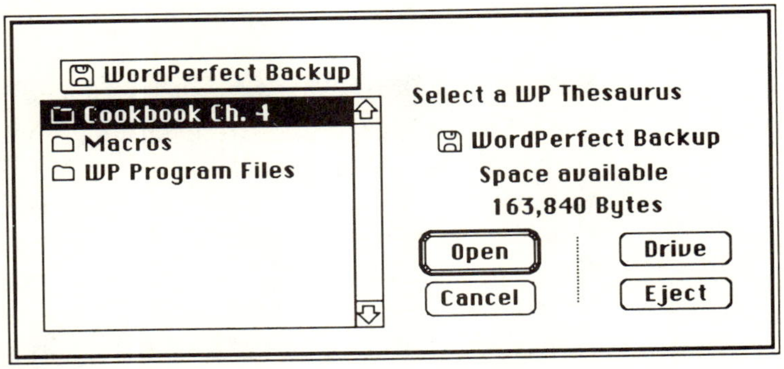

Figure 4-36. The dialog box for the *WordPerfect* Backup disk.

Step 4. Click on Eject. When the *WordPerfect* Backup disk is ejected, insert the Speller/Thesaurus disk. A new dialog box for the Speller/Thesaurus Backup disk will appear on the screen, with *WP Thesaurus* highlighted.

Figure 4-37. The dialog box for the Speller/Thesaurus disk.

Step 5. Click on Open. You will then get this message: *Please insert the disk: WordPerfect Backup,* and the Thesaurus disk will be ejected.

Step 6. Insert the *WordPerfect* Backup disk. Some vertical lines and blank spaces will appear on the screen, and you will see another message saying, *Please insert the disk: Speller/Thes Backup.* The *WordPerfect* Backup disk will be ejected.

Step 7. Insert the Speller/Thesaurus Backup disk. Another message will appear, saying, *Please insert the disk: WordPerfect Backup.* The Speller/Thesaurus disk will be ejected.

Step 8. Insert the *WordPerfect* Backup disk. A list of words will appear at the left-hand side of your screen: the word *stipulate* and five synonyms. This six-step disk swapping routine demostrates how cumbersome it is to run a modern program on the Macintosh relying only on floppy drives. If your time is valuable, a hard disk will pay for itself in a short time. A hard disk is quickly becoming a necessity. Consider buying one.

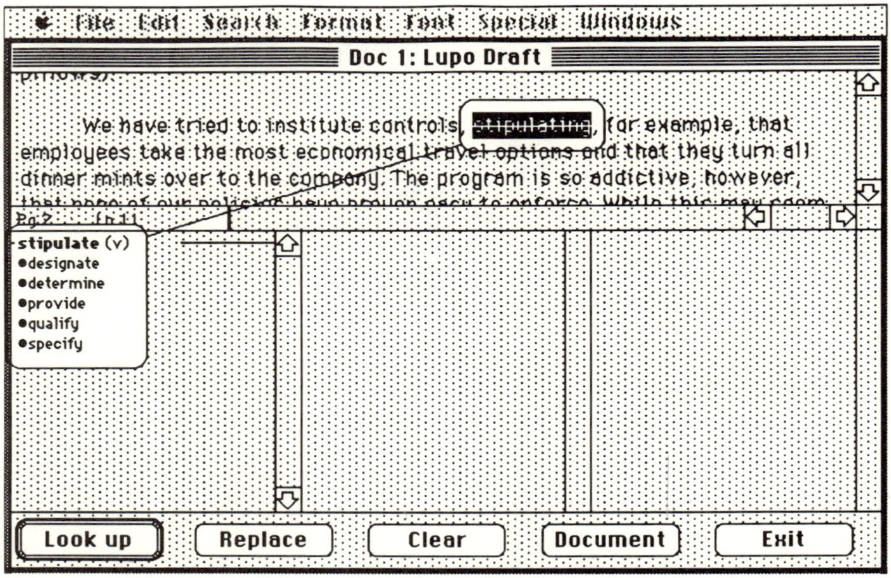

Figure 4-38. The Thesaurus window with a list of synonyms for *stipulate.*

There are also a number of options indicated at the bottom of the screen: Look Up, Replace, Clear, Document, and Exit.

As suspected, *stipulate* is the wrong word. You're looking for a word that has more of the sense of *demand.* Can the Thesaurus provide further help? Let's ask it to look up *demand* and see what happens:

Step 1. Click on Look up. A dialog box appears asking for the word to look up.
Step 2. Type in *demand,* then click on Look Up in the dialog box.

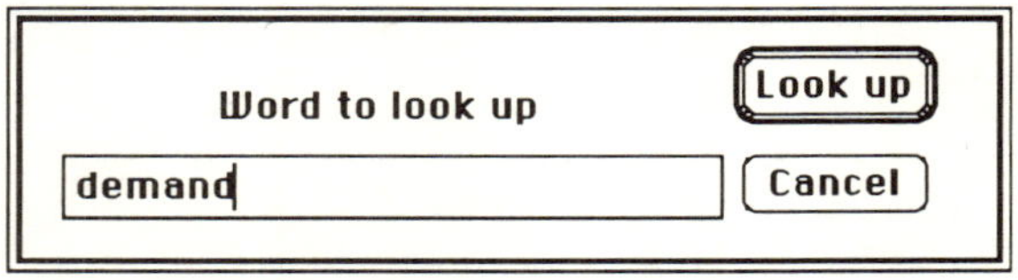

Figure 4-39. The dialog box after you request Look Up in the Thesaurus and type in *demand.*

Run through the disk swapping routine previously described as you are prompted on the screen.

In the Thesaurus section of your screen, a new list of words has appeared under *demand*.

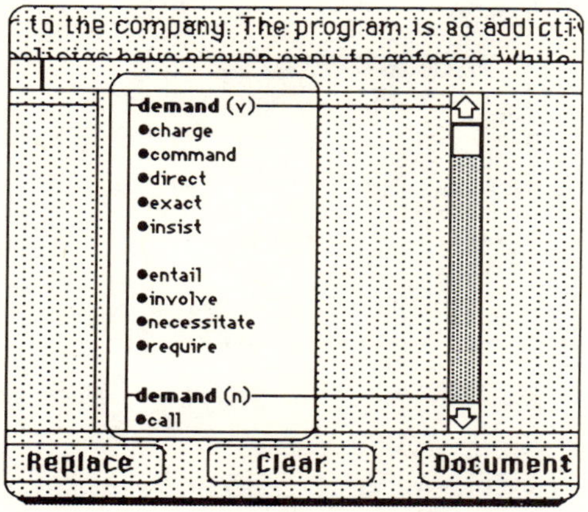

Figure 4-40. The list of synonyms supplied when you asked the Thesaurus to look up *demand*.

Demand is offered both as a verb *(demand(v))* and as a noun *(demand(n))*. There is a scroll bar to the right of the list that enables you to see all of the synonyms.

One of the synonyms is *insist*, and that probably comes closest to the meaning needed in the sentence. Let's replace *stipulating* with *insisting*. Here's how:

Step 3. Click on the word *insist* to select it.

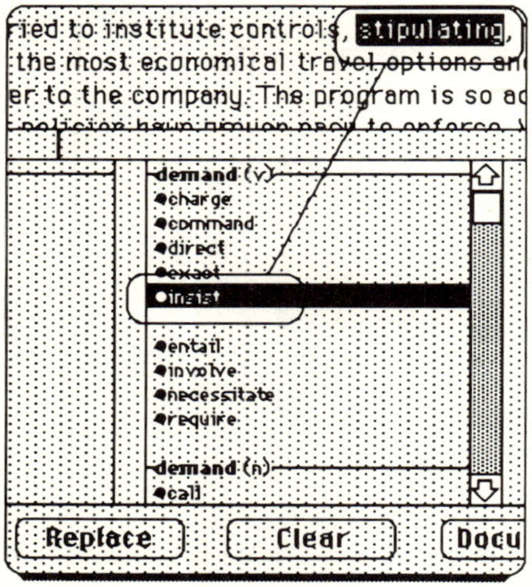

Figure 4-41. The word *insist* selected to replace *stipulating*.

Step 4. Click on Replace. You see now that *stipulating* has been replaced with *insist*.

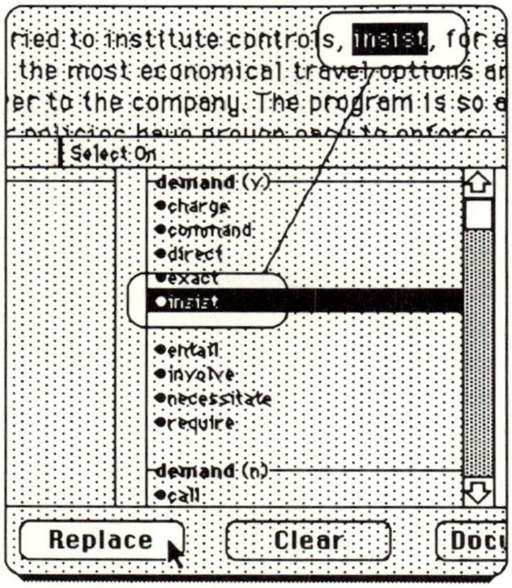

Figure 4-42. The word *stipulating* has been replaced with *insist*.

Let's get out of the Thesaurus.

Step 5. Click on Exit. The job is almost done. To finish it, simply type the word *insisting*. It will replace the selected and struckout *insist*.

The final sentence in this paragraph, beginning *While this may seem . . .*, has an account that's about to *boil over*. Block that metaphor! Let's turn this sentence into two sentences, and make the expression of anger understated, dignified, and icy cold.

Select the phrase *I can assure you that*. Then type *we don't think so* and end the sentence with a period. Now change the next sentence to read *Worldwide Wigwams and the other major hotel chains are engendering in your corporate customers ill will and resentment that will backlash when you most need support*. Simply select the passages you want to remove and type the replacements.

In the final paragraph the sentence beginning *But you cannot endure . . .* is somewhat overwrought. Here is something just as firm but less florid. Try this:

Step 1. Select the sentence.

Like you, we support the idea of free markets and open competition. ~~But we cannot endure a situation where you are permitted to abuse your captive clientele with impunity, while driving competition out of the market with anti-competitive practices that they cannot afford.~~ If you and your industry colleagues can't bring yourselves to find a just remedy for the TDADM problem, we will be compelled to join the rising cry for chocolate regulation and warning labels on all dinner mints. We would rather not do that

Figure 4-43. The overwrought sentence selected for replacement.

Step 2. Type *But*.

Like you, we support the idea of free markets and open competition. But if you and your industry colleagues can't bring yourselves to find a just remedy for the TDADM problem, we will be compelled to join the rising cry for chocolate regulation and warning labels on all dinner mints. We would rather not do that.

Figure 4-44. The new version of the final paragraph.

Use Reveal Codes to remove the strikeout code marking the word *But*. With the offending sentence removed, the paragraph is left with more punch and less perfume.

How to Remove Redlines and Strikeouts

You have two or three more changes to make to this letter. First, let's agree that all the passages that you redlined are to stay in, and all those marked for strikeout are to go. Act on that decision with the command Remove on the Special menu.

Removing Special Editing Marks

Step 1. Select Remove on the Special menu.

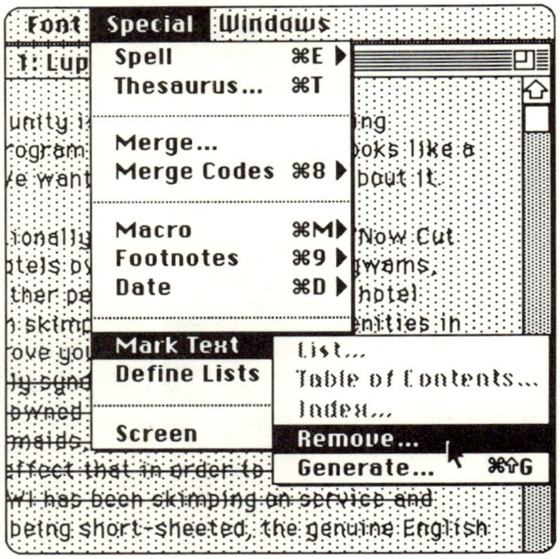

Figure 4-45. Choosing Remove from the Mark Text submenu of the Special menu in order to remove Redline and Strikeout text.

Step 2. You will see a dialog box whose purpose is to double-check that you want to remove the strikeouts and instate the redline text.

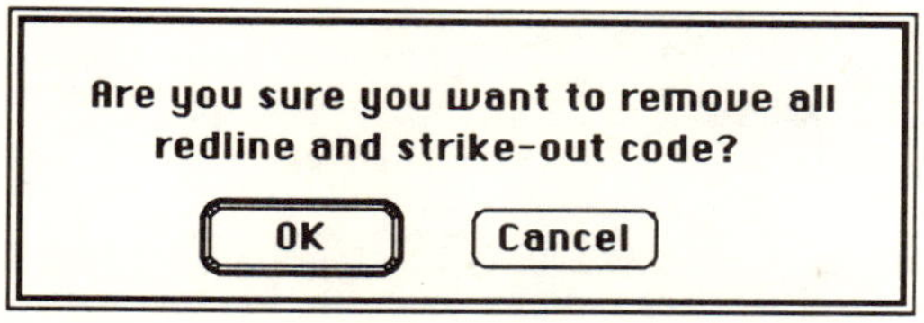

Figure 4-46. The Remove dialog box.

Click on OK.

In what is now paragraph 6, beginning *As corporate travel manager . . .*, Select the passage at the beginning of the second sentence: *At our company, for example, we estimate* and replace it with *My figures show*.

In the next sentence, insert a comma and the word *including* after the word *factors*. Just position the cursor in front of the colon after *factors* and type a comma, a space, and the word *including*.

How to Use Search and Replace

Go back to the beginning of the letter. There are still one or two changes needed:

The first change involves a question of tone. You started out addressing Frank Lupo as Mr. Lupo, and you should be consistent about that throughout the letter. The fourth paragraph begins, *Now Frank . . .*, which sounds flippant, condescending, and altogether inappropriate to the content of the letter. Let's correct it by using the Replace function on the Search menu.

Using Search and Replace

Step 1. Position the cursor in front of *Dear Mr. Lupo*. This is a very important step. The cursor must be located at the beginning of a document before a search and replace maneuver so the computer will search through the whole document.

Step 2. Select Replace from the Search menu.

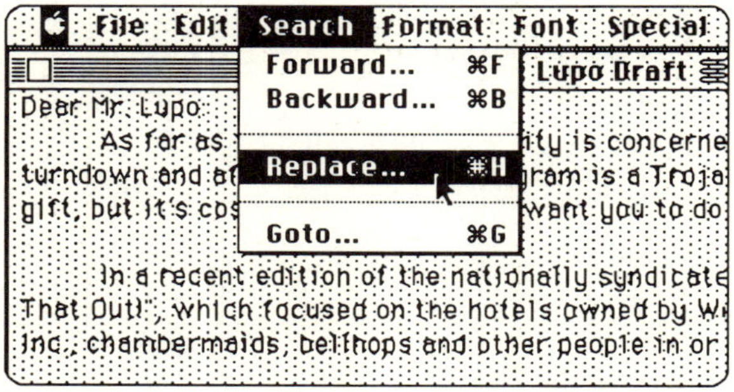

Figure 4-47. Selecting Replace from the Search menu.

The Replace dialog box will appear.

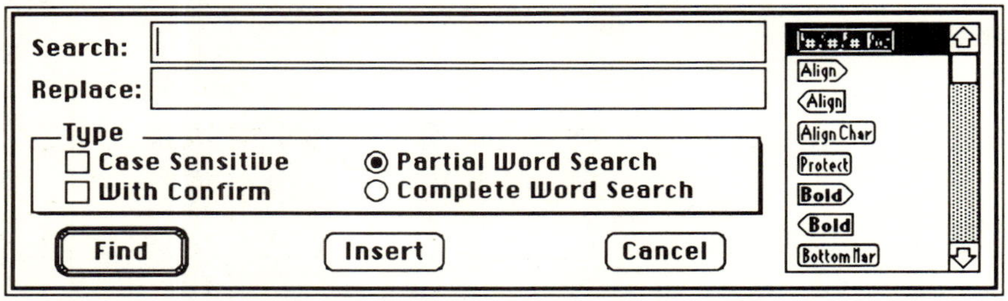

Figure 4-48. The Replace dialog box.

Step 3. Where the cursor is flashing in the Search box, type *Now Frank*. Then hit the Tab key to move to the Replace box and type *Mr. Lupo*.

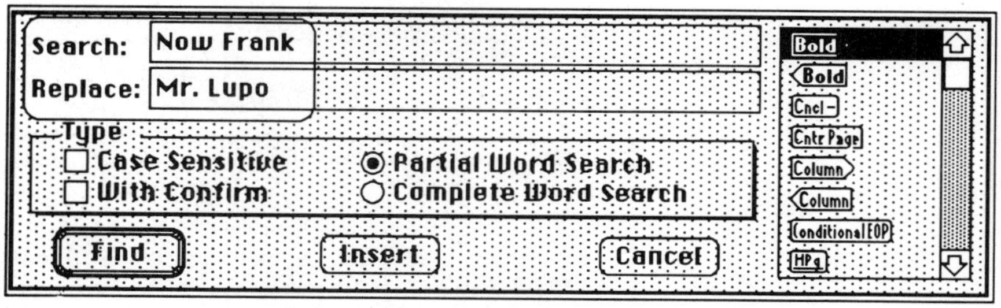

Figure 4-49. The Replace dialog box after you typed in *Now Frank* as the search phrase, and *Mr. Lupo* as the replace phrase.

Step 4. Click on the circle in front of Complete Word Search.

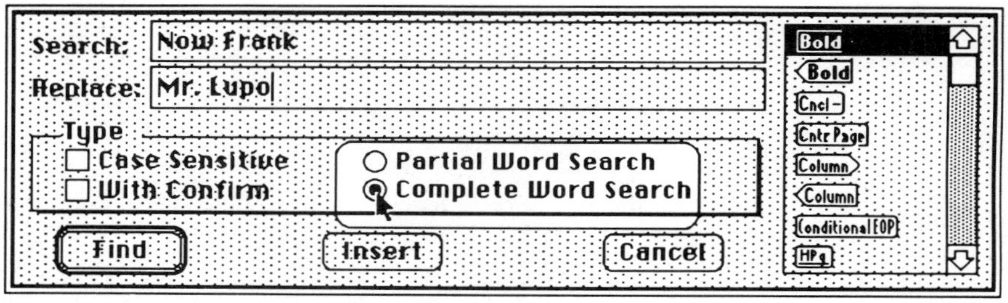

Figure 4-50. Instructing the Mac to Search only for the complete words *Now Frank.*

You're looking for the words *Now Frank* only when they occur as complete words. This is an important distinction. If you intended to change every instance of the word *we* to *you* in a file and you didn't specify complete words, you would find such oddities as *hoyouver* and *youlfare* where you have written *however* and *welfare.*

Step 5. Click the pointer on Find in the Replace dialog box. When the Box goes away, *Now Frank* has been replaced with *Mr. Lupo.*

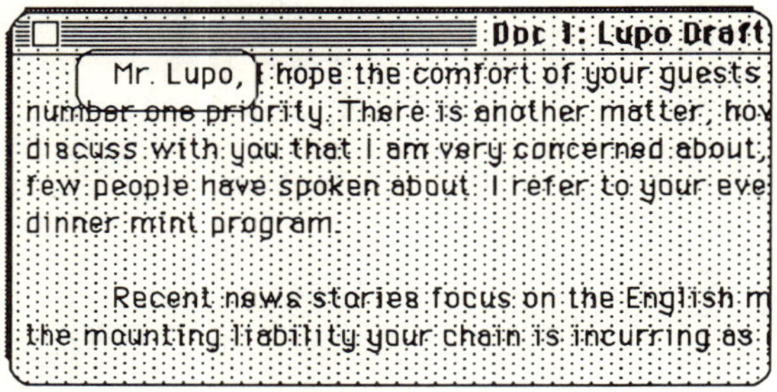

Figure 4-51. The Search and Replace operation has now replaced *Now Frank* with *Mr. Lupo.*

You could work at polishing this letter (or any document) forever. But you will have to admit, it's much better than the original draft.

In the next chapter you'll learn procedures that will help you improve your productivity: formatting, addressing, closing, selecting fonts and type sizes, creating macro shortcuts, and much more.

Chapter 5

Making Your Job Easier with Macros and Other Tricks

Chapter 5

Making Your Job Easier with Macros and Other Tricks

At the end of Chapter 4, you had just finished revising a draft of a business letter. The hardest part of the job has been done: putting the words into place and making them sound right. Now all you have to do is get the letter onto paper, address an envelope, and send it out. That's the simple part of the job. It shouldn't take long at all.

But the truth is that simple jobs eat up more of a day than most people would ever want to admit. Hours are spent looking up addresses, retyping messy pages, getting the address in the right place on the envelope, repeating for Clients B and C the same work already done for Client A.

This repetitive work is no longer necessary in the Mac office.

To discover how to avoid the hardest parts of office work, load up the letter you worked on in Chapter 4. Some work has to be done before the letter is ready to send out into the world. It needs an address and a date, and you need to make some decisions about the font type and size, as well as margins and tabs. Finally, you have to fit the letter onto your letterhead.

This may seem like a lot of detail, but when you're through, you can perform a little magic that will cause your Macintosh to do all of these things automatically from now on.

That magic trick is called a *macro.* By the time you are finished with this chapter you will know how to create and use a macro.

The Letter Macro

Before you enter the address, open a new file or document where you're going to keep it. Here's how:

Opening a New File

Step 1. Click on the File menu and select New (Figure 5-1).

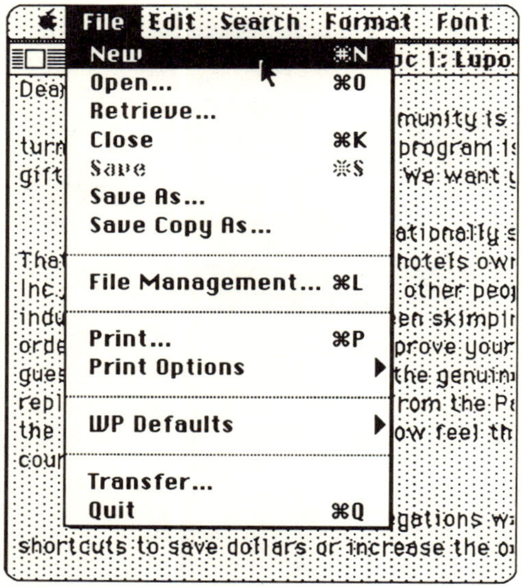

Figure 5-1. Choosing New from the File menu.

Step 2. Release the mouse button. A new, blank, untitled document *(Doc 2: Untitled)* appears on your screen on top of Doc 1.

Figure 5-2. The new document *Doc 2: Untitled* appears on top of Doc 1 when you choose New from the File menu.

Doc 2: Untitled is your address file. You'll give it a title in a minute, but first, enter the address. Type it in right at the cursor on Doc 2. Hit Return at the end of each line in the address, just as if you were using a typewriter and had to make the carriage return.

Mr. Frank Lupo
Chairman and CEO
Worldwide Wigwams, Inc.
1869 Cherokee Plaza
Buxtehude, NC 00909
Check your results against Figure 5-3.

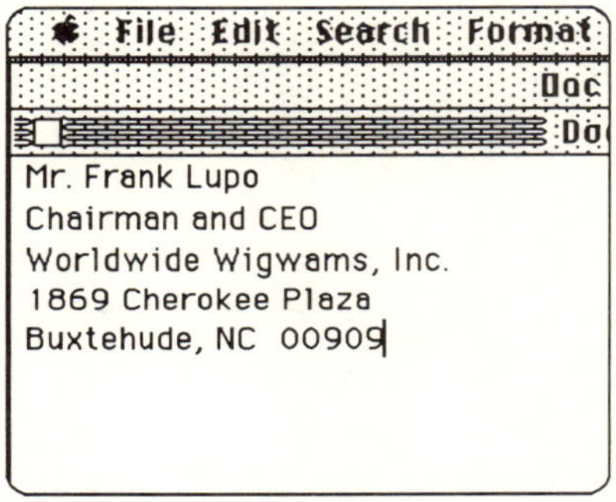

Figure 5-3. The address typed onto Doc 2.

Now, before you do anything else, you should name and save the file with the address. Here's how:

Saving a File Step 1. Choose Save As from the File menu.

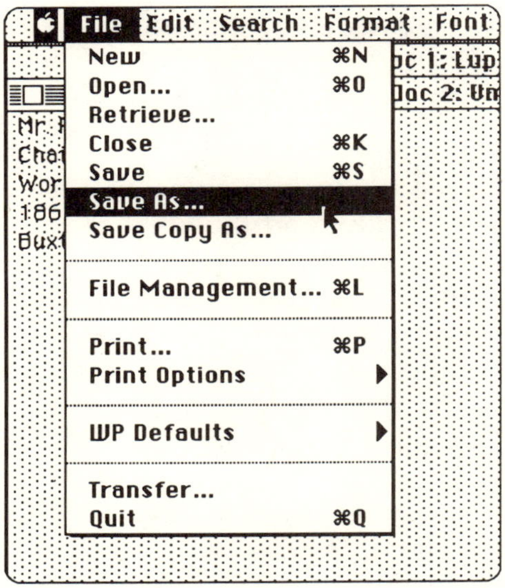

Figure 5-4. Choosing Save As from the File menu.

Step 2. When you see the Save As dialog box, type in *Phone Book.*

Step 3. Click on Save to make Phone Book a permanent file.

You now have a file called Phone Book to contain addresses and telephone numbers. You'll add to it every time you write a letter. This kind of file can be treated as if it were an electronic Rolodex.

To confirm that the file is there, choose File Management from the File menu. You should see a dialog box displaying a listing of the *WordPerfect* files on the *WordPerfect* disk.

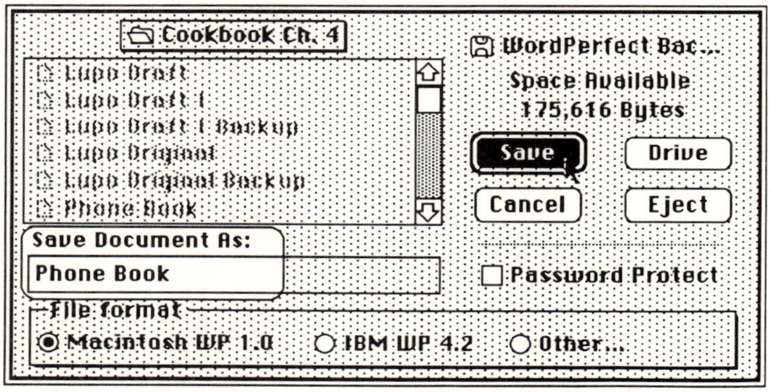

Figure 5-5. The Save As . . . dialog box.

If you don't, and the heading for the file listing says *System* or *System Backup* or something similar, and the folders listed are the System Folder and the Utilities Folder, you are looking at the wrong drive. Change drives by clicking on Drive (the upper right hand button).

Now you will move the address to the letter. The procedure is straightforward, and it's one you'll use over and over. Whenever you have to move a block of copy from one file or document to another, here's what you do:

Copying Information Between Files

Step 1. Select the address. Since it's the only thing on the Phone Book file right now, you can do it by choosing All from the Select submenu of the Edit menu.

Step 2. Make a copy of the address by choosing Copy from the Edit menu. This places a copy of the address in the Clipboard. It will stay in the Clipboard until you Copy or Cut something else. Confirm that the address is in your Clipboard by choosing Show Clipboard from the Windows menu.

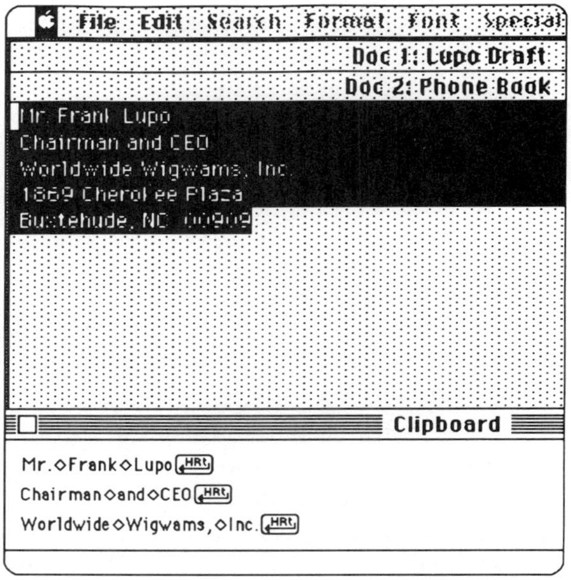

Figure 5-6. The Clipboard showing that the Lupo address has been copied.

Now put the Clipboard away by clicking on the close box on the title bar of the Clipboard, or by choosing Hide Clipboard from the Windows menu.

Step 3. Move back to the Lupo letter by clicking on the title bar of Doc 1: Lupo Draft (if it's visible) or by choosing Doc 1: Lupo Draft from the Windows menu.

Step 4. Move the cursor to the top of the Lupo letter by pressing Enter, Enter, Up Arrow (Enter is on the numeric keypad) or by moving the scroll box to the top of the slide bar with the mouse and then clicking the mouse at the top of the document. Pressing Enter, Enter, Up Arrow will not work on some Macintoshes. In that case, simply use the scroll bar.

Step 5. Insert or *paste* the address at the head of the letter by choosing Paste from the Edit menu.
Step 6. Press Return twice to move the salutation, *Dear Mr. Lupo:,* down to its proper position.

Next, you need the date in the letter. Move the cursor to the top of the letter. Many people position the date and the closing so they begin at the center of the page. It's also perfectly acceptable to put the date and closing at the left margin with everything else. You'll find that this sort of thing varies considerably among individuals and companies. For the sake of this explanation, adopt the style of beginning the date and closing at the center of the page. Here's how:

Press Return three times, then press Enter, Enter, Up Arrow to position the cursor three lines above the address (or use the Up-Arrow key repeatedly, if this key combination doesn't work on your Macintosh). Then tabulate to the middle of the page, or about 4.5 inches. That should take about seven taps of the Tab key, with the default tab settings. (If you can't see your screen position in the lower right hand corner of the screen, turn on the position numbers by choosing Show Position from the Screen submenu of the Special menu.)

The actual center of the screen (or of a standard sheet of typing paper) would be 4.25 inches, but since *WordPerfect* sets the tabs every half inch, it will give you the choice of tabs at 4 inches and 4.5 inches. (Later you'll see how to adjust tabs.) Take 4.5 inches. Now you will enter the date.

Of course, you have the option of simply typing in the date. But that takes extra keystrokes, and many people would have to check the calendar. Since the Mac already knows the date, you can instruct the computer to enter the date for you.

Step 1. Choose Date from the Special menu.

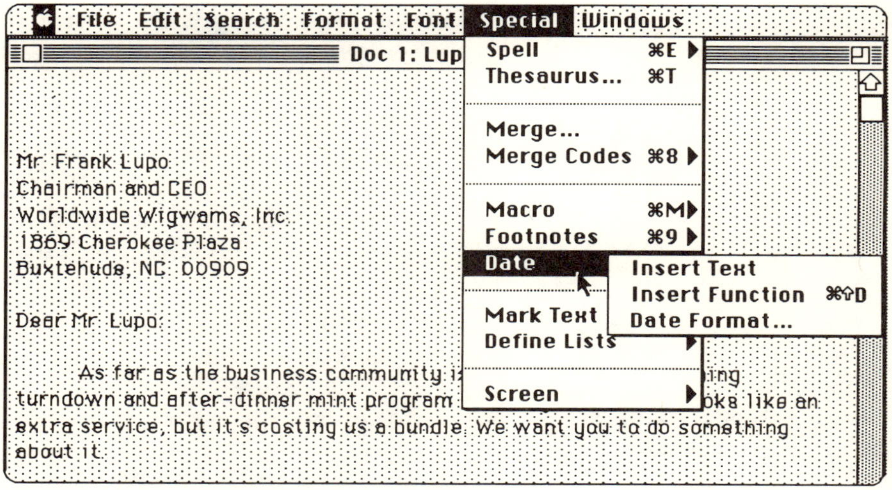

Figure 5-7. Choosing Date from the Special menu.

Inserting the Date into a Document

You will then see a submenu that gives you three choices:

Insert Text
Insert Function
Date Format . . .

The third choice, Date Format . . ., allows you to enter the date in the format you prefer. If you prefer the military style of writing the date (for example, 3Apr58), you can install that format by clicking on Day of Month, then Name of Month, then Two Digit Year, then OK. From then on, whenever you tell *WordPerfect* to enter the date, it will respond with this format until you tell it differently. The default format *WordPerfect* uses if you don't give it a format to use, is Name of Month, space, Day of Month, comma, space, Four Digit Year (for example, April 3, 1958).

Examining the Formatting Codes

The second choice, Insert Function, is useful for a document you will send out several times on different dates. This choice puts a code, rather than a specific date, into your document. Then whenever you retrieve this document, *WordPerfect* will automatically insert the correct date. What you see on the document is always the current date, but if you choose Show Codes from the Edit menu, you will see the document onscreen replicated at the bottom of the screen with all special font and formatting codes printed out. Where you inserted the date function, you will see a code that says *Month Date Year*. This ensures that the current date will always be printed at this point in the document.

The first choice, Insert Text, simply enters the date in the format of your choice. For now, let's use that option.

Step 2. Choose Insert Text from the Date submenu of the Special menu. The correct date appears at the cursor position.

Setting the Date and Time

If your Mac has the wrong date, here's how to change it:

Step 1. Choose Control Panel from the Apple menu.
Step 2. Put the cursor (now shaped like a cross or a plus sign) over the part of the date (month, day, or year) you want to change, and click.
Step 3. Adjust the number by clicking on the arrow sign to the right. Click the up arrow to make the number larger, or the down arrow to make the number smaller.

If your Mac is showing the wrong time, you may also correct that while you're on the Control Panel. Make changes just as you did for the date.

The letter is almost ready. All you have to do now is add a letterhead, or allow space for the letterhead that is already on your stationery. Just for the sake of having something on the page, let's type in a letterhead:

Position the cursor at the top of the page, then press Return three times to create space between the letterhead and the date, then return to the top of the page again.

Now type in the letterhead:

Wanton Widgets, Inc.
2020 Walla Walla Way
Woonsocket, WY 90909

And with that, the text of our letter is complete.

The next step is to format the letter. Formatting refers to setting the margins, the tab stops, the page numbering instructions, and so on.

Our first choice is to do nothing, since *WordPerfect* has already set up a default format. To find out what the default settings are, choose Page from the Format menu.

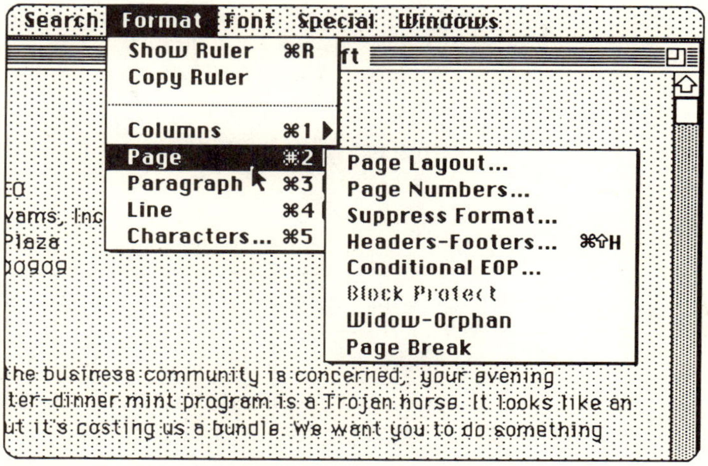

Figure 5-8. Choosing Page from the Format menu.

That gives you the Page Format submenu, which has eight choices. For now, let's click on Page Layout.

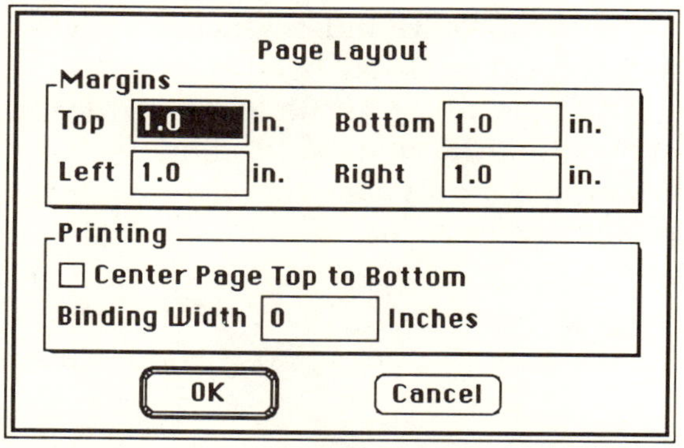

Figure 5-9. The Page Layout dialog box.

Checking and Changing Page Layout Defaults

The default setting gives you one-inch margins at top, bottom, left and right. Those are standard settings, and you might be perfectly happy to leave them alone. But just for practice, here's how to alter these settings:

To create more white space on the paper, let's make the margins 1.5 inches all around. Since the number for the top margin is already selected or highlighted in the Page Layout dialog box when you open it, just type in *1.5*. Hit the Tab key, and move to the left margin number. Type *1.5* again, tab to move to the bottom margin, and so on until you set all four margins at 1.5 inches.

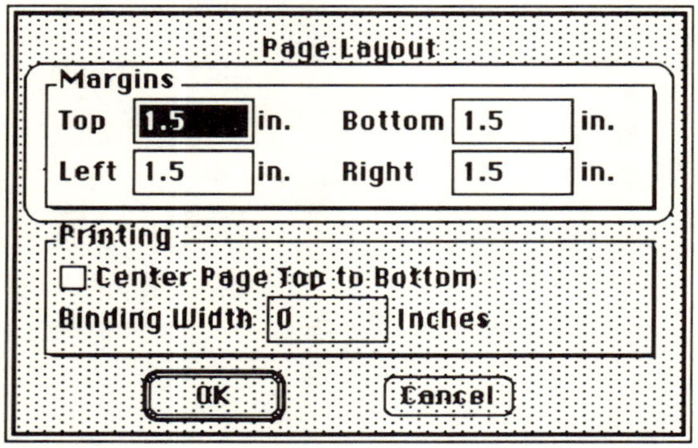

Figure 5-10. The Page Layout dialog box with all margins changed to 1.5 inches.

When you're finished, click on OK. You will return to the letter, and see it has been reformatted automatically. The screen position indicator at the lower right-hand corner of the screen shows that the vertical location of the cursor is about 1.5 inches below the top of the page. (It may actually be 1.67, 1.72, or some other measure close to 1.5, depending on the font you're using at the moment. More about that later.)

Next you'll set the tab stops. Tab stops are preset every half inch. To verify this, choose Show Ruler from the Format menu.

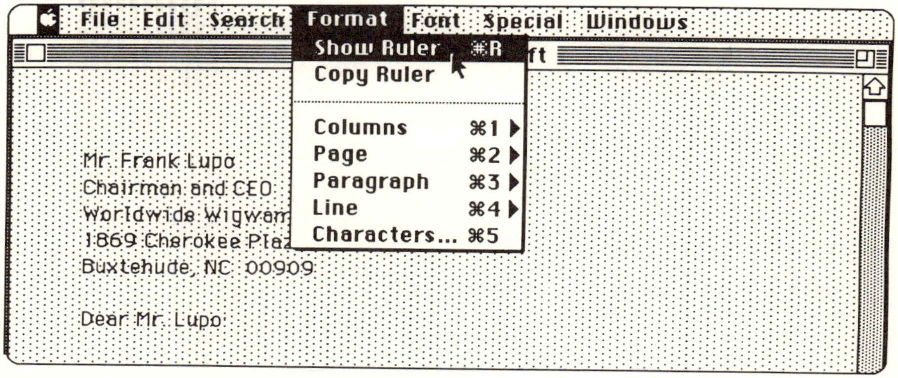

Figure 5-11. Choosing Show Ruler from the Format menu.

Setting Tab Stops

Note that all across the ruler, at half-inch intervals, there are black flags or pennants pointing toward the left. Those are the tab markers. While we're here, notice also the slightly larger black flag or triangle at 1.5 inches and at 7 inches. Those are the margin indicators. You can drag these tab and margin markers around and set up new formats while in the Show Ruler mode. As a rule, however, it's easier to change these settings from the format mode.

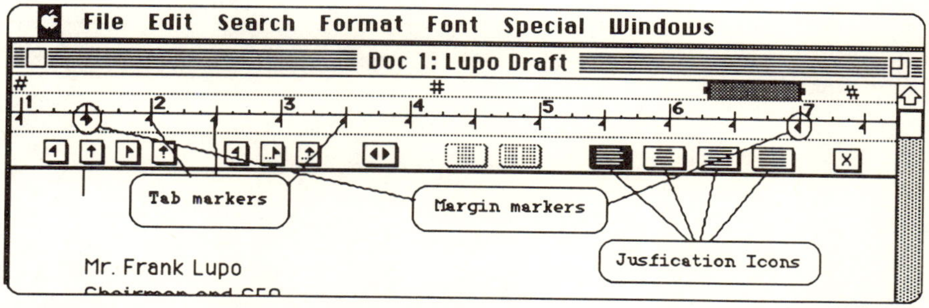

Figure 5-12. The ruler showing tab markers, margin indicators, and justification icons.

Take a look at the ruler and your letter to see where you're going to want tab stops. (You might wonder what the use is of putting tabs in, now that the letter is already set up. This will be explained shortly.)

With the left-hand margin at 1.5 inches, you'll want a tab at 2.0 inches, and, just in case you want two levels of tabbing, one at 2.5 inches. You'll also want to be able to tab quickly to the date location, so you should set a tab at 4.5 inches. (Keep the ruler visible, and watch what happens as you give tab instructions.)

Step 1. Choose Tabs from the Line submenu of the Format menu.

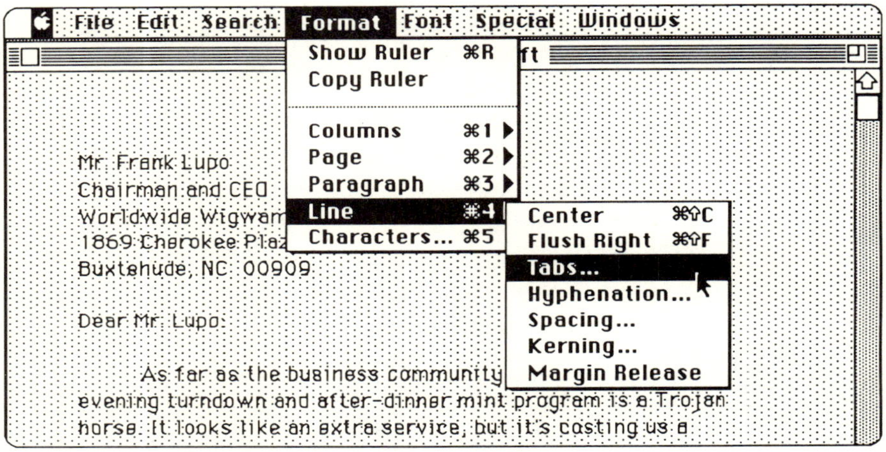

Figure 5-13. Choosing Tabs from the Line submenu of the Format menu.

Step 2. In the Tab Format dialog box, click on Delete to remove all tab stops. Note that all the black flags disappear from the ruler except the large ones marking the margins at 1.5 and 7 inches.

Step 3. Look at the two sides of the Tab Format dialog box. If you're going to set up tabs at regular or uniform intervals, you'll use the Uniform Tabs side of the dialog box. Simply enter the location of the first tab (2.0 inches, for example, if your left-hand margin is at 1.5 inches and you want the first tab 0.5 inch in from the left margin), then enter the interval at which you want the tab repeated. Since for the moment you are interested in nonuniform intervals, go to the Varying Tabs side of the dialog box.

Step 4. Since the cursor is already flashing in the New Tab Position box, type *2* to locate your first tab stop. Then click the mouse button on Set at the bottom of the dialog box.

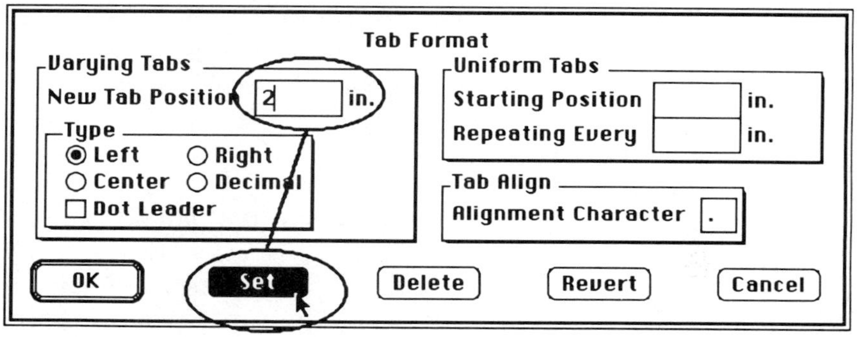

Figure 5-14. Setting the first tab at 2.0 inches.

Notice that a black tab flag appears instantly at 2.0 inches on the ruler. Now set tab stops at 2.5 inches and 4.5 inches in the same way.

Step 5. Click on OK in the dialog box. You're all set. Confirm this by looking at the ruler, which should show black flags at 2.0 inches, 2.5 inches, and 4.5 inches.
Your tabs are set.

What You See Is What You Get

So far, little has been said about how things look on the screen: the typeface, the type size, the readability of the various faces and sizes, and so forth. Nor have we discussed the difference between what you see on the screen and what you will get on the printed page. Now that you are almost ready to print the letter, it's time to cover those subjects.

As a machine with a graphics-based display, the Macintosh running *WordPerfect* shows on the screen a fair approximation of what you will see on paper in the printed copy. In computer jargon this is known as *WYSIWIG* (pronounced WHIZZY-wig), for

What You See Is What You Get. When you enter a character in boldface or italics, you see boldface or italics on the screen. Larger type looks larger, smaller type looks smaller, different typefaces look different. Consequently, looking at a document on your computer monitor gives you a fair idea what you'll see when you print it out.

But it's only a rough approximation of the final result because current computer monitors are limited in their ability to produce high resolution or high quality pictures (although the science and the products are improving every day). Consequently, a typeface that's difficult to read on the computer screen may be perfectly legible when produced on paper by a printer or a computer-driven typesetter.

For that reason, the default typeface or font that is set on your Mac by *WordPerfect* has been selected for its readability on the screen, and not necessarily for its appearance on paper. The default typeface appears to vary from one machine to another. When the program is run on a Macintosh 512E, the default font is Geneva. When run on a Macintosh II the default font is Helvetica.

Selecting a Font

You need to select a font type and size for printing. You want it to be readable, and you want it to be a typeface people will find acceptable in a business letter. (People tend to be very conservative about such matters.) The two most popular typefaces for letters are Times and Courier. Many people prefer Courier because it looks like a typewriter face (that's a little like preferring an automobile body design because it looks like a horse-drawn carriage).

Times is a good, sturdy, readable typeface. That's why it's used by so many newspapers. Here's how to change your document to Times:

Step 1. Position the cursor at the top of the document.
Step 2. Choose Show Codes from the Edit menu.
Step 3. Choose Times from the Font menu.

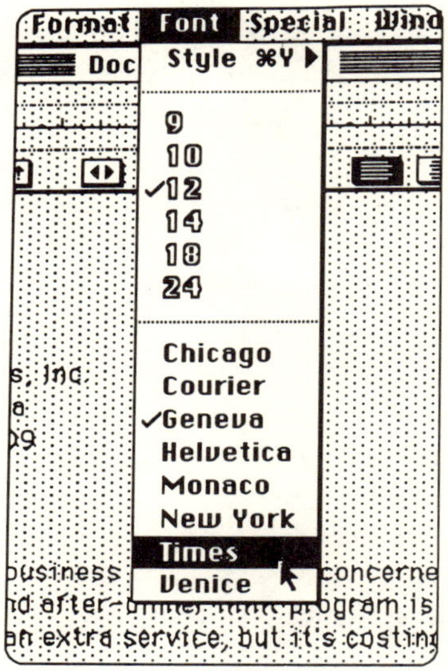

Figure 5-15. Choosing Times from the Font menu.

The type on the screen stays the same. Why? If you look down at the lower part of the screen where the codes are visible, you see that the cursor is between a Times code and a Geneva code (or whatever font you were using before switching to Times: Figure 5-16).

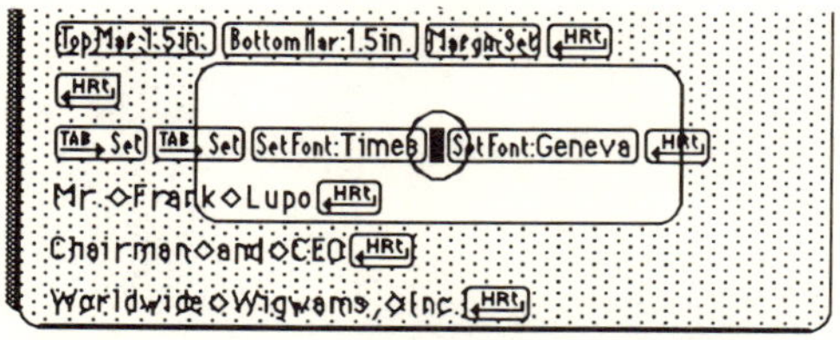

Figure 5-16. After selecting the Times font, the cursor is between the Times code and the code for the previous font.

Apparently *WordPerfect* decided to make things easy for the person who switches fonts in midstream: You tell the Mac to switch, and as you type, everything after the selection will be in the new typeface. Then, when you want to return to the former typeface, simply hit the End key or a Right Arrow and you're back to the original font.

Step 4. In this case, you have two extra keystrokes to enter: Right Arrow, Delete. This jumps the cursor over the old typeface code and deletes it. The letter is immediately reformatted in the new font. As you see, the Times characters are closer together and more difficult to read. But on most printers they print beautifully.

If, after you print the letter, you decide that you want another type size, you may change that just as you changed the font itself, by selecting the Font menu and then dragging the highlight down to the type size you want to use. You'll probably find, however, that 12-point (the default size) is just right.

Page Numbering

If you want to number the pages, there is a simple way to do so. Down the road you'll learn fancier ways to head and number pages. For now you will simply add page numbers at the bottom of each page (after the first). Here's how:

Step 1. Move the cursor to the top of the document.

Step 2. Choose Page Numbers . . . from the Page submenu of the Format menu.

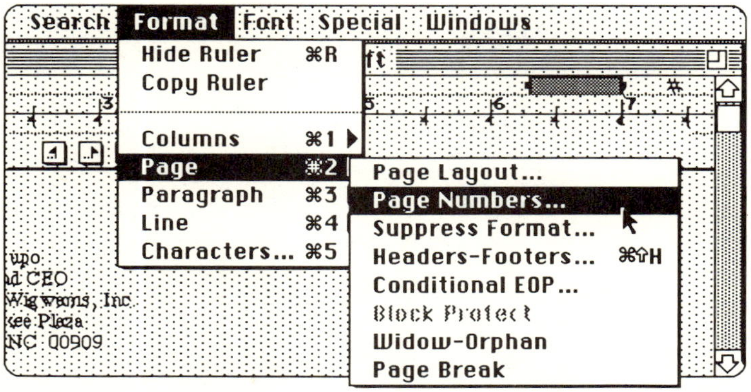

Figure 5-17. Choosing Page Numbers . . . from the Page submenu of the Format menu.

You'll see a big dialog box full of choices. You will have your choice of Arabic or Roman numerals, and you can select the location of the page number on the page.

Step 3. Click on the small circle indicating Bottom Center.

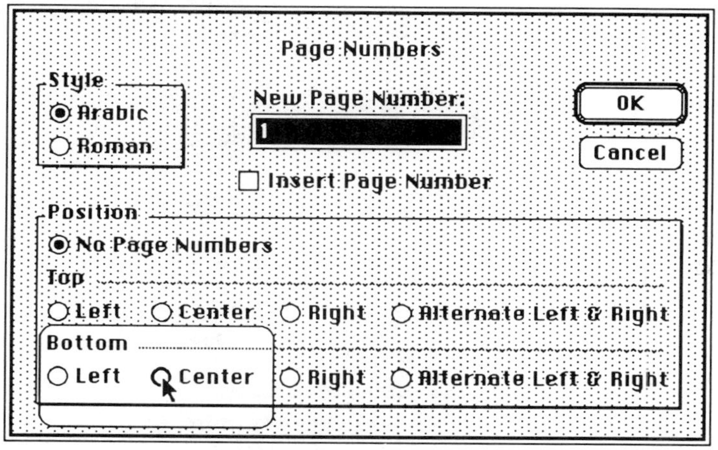

Figure 5-18. Choosing Bottom Center for the page number location in the Page Numbers dialog box.

That tells *WordPerfect* to put a page number at the bottom of every page, in the center. But what about the first page? You won't want a number there. Here's how to let your Macintosh know you want a number on every page, beginning with the second page:

Step 1. From the Page submenu of the Format menu, choose Suppress Format . . .

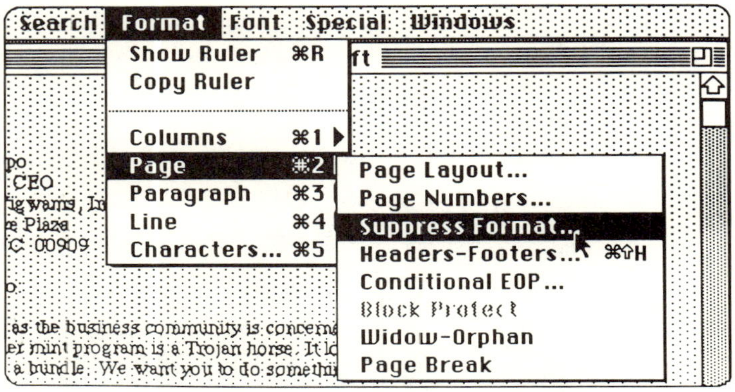

Figure 5-19. Choosing Suppress format . . . from the Page submenu of the Format menu.

You'll see a dialog box offering several choices.

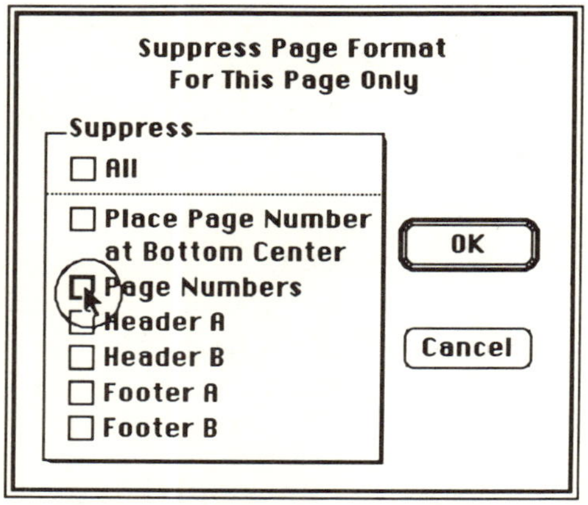

Figure 5-20. Instructing the Suppress Page format dialog box to omit page numbers for the first page.

Step 2. Click on the box next to Page Numbers. This tells the Mac to ignore page number instructions for this page only.
Step 3. Click on OK to return to the letter.

Spelling Checker

That concludes the cosmetic work on this letter. Before we go any further, however, you have a job to do that *WordPerfect* makes very easy: Checking the spelling. This is always an important final step for at least two reasons:

First, it ensures that your spelling is correct. People react strongly to misspelled words and names. Even one misspelling may completely undermine the purpose of the document.

Second, it gives you the chance to add special words and frequently-used names to your own User's Dictionary. If a client has a name that's difficult to spell, enter it carefully once. After that, *WordPerfect* will check it for you to be sure it's correct. Here are the steps for checking the spelling of a document:

Check Spelling

Step 1. Move to the top of the document.

Step 2. From the Spell submenu of the Special menu, choose Check Document. . . .

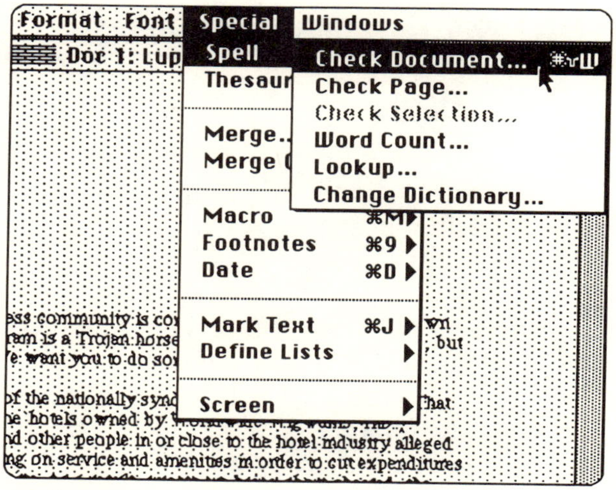

Figure 5-21. Choosing Check Document . . . from the Spell submenu of the Special menu.

WordPerfect will then begin looking through the letter, highlighting each word it can't find in its active dictionaries. As the words are highlighted one at a time, you will be given several choices for correcting the word or adding it to your private dictionaries. In this case, it makes its first stop at the word *Widgets*.

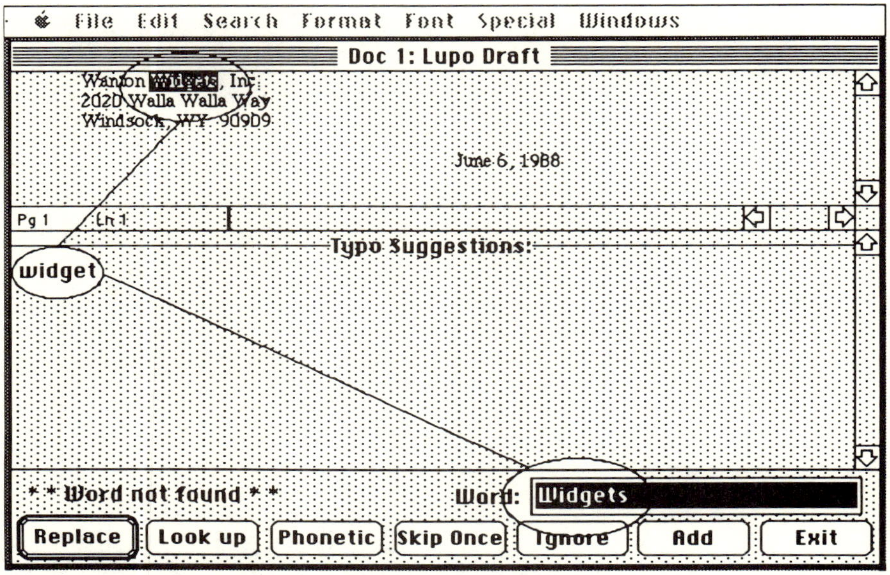

Figure 5-22. The Spelling dialog box asking if the word *widgets* should be *widget*.

In the middle of screen is the heading *Typo Suggestions*. Under this heading, *WordPerfect* will list the words it suspects you meant to use.

Step 3. Since *widget* isn't the word you meant to use, tell your Macintosh to add the word *Widgets* to your own dictionary by clicking on the box labeled Add. This is part of your company's name, so you'll use it frequently. Once you have entered it into your own dictionary, *WordPerfect* won't query you about it anymore. The program now moves on to the next word that is not in its dictionary: *Walla*. This time it gives you four columns of alternate choices, including *waylay*, *walleye*, and *williwaw*.

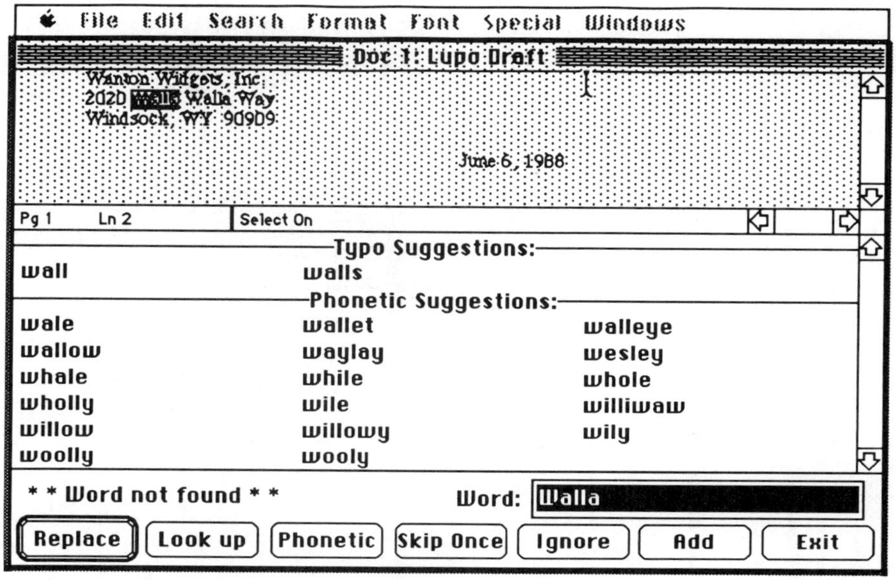

Figure 5-23. When the Speller program can't find *Walla,* it offers three columns of alternative words.

Once you are absolutely sure the spelling of *Walla* is correct, tell *WordPerfect* to add it to your dictionary, and go on to the next word.

Continue as the program checks words it doesn't recognize. Sometimes it will give you extra help by alerting you to duplicate words—as in *Walla Walla.* It waits for you to decide whether you want to continue or delete the duplicate word. This is useful in eliminating the duplication of words like *the,* which even close proofreaders may miss, particularly if the first instance falls at the end of one line and the next instance falls at the beginning of the next line.

If *WordPerfect* locates a real misspelling or typo, you have several choices. Let's say the next word that the Mac stops on is Woonsocket. When you see it highlighted, you realize it's an error. You really meant *Windsock,* Wyoming. This time *WordPerfect* is stumped; it has no Typo Suggestions at all. Here's how to make the correction:

Step 1. Type *Windsock*. It will appear in the Word box.
Step 2. Click on the Replace box. (Apple calls these boxes *buttons*.)

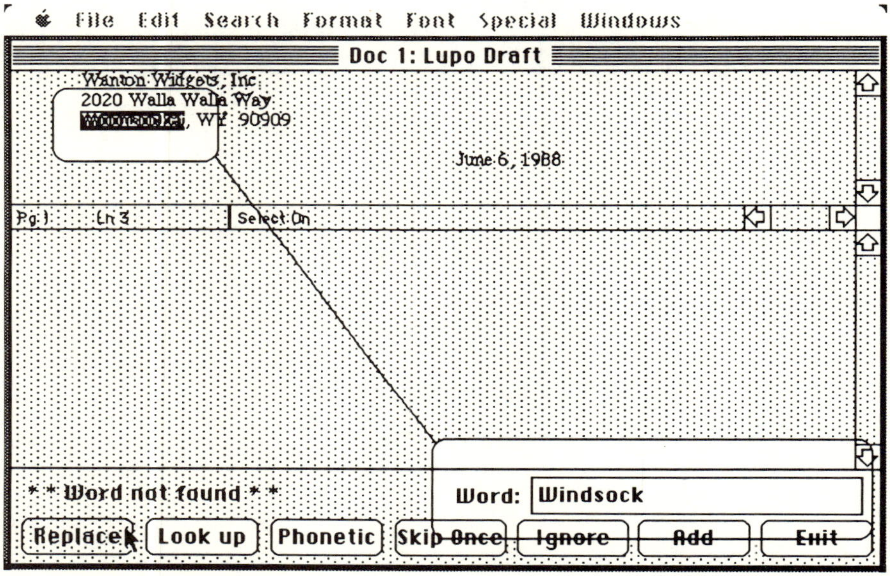

Figure 5-24. Replacing the word *Woonsocket* with the word *Windsock*.

WordPerfect instantly replaces *Woonsocket* with *Windsock* and is now worrying about *Lupo*.

This time the program has no possible typos to suggest, but has come up with a number of Phonetic Suggestions for you to consider. The Macintosh is suggesting that you intended to use a word that sounded a little like *Lupo*. Like *lippy*, or *loupe*, or *lappa* (*lappa* is another name for burdock).

Moving along, *WordPerfect* discovers that you have duplicated the word *program*. Tell it to delete the second appearance of *program*.

A bit further on, *WordPerfect* balks at the phrase *short-sheeted*, suggesting that you consider instead such combinations as *short-chatted*, *short-shadowed*, and *short-shootout*. This suggestion tells you that grammar isn't *WordPerfect's* strong suit. Because *short-sheeted* is either past tense or a past participle, *WordPerfect* is correct in offering *short-chatted* and *short-shadowed* as possible substitutions. But *short-shootout* is a noun. It's important to be cautious when using *WordPerfect's* spelling checker. The Mac is limited in its intelligence by what is in memory, what is on disk, and what it is programmed to do.

WordPerfect can check your spelling. It can help you find synonyms for words. It can spot words that are duplicated and words that have numbers in the middle. But it cannot correct your grammar, nor can it help you with word usage or diction. In that perilous country, you're on your own.

To return to spelling for a moment: If you have misspelled a word, and *WordPerfect* offers you a Typo Suggestion or Phonetic Suggestion that's the correct version of the word you intended, you can replace your version with the correctly spelled version simply by clicking on the suggested word where it appears on your screen, then clicking on the Replace box at the bottom.

Finally, note that *WordPerfect,* just to be helpful, gives you a word count at the end of the spelling procedure. (You can ask for the word count alone, without going through a spelling check.)

Printing Your Work

If you are weary of electronic information and yearn for the touch of hard copy that can be folded, spindled, and mutilated, it's time to turn to your printer and see what your letter looks like in the flesh.

First of all, be sure to review your Mac instruction manual about printers and printing. Take these precautionary steps:

Using Your Printer

Step 1. Select Chooser from the Apple menu. When the Chooser file appears, you should see at least one printer icon at the left-hand side of the Chooser file. Either the ImageWriter icon or the LaserWriter icon should be there. If you're in a network with two or more printers, they might both be there. If you're hooked up to Appletalk (as you must be if you are using a LaserWriter or are in a network with two or more printers), you need to select the correct printer by clicking the appropriate icon.

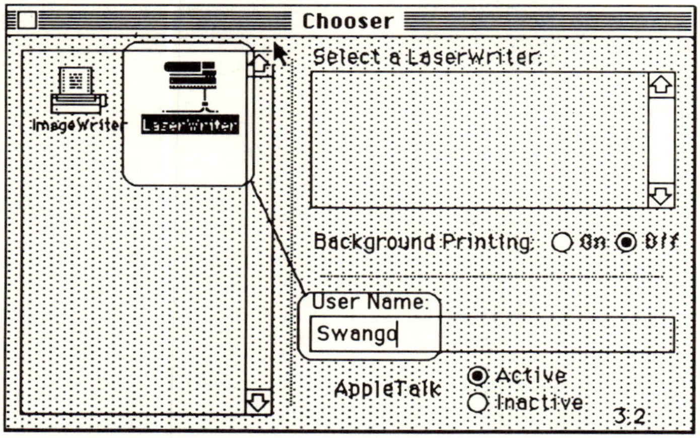

Figure 5-25. Selecting the LaserWriter printer in the Chooser on the Apple menu.

Type in your user name. Click in the Select Box on the specific machine you want to use (if more than one choice is involved). Exit Chooser by clicking on the close box.

Step 2. Choose Page Setup from the Print Options submenu of the File menu.

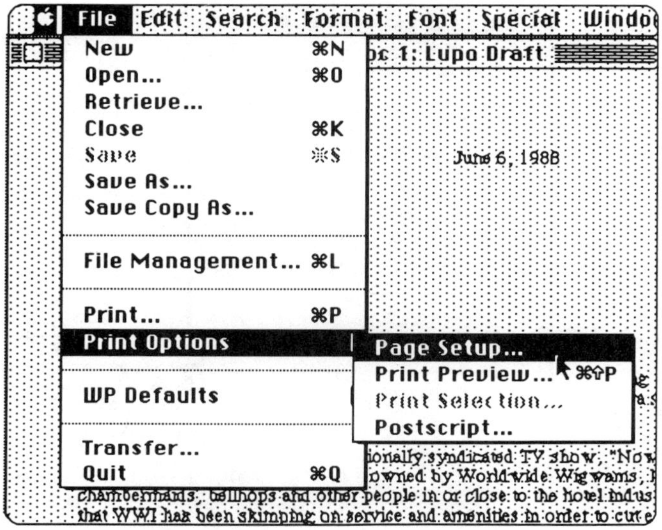

Figure 5-26. Choosing Page Setup from the Print Options submenu of the File menu.

The Page Setup dialog box gives you a number of options; the specific options vary according to which printer and which version of the system you are using. On a system with a Mac II and a LaserWriter II NT, there are four choices of letter size, two paper orientations, three printer effects, and a box for telling the Mac whether to reduce or enlarge, and by how much. (Two of the options here deserve explanation: An A4 letter is printed on paper $8\frac{1}{4} \times 11\frac{2}{3}$ inches—common in Europe—and a B5 letter is 9.8×7 inches.)

Step 3. If everything on the Page Setup dialog box is agreeable to you, click on OK.

Just to be sure that things are set up as you want them, use the Print Preview . . . selection on the Print Options submenu of the File menu.

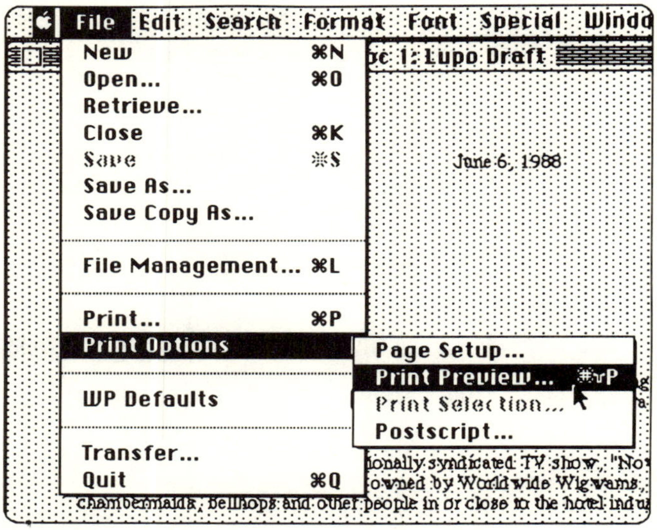

Figure 5-27. Choosing Print Preview from the Print Options submenu of the File menu.

When you choose Print Preview . . ., you'll get a picture of what the full pages of the document will look like on the paper, page by page.

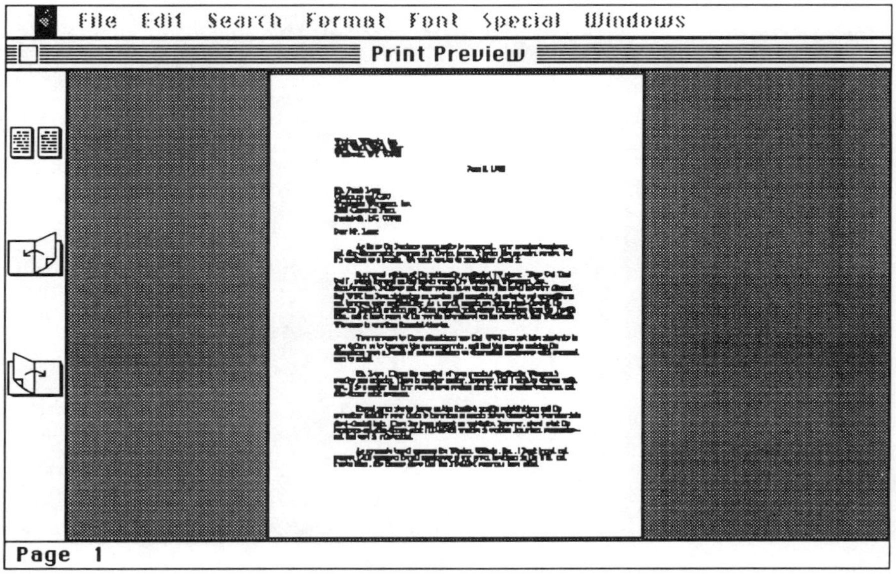

Figure 5-28. The page picture you get from Print Preview.

It's nearly impossible to read the text, but you can see the margins and the relationship of the various elements to each other, while you can also check whether the page numbers look right, and so on.

Here's how to print the document on paper:

Step 1. Choose Print from the File menu.

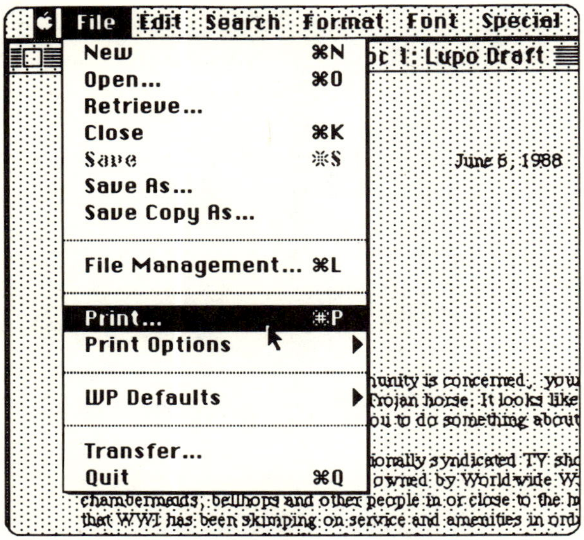

Figure 5-29. Choosing Print from the File menu.

A dialog box with the name of your printer will appear.

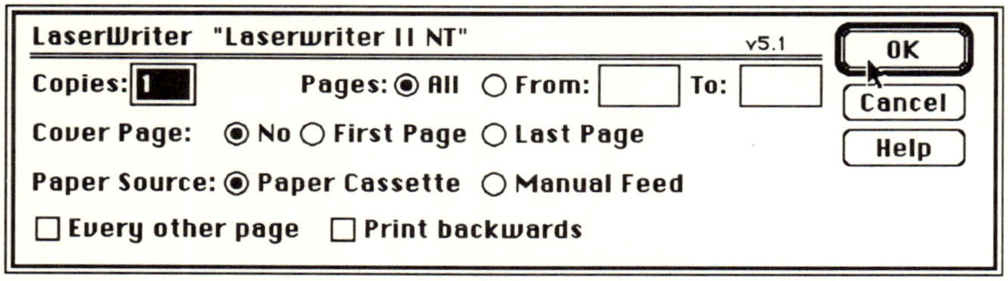

Figure 5-30. The Print dialog box.

Step 2. From the various options in the Printer dialog box, make your choices: number of copies to print, which pages to print, and so on.

Step 3. Click on OK. If all instructions have been properly given, if all hookups were properly made, if the printer is working properly with a sufficient supply of paper, you will get a proper printout of the letter. If there seem to be too many *ifs* in the previous sentence, it's only because printers are more subject to Murphy's Law than any other piece of computer equipment.

Remove the letter from the printer and look it over. If it's like most computer printouts, you will discover at least one error you missed on the screen. Make corrections using *WordPerfect* and reprint if necessary. This, your first *WordPerfect* document, took a lot of talk and many maneuvers to produce, but the beauty of it is that these procedures are easily repeated and many can be automatically set for the computer to perform for you.

Macros

This brings us to the magic of macros. A macro is a small program that condenses a number of keystrokes, and often a number of routines, into a much smaller number of keystrokes or routines. You should consider creating a macro for any keyboard routine that is repeated frequently and that involves more than five or six keystrokes. Macros multiply the power of your computer, increasing your efficiency by saving time and reducing errors. In the remaining portion of this chapter, you are going to learn to create macros that can be customized for your own tasks. You will see a formatting macro, a closing macro, and a printing macro.

Begin by doing a macro of your name as an example of how to create and recall macros. The basic procedure outlined here will be repeated for every macro you create:

Step 1. Tell *WordPerfect* you want to create a macro.
Step 2. Give the macro a filename.
Step 3. Define or create the macro.
Step 4. End defining and save the macro.

Writing a Macro

Now you will see step-by-step how to write your first macro. Clear the screen by choosing New from the File menu. Then:

Step 1. Choose Define Macro from the macro submenu of the Special menu.

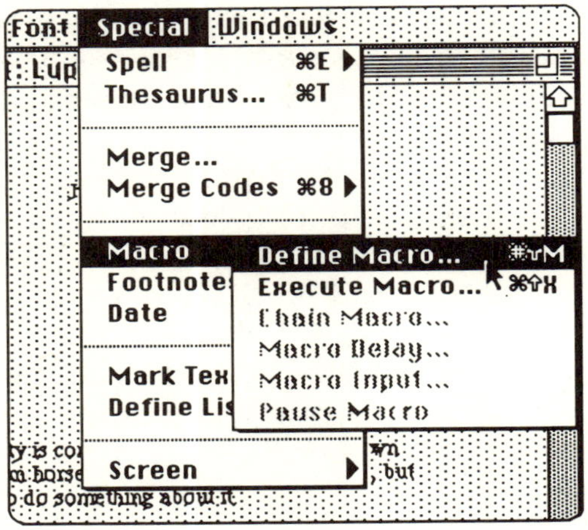

Figure 5-31. Choosing Define Macro from the Macro submenu of the Special menu.

A dialog box appears, asking you for the filename under which you want to save the macro.

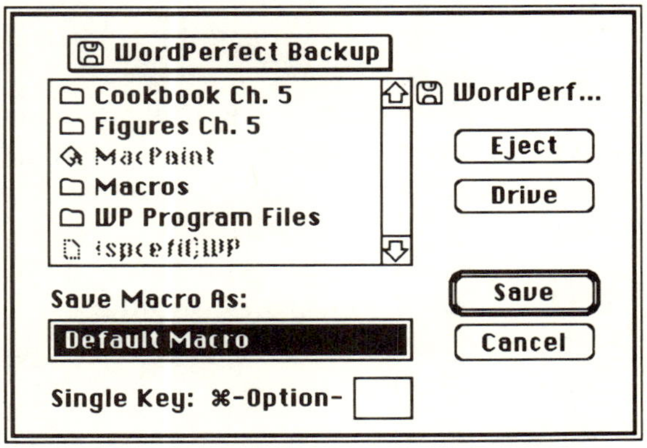

Figure 5-32. The dialog box for naming the macro.

This can be a single letter, number, or character. You may also choose to make this a single-key macro, which means that after the macro is created, you can start it at any time just by typing Command-Option-*key*, where *key* represents any single key on the keyboard. Let's try a single-key macro first.

Creating a One-Key Macro

Step 2. Give your macro a name. Since this will be a single key name, you should first click in the Single Key box. This is your first macro. As mentioned earlier, it will print your name at the press of a single key. Since it is first, use the 1 key. Type the number 1 in the Single Key box.

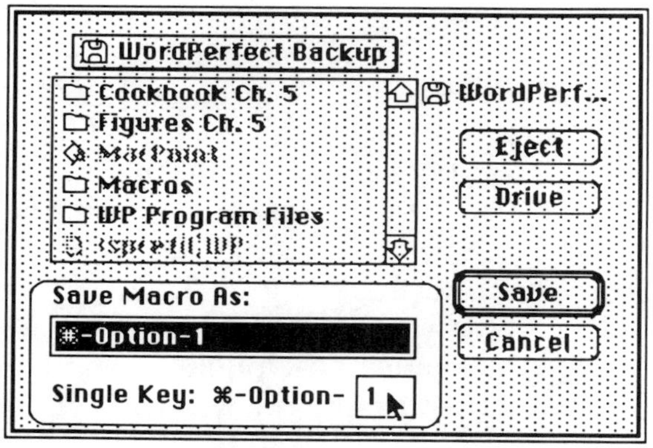

Figure 5-33. Naming the macro Command-Option-1.

Note that as soon as you hit 1, the full macro name appears in the Save Macro As box: *Command-Option-1*.

Step 3. Click on Save to save the macro name. At this point, the phrase Macro Def appears in the status line at the bottom of your screen, and you are ready to go through the procedure, or the series of keystrokes, that the macro Command-Option-1 is going to replace.

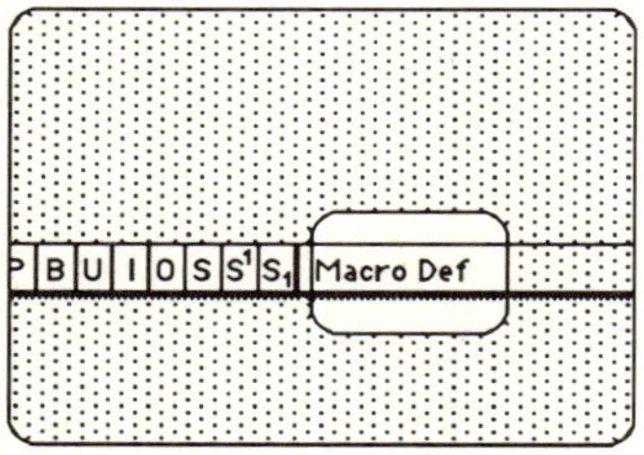

Figure 5-34. As long as Macro Def appears at the bottom of the screen, you're in the process of defining a macro.

Step 4. In this case you want the macro to type your name. Therefore, type your name exactly as you want the macro to reproduce it.

Step 5. End creating/defining the macro by choosing Define Macro from the Macro submenu of the Special menu.

Executing a One-Key Macro

That's all there is to it. Let's test it to make sure it works. Here's how you execute a single key macro:

Press Command-Option-1. That is, hold down both the Command and Option keys while you hit 1.

Your name should appear in the document at the current cursor location. If your name is 19 keystrokes long (including spaces, punctuation, and so on) and you have reduced it to three keystrokes, you have already increased your productivity by 533 percent!

You may want to change a macro at some point. Macros are easily changed, which makes them a very flexible tool for text editing. Let's make a new macro that won't be a single-key model. The macro you write next is a macro for your standard letter closing. You should be able to use it from now on.

Writing an Ordinary Macro

Step 1. Choose Define Macro . . . from the Macro submenu of the Special menu.

Step 2. Let's call this macro Closing. Type *Closing* in the Save Macro As box.

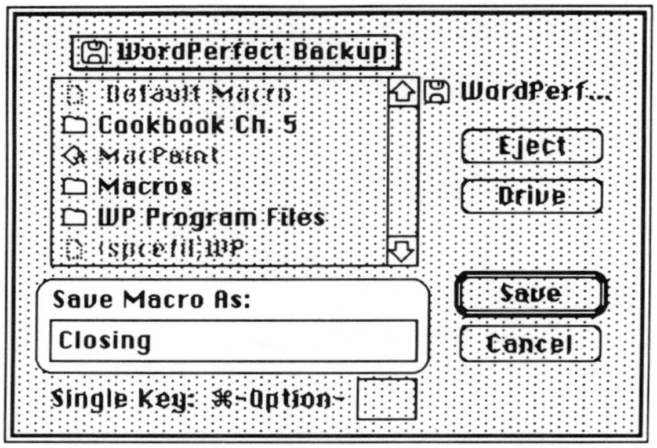

Figure 5-35. Giving the macro the name Closing.

Step 3. Hit Return, or click on Save. You now should see the Macro Def phrase in the status line at the bottom of your screen.
Step 4. If you place your closing at the center of the page, hit three tabs. (When you set the tabs in the letter format macro later, three tabs will take you to the center of the page.) If you place your closing at the left margin, skip this step.
Step 5. Type *Sincerely,* or *Yours truly,* or whatever your usual closing phrase is. Be sure to include the comma.
Step 6. Press Return four times.
Step 7. Enter three tabs if you place your closing at the center. If not, skip this step.
Step 8. Type your name.
Step 9. Press Return.
Step 10. Enter three tabs if you place your closing at the center. If not, skip this step.
Step 11. Type your title.
Step 12. To end defining the macro, choose Define Macro from the Macro submenu of the Special menu.

To see whether the macro performs as it should, close this document and open a new one. Now execute the macro, as explained below (it's only slightly more complicated than the single-key macro.

Executing an Ordinary Macro

Step 1. Choose Execute Macro . . . from the Macro submenu of the Special menu (Figure 5-36).

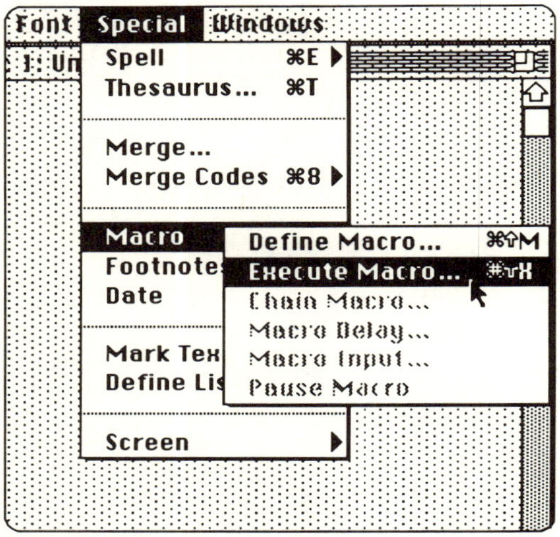

Figure 5-36. Choosing Execute Macro . . . from the Macro submenu of the Special menu.

You will see a dialog box asking you which macro you want to invoke, and showing a listing of folders and macros. On this listing, macros look like regular files, but you'll note that no regular files appear. When you leave *WordPerfect* and go back to the listing for the *WordPerfect* folder, you'll see that the icon for a macro is different from that for a regular file: It looks like a tape cassette. Your closing macro should be listed.

Step 2. Invoke the macro by clicking twice on Closing, or by clicking once on Closing and once on Execute, or by clicking once on Closing and pressing the Return key.

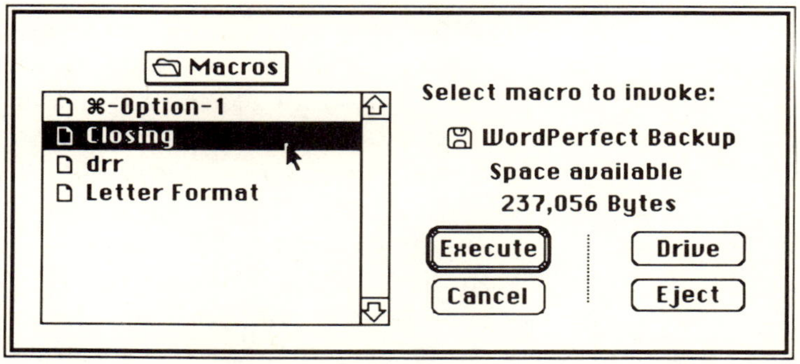

Figure 5-37. Choosing Closing in the Execute Macro dialog box.

Your closing should now appear in its correct form on the screen. If it isn't correct, go back through the steps again to see if you can spot your mistake.

A Letter Format Macro

The Closing macro is a just a one-action macro—a micromacro. Next, you'll attempt a minimacro. Let's write a macro that will set up a business letter on your company's $8\frac{1}{2} \times 11$ inch letterhead stationery. It will (among other things) set the margins and the tabs, give page numbering instructions, select the font, enter the correct date, and leave the cursor in the right place to start your letter.

Step 1. Open a new document. Choose New from the File menu, or type Command-N.
Step 2. Start the new macro. Choose Define Macro from the Macro submenu of the Special menu.
Step 3. Give the new macro a name. Type *Letter format,* then hit Return or click on Save.
Step 4. Now you're entering the procedures that will constitute the macro. First, format the page. Pull down the Format menu, highlight Page, slide across to Page Layout. The Page Layout dialog box appears and asks you to set the margins.

It's important to account for your letterhead. Where is it located on the page? Top? Side? Do you have an address footer at the bottom of the page? You have to make allowances for the location of the letterhead and any other printed information on your stationery. Usually pages after the first page are printed on standard stationery, so you only have to allow for the letterhead on the first page.

In this macro, enter the margins that are appropriate for your stationery. Values are entered here that may not be correct for your paper. Simply substitute the correct values for your stationery.

Setting New Margins

Step 5. Enter the figure for your Top Margin. Remember, if you have a top letterhead that appears only on the first sheet and not on subsequent sheets in a letter, you should set the top margin for the plain sheets. Account for the letterhead later. Accept the default top margin, 1.0 inch, so you don't have to enter anything.

Step 6. Hit the Tab key to move to the Left Margin box.

Step 7. Enter the figure for your Left Margin. If you have printed matter down the left side of your stationery, you'll have to allow for it when you set your left margin. If it takes up about 1.5 inches of the left side of your paper, you'll want to set the left margin at 2.0 inches or more. Once again, accept the default margin, 1.0 inch, by entering nothing.

Step 8. Tab to Bottom Margin.

Step 9. Enter the figure for your Bottom Margin. If you have the company address or other information at the bottom of your stationery, you will want to measure up from the bottom and add 0.5 inch or more. If not, select the default bottom margin and enter nothing.

Step 10. Tab to Right Margin.

Step 11. Enter the figure for your Right Margin. If there is no compelling reason not to do this, allow the default 1.0 inch margin to stand.

Step 12. Click on OK. Next, set the tab stops.

Step 13. From the Line submenu of the Format menu, choose Tabs. . . .

Step 14. Clear the tabs by clicking on Delete. Now install three tab stops. The first will be 0.5 inches from the left margin, the second will be 1.0 inch in from the left margin, and the third, an optional tab, will be at 4.25 inches.

Step 15. Type in the location of your first tab. It should be at LM + 0.5 inches, where LM is the position of the left margin in inches. Since the example let the left margin remain at 1.0 inch, type 1.5 inches as your first tab position.
Step 16. Click on Set.
Step 17. Type in the location of your second tab. It should be at LM + 1.0 inches, where LM is the position of the left margin in inches. Type 2.0 inches as your second tab position.
Step 18. Click on Set.
Step 19. If you prefer to put the date and the closing at the left margin, you can skip this step. If your practice is to start the date and the closing at the center of the page, you should enter 4.25 inches as the position of the third tab.
Step 20. If you entered a third tab setting in Step 19, click on Set. If not, go to Step 21.
Step 21. Click on OK to confirm the new tab settings.

Inserting Page Numbers

Step 22. Now tell *WordPerfect* what you want to do about page numbers. Choose Page Numbers from the Page submenu of the Format menu.
Step 23. Answer the questions on the Page Numbers dialog box by clicking in the appropriate circles. I prefer page numbers at the bottom center of each page, so I will click the Bottom Center circle.
Step 24. Confirm your page number selections by clicking on OK.

Next, make a decision about justification. Do you want the text of your letters fully justified (even at the right and left margins) or do you prefer the copy to be ragged-right (like most typewritten documents)? Either option will result in a good looking document, but fully justified documents look more formal.

Setting Justification

Step 25. Choose Show Ruler from the Format menu. When the ruler appears, you will see four justification icons just to the right of center.

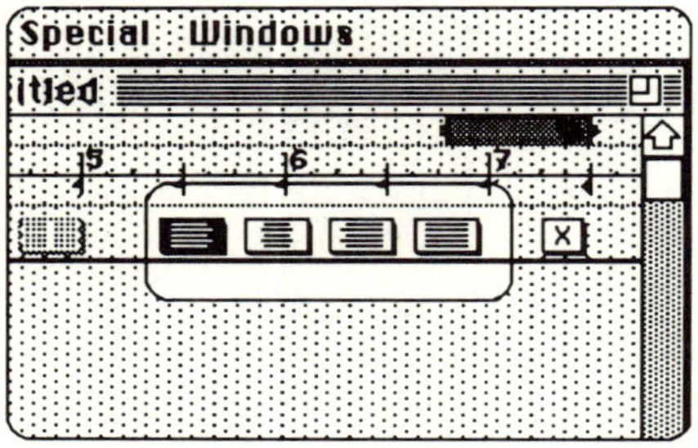

Figure 5-38. The four justification icons.

From left to right, they represent left justification only, center justification (every line centered), right justification only, and full justification (left and right margins are smooth). The default setting is left justification only.

Step 26. Click on the justification icon you prefer. If you prefer left justification only, do nothing. If you prefer to have your right margins justified as well, click on the full-justification icon.

Step 27. Hide the ruler by choosing Hide Ruler from the Format menu or by typing Command-R.

What about hyphenation? Do you want *WordPerfect* to handle it for you? It's your decision.

Automatic Hyphenation

Step 28. Choose Hyphenation . . . from the Line submenu of the Format menu.

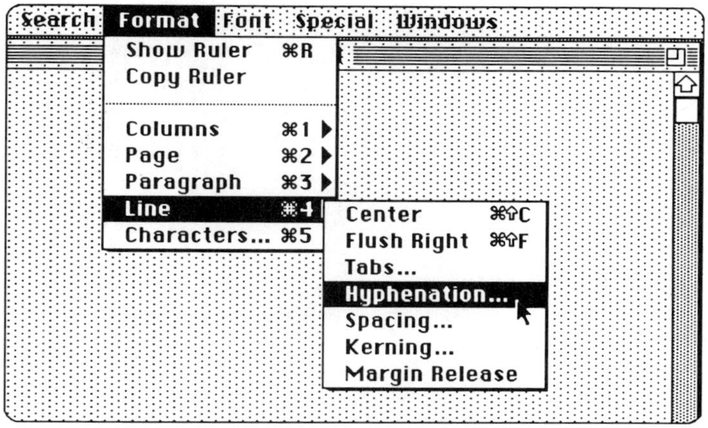

Figure 5-39. Choosing Hyphenation from the Line submenu of the Format menu.

A Hyphenation Control dialog box appears. You may choose whether to turn Hyphenation on, and if so, whether you want hyphenation to be Automatic or Auto-Aided.

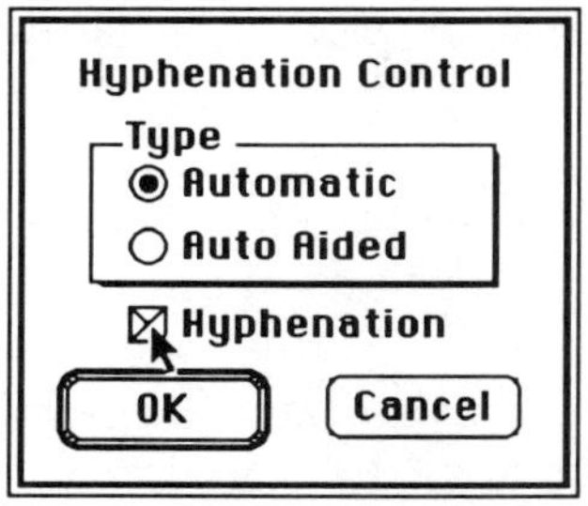

Figure 5-40. The Hyphenation dialog box, with Hyphenation selected.

In the Automatic mode, *WordPerfect* will hyphenate for you according to a set of built-in rules. Whenever the program runs into a word it doesn't know how to hyphenate, it will stop and ask how you want to handle that word.

Auto-Aided Hyphenation

In the Auto-Aided mode, the program will stop at every word it thinks should be hyphenated and ask you how you want to hyphenate it or whether you would prefer not to hyphenate it at all. For example, if you tell the program to hyphenate the Frank Lupo letter in the Auto-Aided mode, the first word it might bring to your attention is *chambermaids.* It will show the word hyphenated between *chamber* and *maids,* and it will give you three choices.

- You can click on OK and the word will be hyphenated as it appears in the box.
- You can click on Cancel and the word will not be hyphenated at all.
- You can click on the left and right arrows to move the hyphen in either direction.

Step 29. If you want hyphenation, click on Hyphenation, and an *X* will appear in the box. If you don't, skip the next step and go on to Step 31.

Step 30. If you want hyphenation, choose Automatic or Auto Aided. Most people prefer Auto Aided, because it's better to know where the program is hyphenating. Sometimes you may not care for the choices built into *WordPerfect.* For example, the program will suggest *approximate-ly* as the hyphenation of *approximately.* Most people would prefer to hyphenate a word closer to the middle.

Step 31. Click on OK to confirm your hyphenation choices. Now you will want to select the font and its size.

Step 32. Pull down the Font menu and choose the font you prefer. For the sake of this example, select Times.

Step 33. The default type size is 12-point. If you prefer a different size, pull down the Font menu again and choose the size you want. If you are happy with 12-point, skip this step and go on to Step 34.

Step 34. Choose Show Codes from the Edit menu and be sure there are no font or font size codes after the cursor. If there are, just use the Right-Arrow key to move the cursor in front of those codes, then use the Delete key to erase them.

Step 35. Choose Hide Codes from the Edit menu.

Entering the Date

The final step is to enter the date. First choose where to locate it vertically on the page (how far down from the top). That will usually be determined by your letterhead, which (for most firms) takes up some room at the top of the first sheet of a letter. (But only the first sheet, which is why you don't set the top margin to conform to the letterhead. After the first page, all subsequent pages are usually blank at the top, so use your usual 1.0 or 1.5 inches top margin.)

Step 36. Press Return (which is the same as moving down a line) until the cursor is the correct distance from the top.

Step 37. If you put the date of a letter at the center of the page, hit three tabs to position the date. If you put it at the left margin, skip this step and go on to Step 38.

Step 38. Choose Date from the Special menu. Look at the Date submenu. Earlier, when you entered a date from this menu, you used the Insert Text option. That was because it was a one-time need: today's date on today's letter. This time, however, you are creating a macro to be used many times in the future, on many different dates. For that reason, use the Insert Function option, which checks with the Mac's internal calendar each time the macro is invoked and enters the correct date. If you use the macro to format a letter tomorrow, it will enter tomorrow's date.

Step 39. Choose Insert Function from the Date submenu of the Special menu.

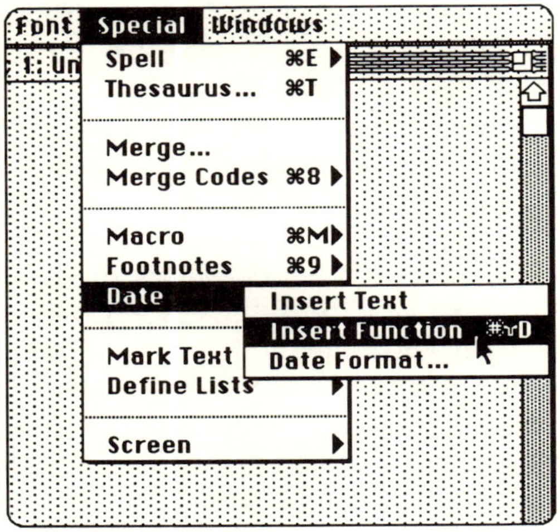

Figure 5-41. Choosing Insert Function from the Date submenu of the Special menu.

Today's date should appear on the screen. (If the date is wrong, go to the Control Panel option on the Apple menu and enter the correct date and time.)

Step 40. Press Return three times. This places the cursor where you want it to start entering the inside address.

Step 41. Choose Define Macro from the Macro submenu of the Special menu.

Running the Letter Format Macro

And that's it. A 41-step macro. Over the course of a few months, it will save you hours of formatting and hundreds (perhaps thousands) of keypresses and mistakes. Finally, call up the macro to be sure it works. Then quickly review what you just did.

Step 1. Open a new file by choosing New from the Edit menu or by typing Command-N.

Step 2. Invoke the macro by choosing Execute Macro from the Macro submenu of the Special menu, or by typing Command-Shift-X.

Step 3. Click twice on the Letter Format icon, or click once on the Letter format icon and then click on Execute.

With two quick steps you have a completely formatted and dated file in front of you, ready for you to type the inside address at the cursor. The two-step macro has accomplished all of these tasks:

- Set the top, left, bottom and right margins.
- Set the tab stops.
- Gave page numbering instructions.
- Gave margin justification instructions.
- Gave hyphenation instructions.
- Selected a font and a font size.
- Entered a date code.

At this point you have written a complete business letter and created three macros: one for your name, one for your letter closing, and one for formatting a business letter. Keep these macros. You can use them endlessly. You can also use them as models to create similar macros: Your boss's name and closing, for example.

Chapter 6

More Features, More Macros, More Sleight of Hand

Chapter 6

More Features, More Macros, More Sleight of Hand

The last two chapters have been spent preparing a letter to Frank Lupo. To get it into the mail, you'll need an envelope. Here are two envelope formats that you can store permanently as macros.

You need to put a return address in the upper left-hand corner if this is not a printed company envelope. If it is, you need to account for the location and size of that printed address. First, let's assume you're using a company envelope.

A standard #10 business envelope measures 9.5 × 4.125 inches. If the Wanton Widgets logo and address extend out about 3.5 inches from the left edge, and about 1.25 inches from the top edge, you will probably want to start the outside address about 3.5 inches from the left side and about 2 inches from the top.

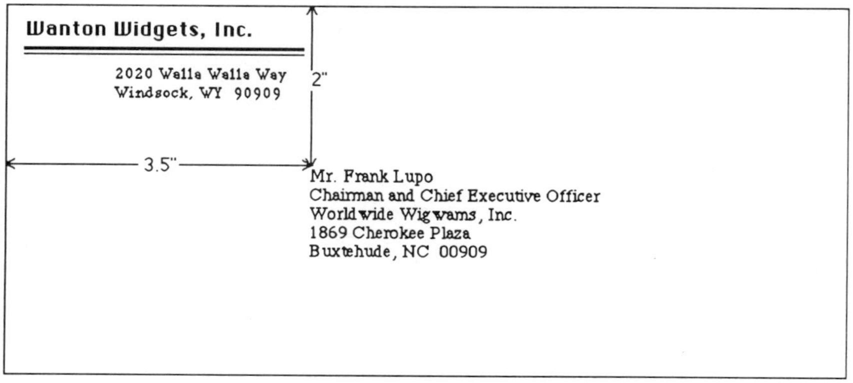

Figure 6-1. The envelope layout with a good location for the outside address: 2.0 inches from the top, 3.5 inches from the left.

In terms of your position display on the status line at the bottom of your screen, you want to start the address approximately at a horizontal position of 3.5 inches and vertical position of 2 inches. In other words, you want to set the left margin and top margins at those values. Here you go:

Step 1. Set up the envelope format by choosing Page Layout from the Page submenu of the Format menu.

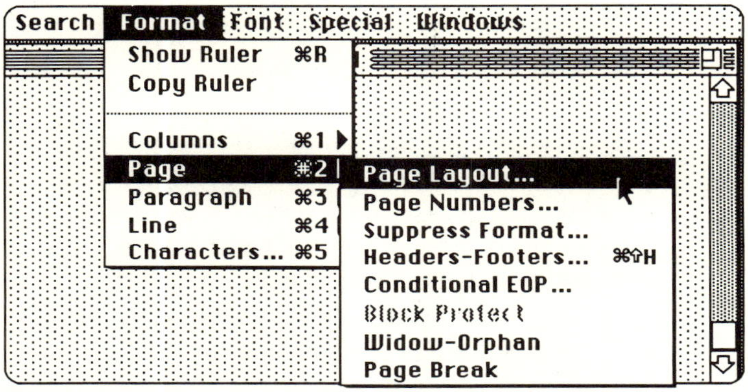

Figure 6-2. Choosing Page Layout from the Page submenu of the Format menu.

Step 2. In the Page Layout dialog box, set the margin values as follows:

Margin	**Value**
Top	2.0 inches
Left	3.5 inches
Bottom	0.0 inches
Right	0.0 inches

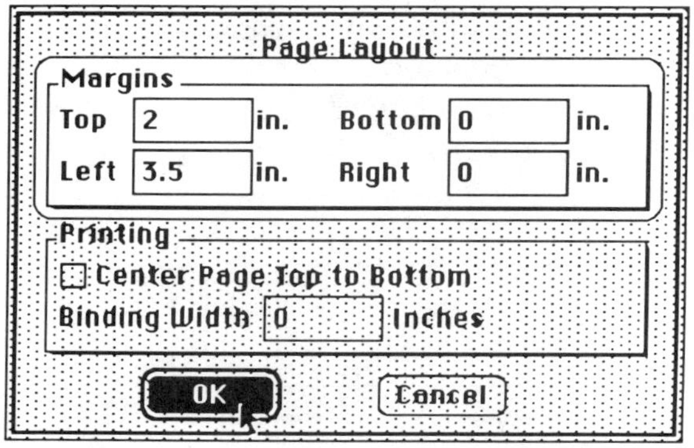

Figure 6-3. The new margin values set in the Page Layout dialog box.

Step 3. Click on OK in the dialog box.
Step 4. Turn on Show Position from the Screen submenu of the Special menu.

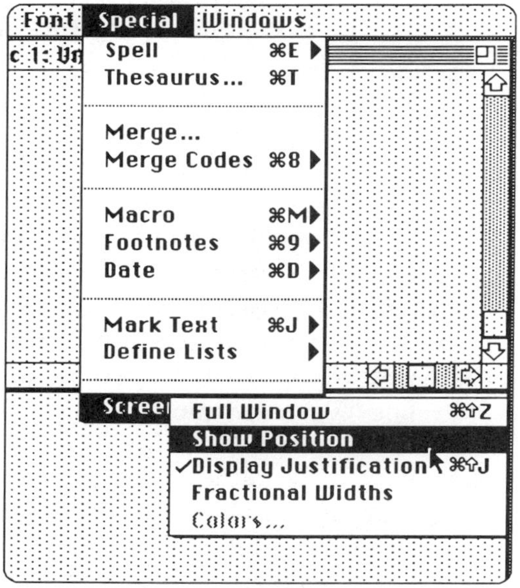

Figure 6-4. Turning on Show Position from the Screen submenu of the Special menu.

You see that after formatting the page (envelope), the position of the cursor is:

v 2.25 inches
h 3.5 inches

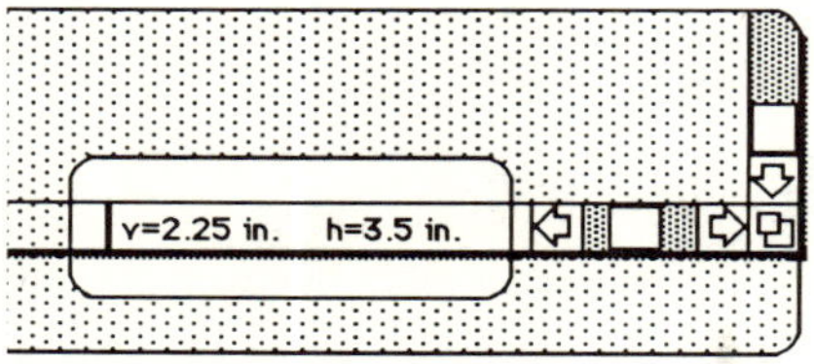

Figure 6-5. The position indicators show that the cursor location is at v = 2.25 inches (from the top), h = 3.5 inches (from the left side).

That's the format. Now retrieve the address from the Phone Book file.

Step 1. Select Open from the File menu.
Step 2. Locate the Phone Book file and open it.
Step 3. Select the Lupo address by dragging the cursor across it.
Step 4. Copy the Lupo address to the Clipboard by choosing Copy from the Edit menu.
Step 5. Close the Phone Book file.
Step 6. Paste the address onto your blank screen by choosing Paste from the Edit menu.

Now you're ready to print. The whole procedure so far presumes that you'll be printing your envelope on an ImageWriter dot-matrix printer. Despite all the other wonderful things they do, I have yet to find a laser printer that doesn't mangle envelopes. (If your laser printer works on envelopes, you may want to select the LaserWriter when you get to the Chooser, and you will probably want to select the Landscape mode in Page Setup (printing lengthwise rather than crosswise).

To automate this whole procedure for future use, you're going to create three envelope macros. In addition to the steps you have already taken, you will include the print steps. You will also see demonstrated the use of a terrific new macro option: the Pause option. Using the Pause device, you can stop in the middle of executing a macro, insert some material, then start up the macro again.

The #10 Envelope Macro

Here is the first envelope macro.

Step 1. Open a new file by choosing New from the File menu.
Step 2. Start creating the new macro by choosing Define Macro from the Macro submenu of the Special menu.

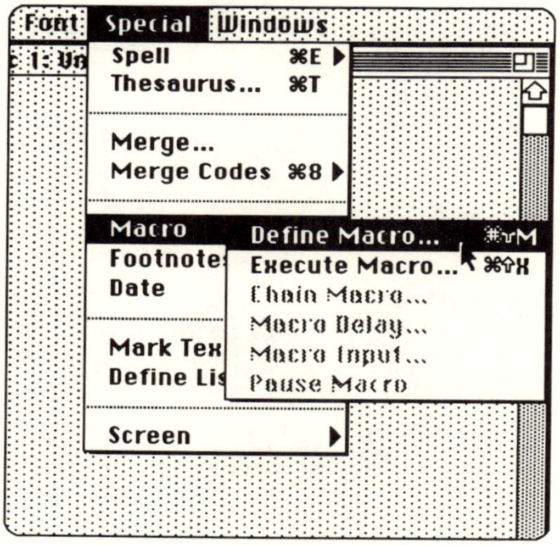

Figure 6-6. Choosing Define Macro from the Macro submenu of the Special menu.

Step 3. When the Macro dialog box appears, type *#10 Envelope* as the name under which you want to save the macro. Press Return.

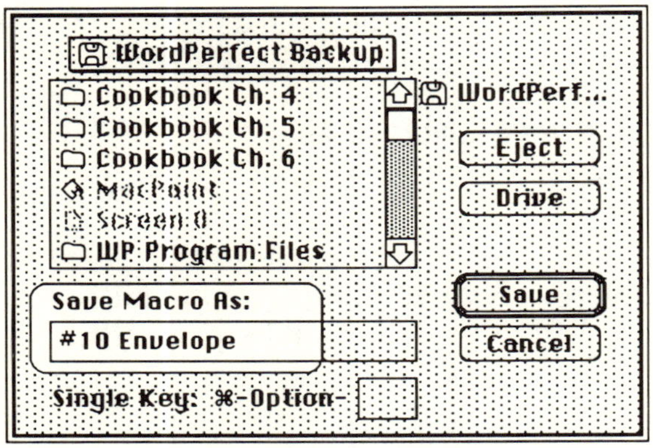

Figure 6-7. The Macro Title dialog box, with *#10 Envelope* entered as the title.

Step 4. Choose Page Layout from the Page submenu of the Format menu.

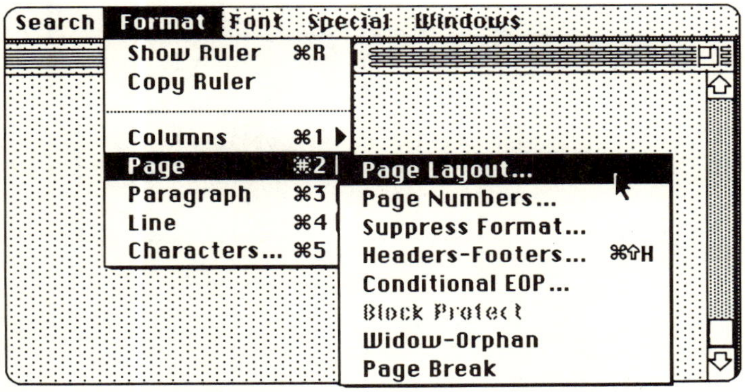

Figure 6-8. Choosing Page Layout from the Page submenu of the Format menu.

Step 5. Enter the Page Layout numbers in the Page Layout dialog box:

Margin	Value
Top	2.0 inches
Left	3.5 inches
Bottom	0.0 inches
Right	0.0 inches

Use the Tab key to move from one margin box to another.

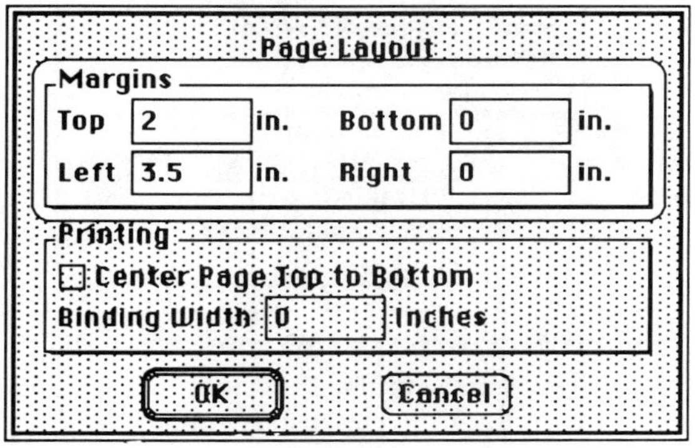

Figure 6-9. The Page Layout dialog box with the margin data entered.

Step 6. Click on OK, or press Return.
Step 7. Choose Show Position from the Screen submenu of the Special menu to confirm that the cursor is positioned where you want to start the address.

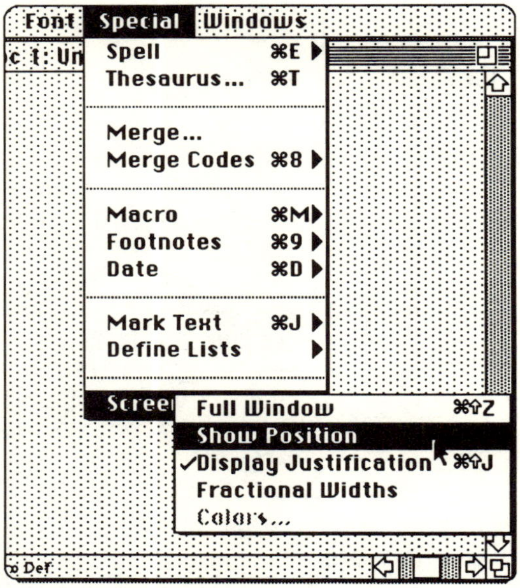

Figure 6-10. Choosing Show position from the Screen submenu of the Special menu to confirm the cursor position.

It should be at approximately
v 2.25 inches
h 3.5 inches

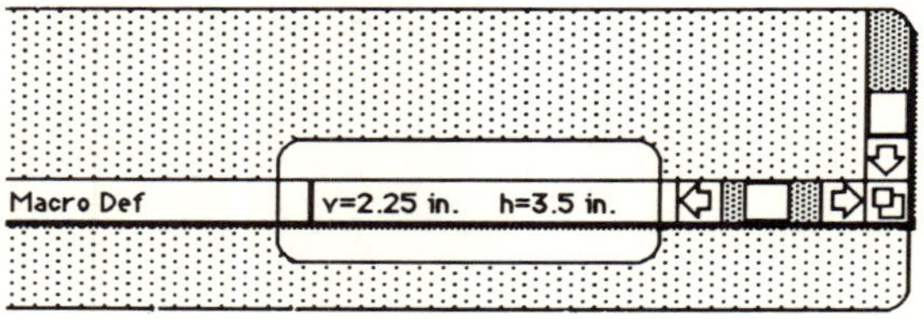

Figure 6-11. The position coordinates showing that the cursor is located 2.25 inches from the top, 3.5 inches from the left side.

Step 8. Select the font you prefer from the Font menu.

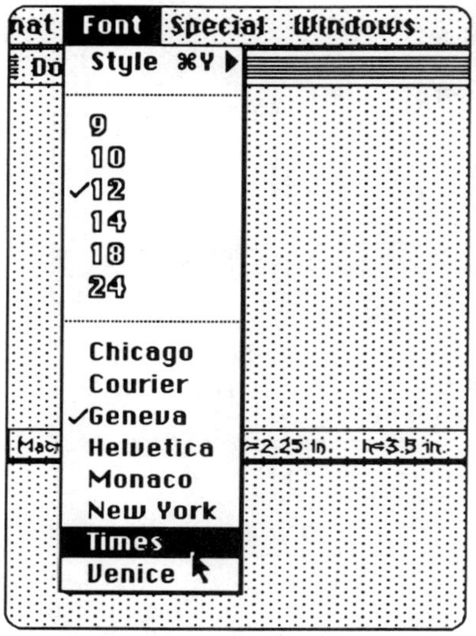

Figure 6-12. Choosing the Times font from the Font menu.

At this point the envelope is formatted and you're ready to enter the address. Close the Macro.

Step 9. Choose Define Macro again from the Macro submenu of the Special menu to end defining the macro. (Actually, you are toggling the Macro switch off after turning it on at the beginning. Perhaps in a future version *WordPerfect* will change this to End Macro Definition

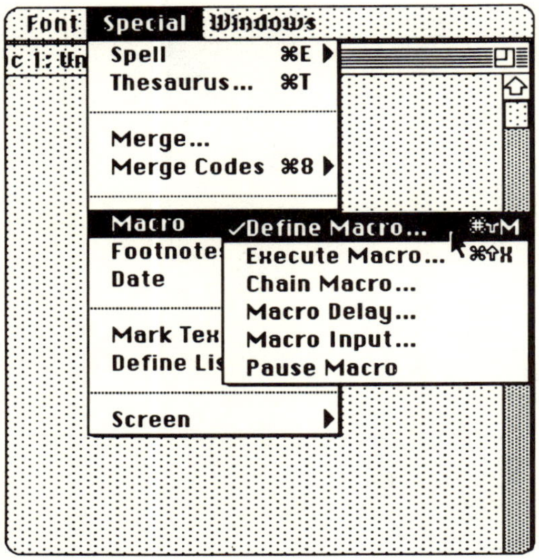

Figure 6-13. Ending the macro definition by choosing Define Macro from the Macro submenu of the Special menu.

The #10 Envelope macro you just created is a general-purpose macro for formatting a business envelope.

The Letter/Envelope Macro

Suppose you have just finished a business letter to someone. You want to address an envelope to that person and print it. That's very similar to the #10 Envelope Macro, with a couple of extra steps.

Here is an outline of the next macro:
Open a new file.
Give formatting instructions for the envelope.
Select the font.
Go to the letter to get the address.
Copy the address and bring it back to the new file.
Paste the address into the new file.
Print the envelope.

Nesting Macros Steps 2 and 3 in the following macro make up the #10 Envelope Macro you just created, so you can substitute that existing macro for those steps. That macro-inside-a-macro technique is called *nesting macros.* The nesting macros technique lets you use macros you have already written within new macros. It's like modular construction. Once you've built a module, you don't have to build it again to use it inside another unit. You simply insert the module.

You're also going to use a maneuver called *Pause* (mentioned earlier), which will stop definition of the macro while you type in the address, then continue when you tell it to resume.

This macro is going to open a new file, format an envelope, retrieve the address from the letter, copy it on the envelope, and print the envelope. Open your final version of the Lupo letter again and follow these steps:

Step 1. Open the macro by choosing Define Macro from the Macro submenu of the Special menu. (See Figure 6-6.)
Step 2. Type the name of the macro in the dialog box. Call it *Letter/Envelope.*
Step 3. Press Return, or click on Save.
Step 4. Open a new file by choosing New from the File menu.
Step 5. Here, the nesting macro maneuver is used. Execute the macro that formats a #10 envelope by choosing Execute Macro from the Macro submenu of the Special menu.

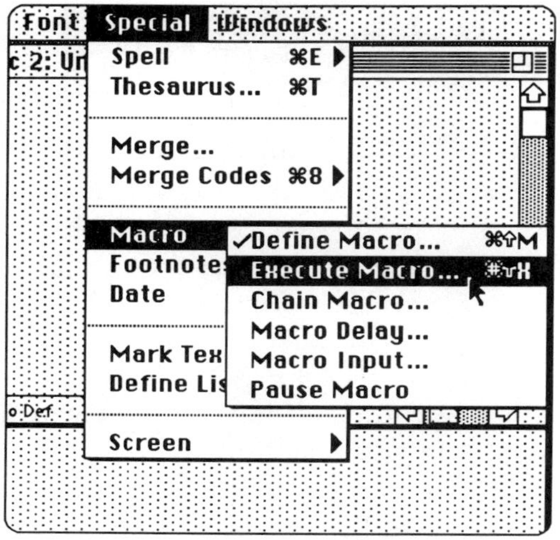

Figure 6-14. Choosing Execute Macro from the Macro submenu of the Special menu.

Step 6. Select the Format #10 Envelope macro in the dialog box.

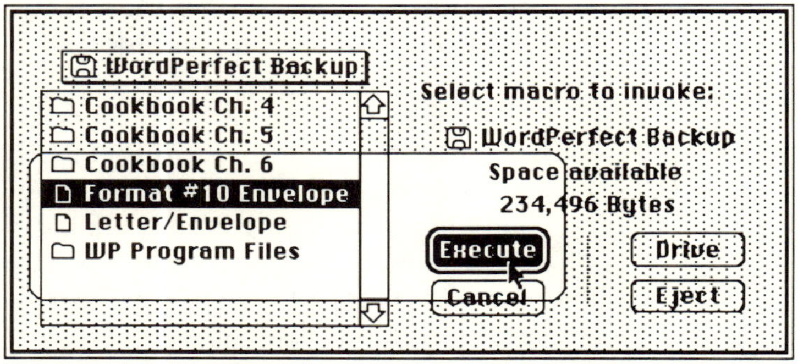

Figure 6-15. Executing the Format #10 Envelope Macro in the dialog box.

Step 7. Click on Execute or press Return. That takes care of formatting the envelope. Next, you have to retrieve the address from the Lupo letter.

Step 8. Return to the Lupo letter by choosing Cycle Windows from the Windows menu.

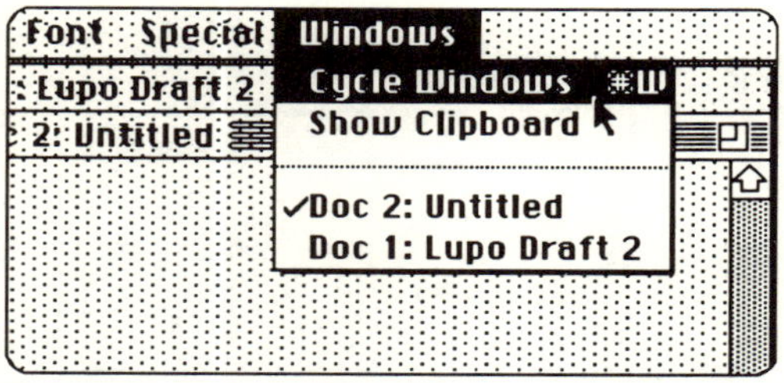

Figure 6-16. Choosing Cycle Windows from the Windows menu to return to the Lupo letter.

At this point you have to Pause while you locate the address and Select it.

Using Pause Macro

Step 9. Choose Pause Macro from the Macro submenu of the Special menu.

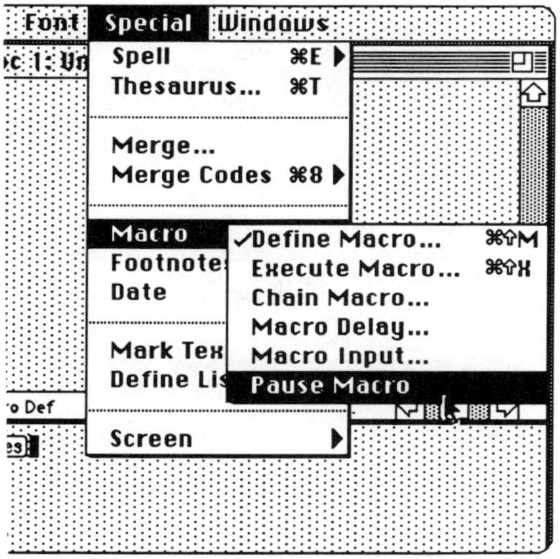

Figure 6-17. Choosing Pause Macro from the Macro submenu of the Special menu.

Note that *Macro Pause* appears in the status line at the bottom of the screen and remains there until you give the Resume Macro command.

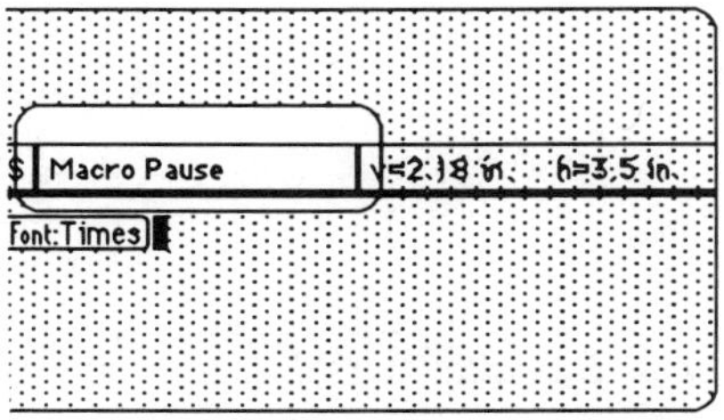

Figure 6-18. The phrase *Macro Pause* remains in the status line until the Resume Macro command is given.

Step 10. Now you're in the Pause mode. You can do anything you want without affecting the macro. You want to move the cursor to the inside address and select it.

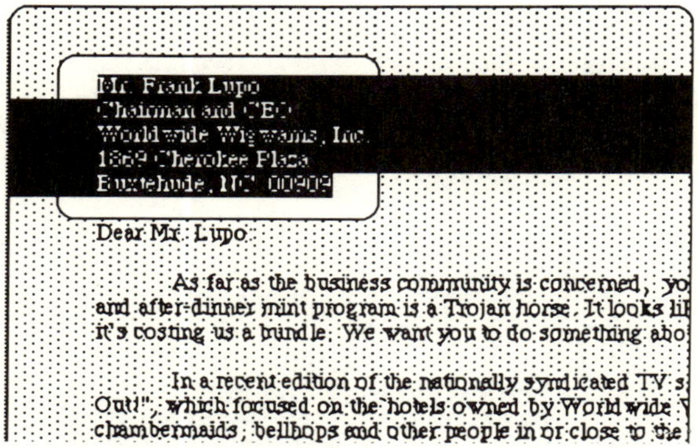

Figure 6-19. The inside address selected for copy and transfer to the envelope.

Step 11. Resume definition of the macro by choosing Resume Macro from the Macro submenu of the Special menu.

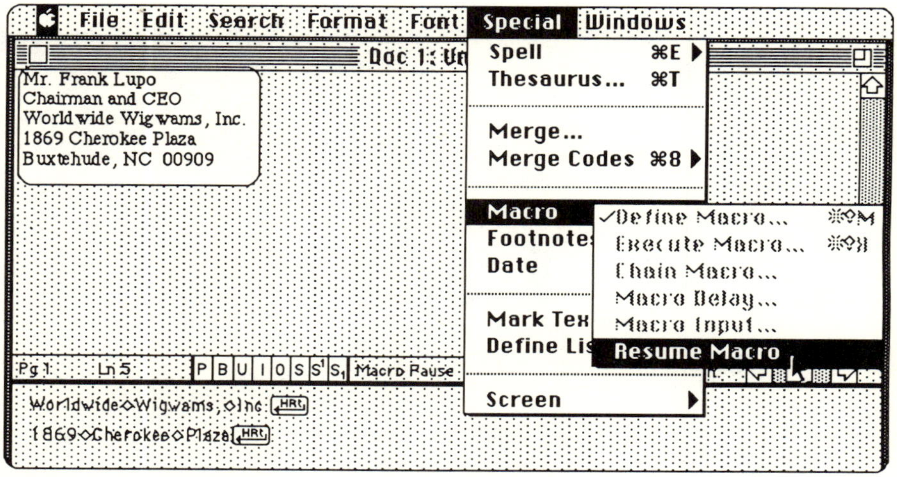

Figure 6-20. Choosing Resume Macro from the Macro submenu of the Special menu.

Step 12. Copy the address by choosing Copy from the Edit menu.

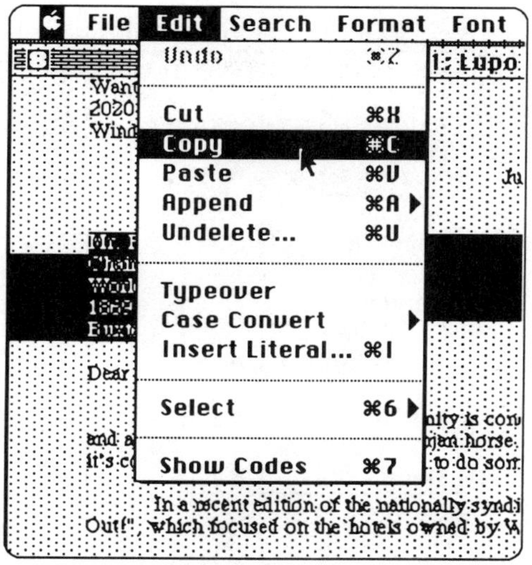

Figure 6-21. Copying the address by choosing Copy from the Edit menu.

Using Cycle Windows

Step 13. Return to the envelope by choosing Cycle Windows from the Windows menu.

Step 14. Paste the address onto the envelope by choosing Paste from the Edit menu.

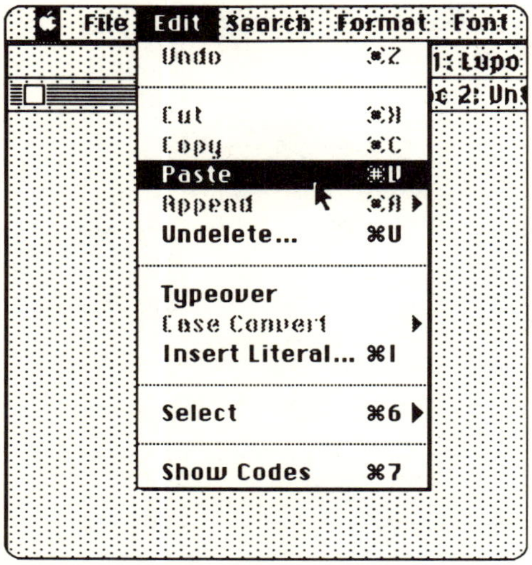

Figure 6-22. Pasting the address onto the envelope by choosing Paste from the Edit menu.

Step 15. Choose Print from the File menu to print the envelope.

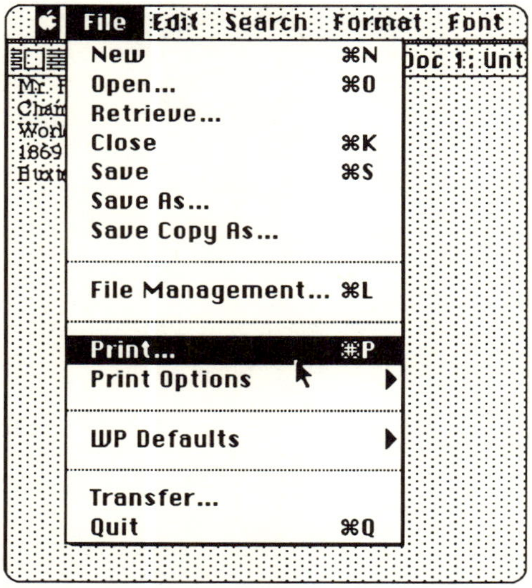

Figure 6-23. Choosing Print from the File menu to print the envelope.

Step 16. If you're using the ImageWriter, click on the Best button in the Print dialog box to get the best print quality, then click on OK or press Return to print the envelope. If you are using a LaserWriter, simply click on OK or press Return. If your printer is turned on and set up properly, the envelope should print.

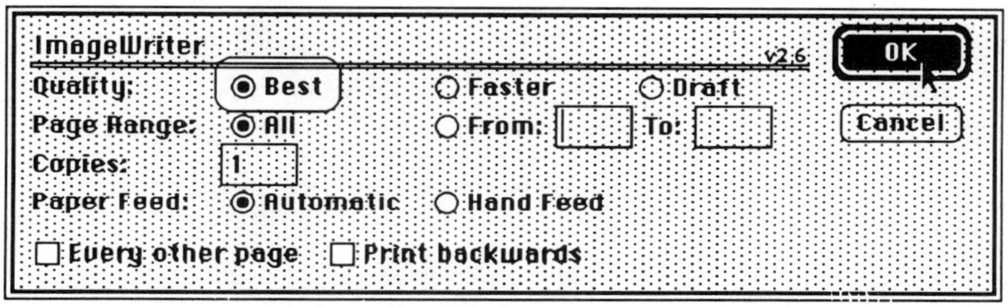

Figure 6-24. The Print dialog box for the ImageWriter, with Best print quality selected.

Step 17. Choose Cycle Windows from the Windows menu to return to the Lupo letter.
Step 18. Click once to Unselect the address.
Step 19. End definition of the macro by choosing Define Macro from the Macro submenu of the Special menu.

This is a handy macro. You can use it every time you write a letter. If you want to change the name of a macro, just pull down File Management from the File menu, click on the macro files, and change the name to whatever you find easiest to use.

The Memo Macro

Here's a fetching macro in about 40 steps that will set up a standard memo form for you. You only have to type the name of the addressee and the subject of the memo. Your name and the date will be automatically entered, along with the memo heading (*To, From,* and so on). Begin by opening a new file.

Step 1. Choose Define Macro from the Macro submenu of the Special menu.
Step 2. Type *Memo* as the name of the macro.

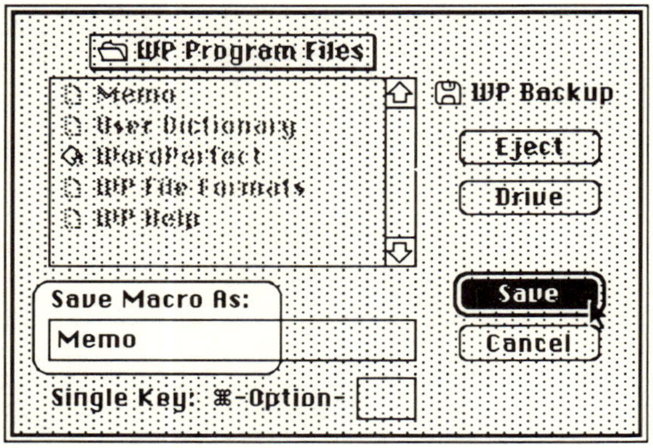

Figure 6-25. Naming the new macro *Memo.*

Step 3. Click on Save or press Return.
Step 4. Select the font from the Font menu.
Step 5. Select the font size you want.

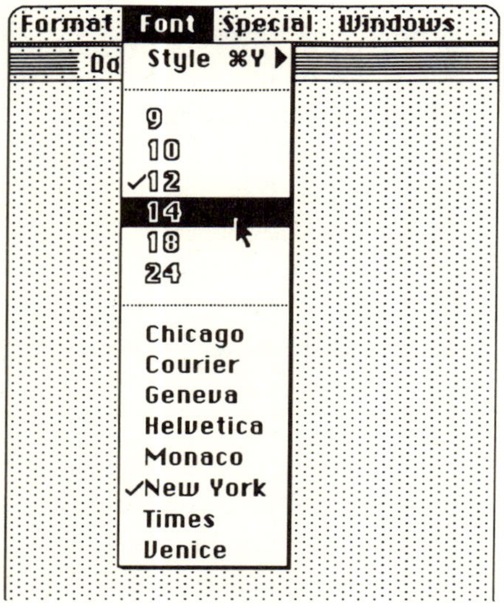

Figure 6-26. Choosing 14-point type in the New York font from the Font menu.

Step 6. Center the heading by choosing Center from the Line submenu of the Format menu.

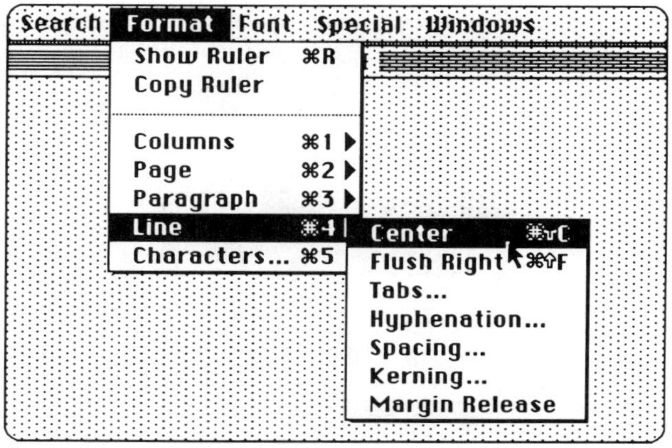

Figure 6-27. Choosing Center from the Line submenu of the Format menu.

Step 7. Turn on Bold by clicking on the *B* in the status line.
Step 8. Set up for uppercase letters by pressing the Caps Lock key at the left end of your keyboard. *WordPerfect* has no screen indicator when Caps Lock is on.
Step 9. Type *MEMO*.
Step 10. Press the Caps Lock key again to turn uppercase off.
Step 11. Press four Returns.

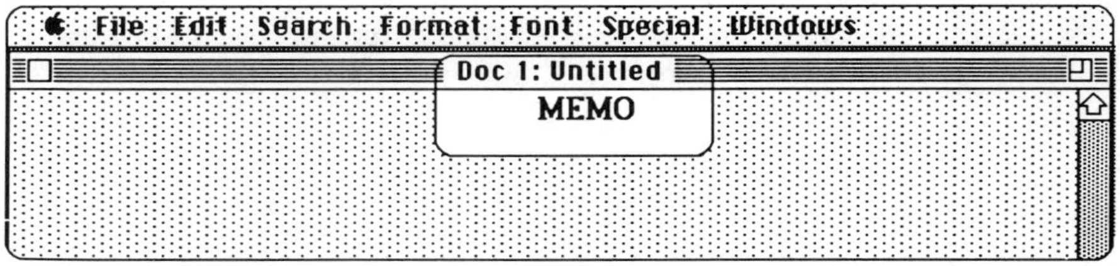

Figure 6-28. Type *MEMO*.

Step 12. Change to a smaller font size by choosing 12-point from the Font menu.
Step 13. Type *To:* and press Tab twice.
Step 14. Turn off Bold by clicking on the *B* in the status line.

Using Macro Input

Step 15. Here comes a new macro trick: Choose Macro Input from the Macro submenu of the Special menu. An Input dialog box will appear, prompting you to enter the input prompt.

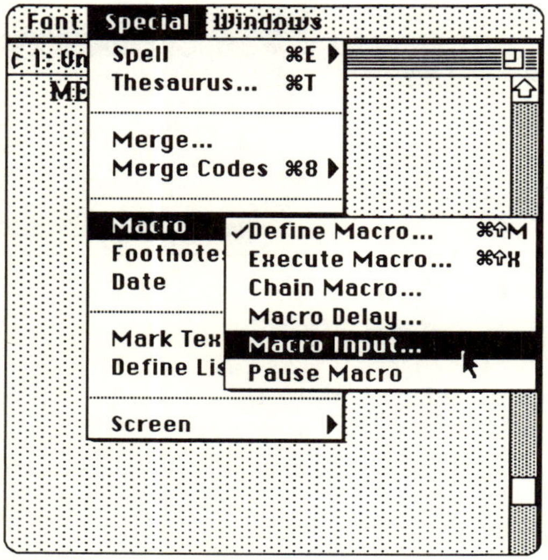

Figure 6-29. Choosing Macro Input from the Macro submenu of the Special menu.

In other words, type in the words that will prompt you or any other user to make the needed entry at this point. Now the macro needs the name of the person to whom this memo is being addressed.

Step 16. Type *Enter name of addressee* in the Input dialog box.

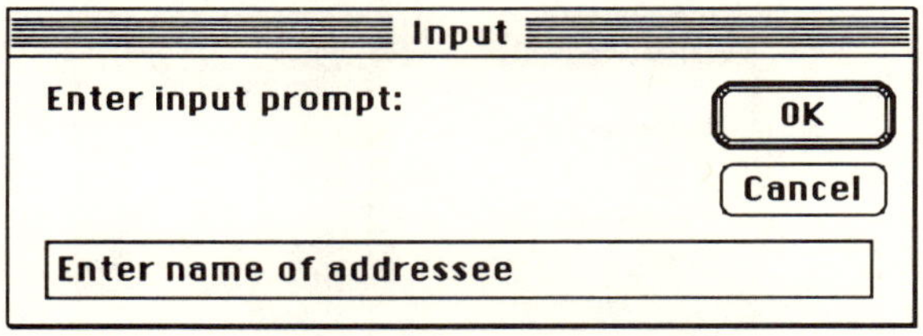

Figure 6-30. The Input dialog box with *Enter name of addressee* entered as the input prompt.

Step 17. Click on OK, or press Return.
Step 18. Press Return again.
Step 19. Turn on boldface by clicking the *B* in the status line.
Step 20. Type *From:* and press Tab.
Step 21. Turn off boldface by clicking on *B* in the status line.
Step 22. Type your name.

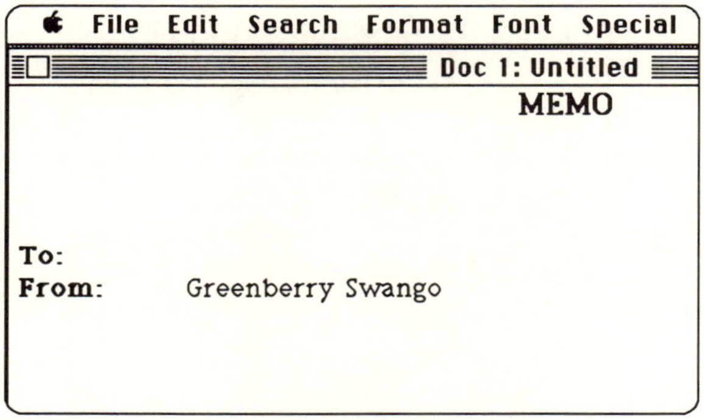

Figure 6-31. The appearance of the screen after Step 22.

Step 23. Press Return again.
Step 24. Turn on boldface by clicking on the *B* in the status line.
Step 25. Type *Date* and press Tab twice.
Step 26. Turn off boldface by clicking on *B* in the status line.
Step 27. Put in the Date code by choosing Insert Function from the Date submenu of the Special menu.

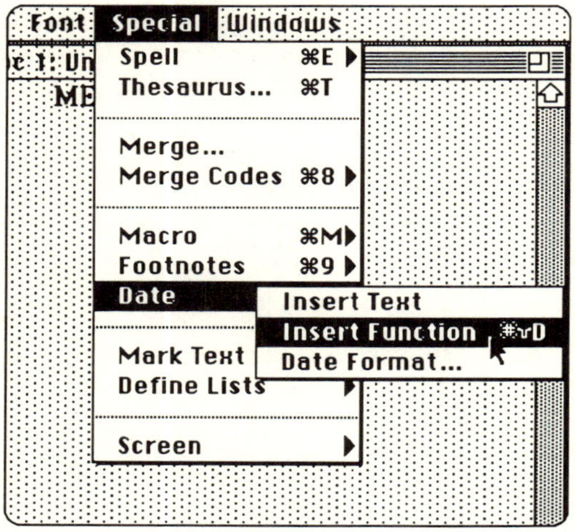

Figure 6-32. Choosing Insert Function from the Date submenu of the Special menu.

Step 28. Press Return.
Step 29. Turn on boldface. (An alternate way of turning on boldface is by pressing Command-Shift-B.)
Step 30. Type *Subject:* and press Tab.
Step 31. Turn off boldface.
Step 32. Choose Input Macro from the Macro submenu of the Special menu.
Step 33. Type in your input prompt for Subject: *Enter memo subject*

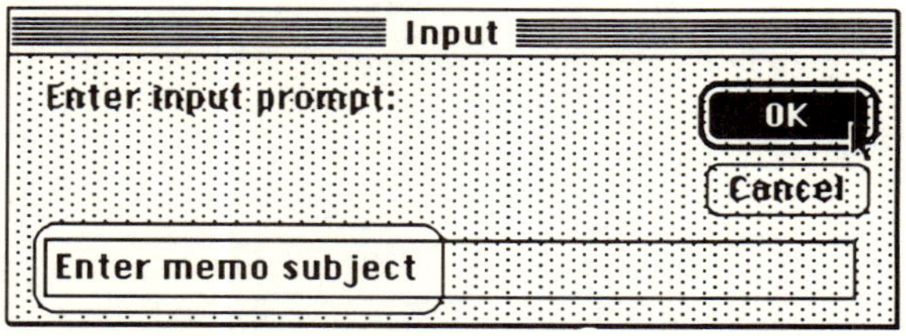

Figure 6-33. The Input dialog box with *Enter memo subject* inserted as the Subject prompt.

Step 34. Click on OK or press Return.

Automating Keystroke Repetitions

Step 35. Press Return twice. You are now going to put a horizontal line or divider across the page in approved memo style, and to do it you'll use a little trick you haven't pulled out of the toolbox before. If you press the Escape (Esc) key, you'll see that this is a way of instructing the Mac to repeat a keystroke or maneuver multiple times. You'll see how it works as we go along.

Step 36. Press Esc (if you have an older Macintosh without an Esc key, press Clear). You'll see the Repeat Count dialog box. The default number, 8, is highlighted. To change it, simply type in another number.

Step 37. Type in the number 65.

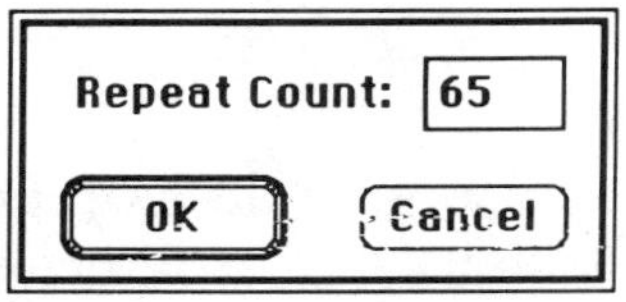

Figure 6-34. The Repeat Count dialog box with 65 entered as the number of times to repeat the function.

Step 38. Press the equal key (=). Don't click on OK or press Return before you press the equal key, or you will change the default setting to 65 repeats, which would be an inconvenient default. If you are using the default margin settings, 65 repeats should make a line from one margin to another. If it doesn't work, use more or fewer repeats.

Step 39. Press Return twice.

Step 40. End programming this macro by choosing Define Macro from the Macro submenu of the Special menu.

This memo macro will quickly format memos for you whenever you need to send one out into the world.

Test the macro by executing it. Type in *Charlie Tuna* as the name of the addressee and *Bumblebee merger* as the memo subject. When you're finished, the memo should look like Figure 6-35.

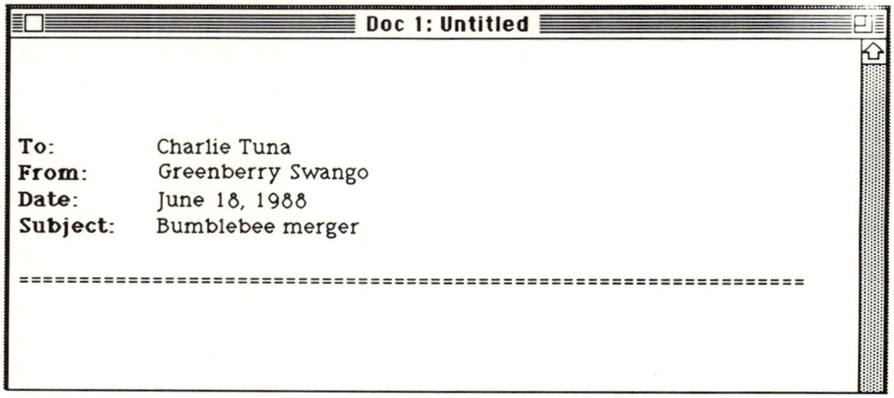

Figure 6-35. Here's what your screen should look like after you execute the Memo macro.

Writing in Columns

Although not a sophisticated desktop publishing package, *WordPerfect* is moving steadily in that direction. It gives you many of the page-layout features of desktop-publishing software, including the ability to create pages in column format.

WordPerfect permits the use of two types of columns: newspaper columns and parallel columns.

Newspaper columns *snake* from top to bottom: You read the left-hand column from top to bottom, then you go to the top of the next column to the right and read it from top to bottom, and so on.

Parallel columns are read in blocks from left to right. You start with an entry in the left-hand column, move to a related entry in the second column, then the third, and so on. This format is often used with interviews. The questions would be in the left column and the replies would be in (usually) larger blocks to the right of the questions.

First, let's practice each type. Later you'll set up macros for using both column formats.

Newspaper Columns

The newspaper column format might be particularly useful for you if you turn out a newsletter for employees, clients, or club members. In setting up a page with columns, you're going to be asked how many columns you want on the page, how much separation you want between columns, whether you want the columns to be the same size and evenly-spaced, and so on.

Let's set up a simple newsletter format on an 8.5 × 11 inch sheet. You're going to have to make some of the same decisions about page format that you did with the business letter. Among the specifications you will have to make are:

Width of right, left, top, and bottom margins
Font style and size
Justification
Hyphenation

Use a three-column format, evenly-spaced, with half-inch margins around the outside to give a bit more room for text on the sheet. Those outside margins have to be set up in the Page Layout dialog box, just as they were for the letter. Start by creating a macro that will set up a newsletter page.

Step 1. Choose Define Macro from the Macro submenu of the Special menu.
Step 2. Type in *3-column format* as the name of the macro.

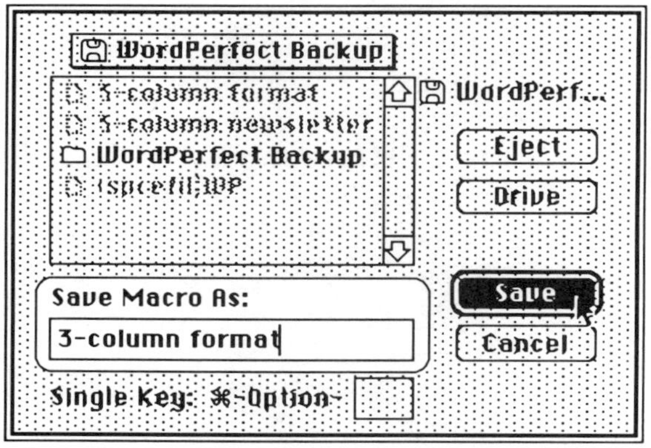

Figure 6-36. Saving the macro under the name *3-column format*.

Step 3. Press Return or click on Save.
Step 4. Choose Show Codes from the Edit menu. This is not an

essential part of this macro, but it is a good technique for following what you are doing step by step. If you can see each code appear as you enter commands, you'll have a better sense of how the program is responding. And you'll feel more confident about what you're doing if you see a visual confirmation of each step. Hide the codes again just before you finish defining the macro.

Step 5. To create smaller outside margins, choose Page Layout from the Page submenu of the Format menu.

Step 6. Type .5 and then press the Tab key. Do this step four times to set all outside margins at 0.5 inches.

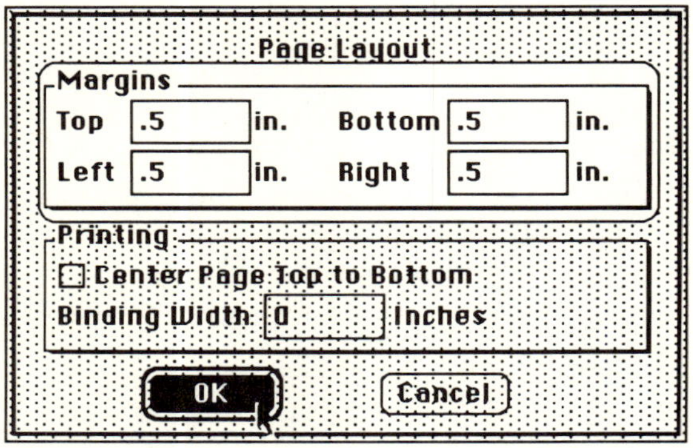

Figure 6-37. The Page Layout dialog box with all margins set at 0.5 inches.

Step 7. Press Return or click on OK.

Using Snaking Columns

Step 8. Choose Column Options from the Columns submenu of the Format menu.

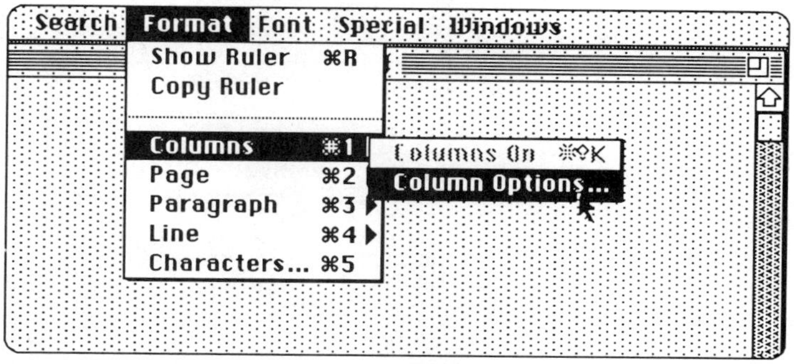

Figure 6-38. Choosing Column Options from the Columns submenu of the Format menu.

Step 9. Type 3 as the number of columns. Accept the default figure of 0.25 inches between columns, so leave the Space Between Columns box alone.

Step 10. Click on the Evenly Spaced Columns box. At this point the Column Margins table will automatically be filled in. The table will show that the first column has a left-hand margin at 0.5 inches and a right-hand margin at 2.83 inches. The second column has a left-hand margin at 3.08 inches (that's 2.83 inches, plus the intercolumn spacing of 0.25 inches) and a right-hand margin at 5.43 inches. The third column has a left-hand margin at 5.68 inches and a right-hand margin at 8.03 inches. (Your values may vary somewhat.)

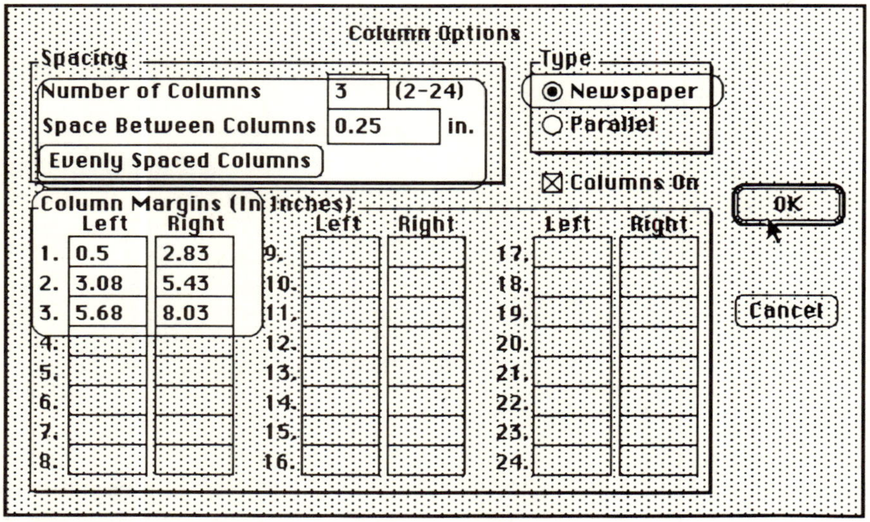

Figure 6-39. The Column Options dialog box with columns and margins described.

Step 11. Press Return or click on OK. You can confirm that the Column feature is turned on by looking at the status line in the lower left-hand corner of your screen. In addition to the page number and line number, it now displays *Col 1*.

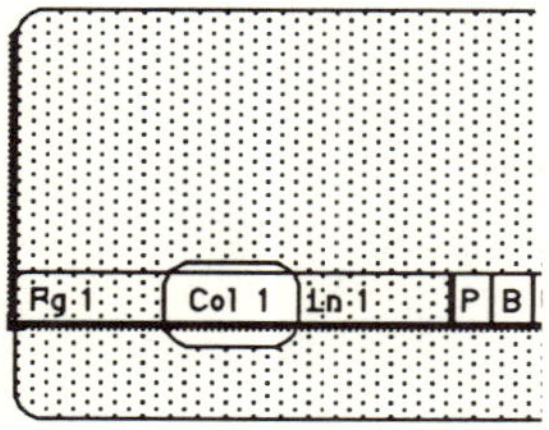

Figure 6-40. The *Col 1* indicator in the status line shows that columns are turned on.

Step 12. Select the font you prefer from the Font menu. (For this exercise, choose Venice, if it's available.)
Step 13. Select the font size you prefer from the Font menu.
Step 14. Newspaper-style columns look better with the right margins justified, so choose Full Justification. Haul out the ruler

by choosing Show Ruler from the Format menu. (Note that the Column icon is highlighted as further confirmation that you are in the Column mode.)

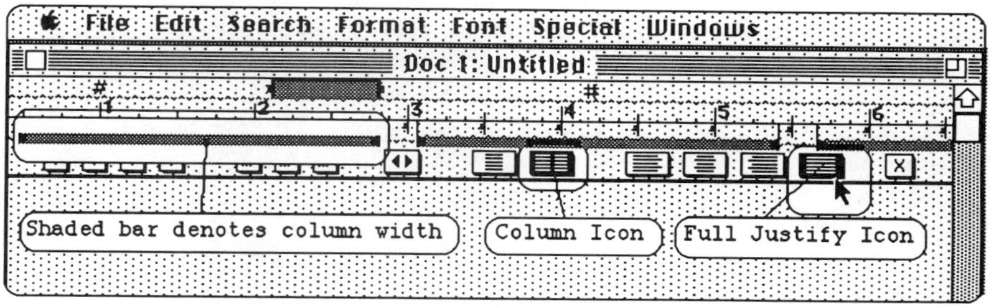

Figure 6-41. The ruler, showing that the Column icon is on and the Full Justification icon has been selected.

Step 15. Click on the Full Justification icon. (While you're looking at the ruler, note the shaded strips just above the icons which mark the column boundaries.)

> When you execute this macro, you may find that your text is not right-justified even though you have included the Full Justification command in your macro. A bug or deficiency in early versions of the software prevents the correct encoding of certain mouse commands into macros. At the time of this writing, the bug is still there, but *WordPerfect* says it will be corrected for later releases. Presumably, by the time this book is published, the bug will no longer be a problem. If you find that your text is not right-justified after you invoke this macro, however, simply go to the head of the text, bring out the ruler, and click on the Full Justification icon.

Step 16. Put the ruler away by choosing Hide Ruler from the Format menu.

Step 17. Choose Hyphenation from the Line submenu of the Format menu.

Step 18. In the Hyphenation Control dialog box, click on Hyphenation.

Step 19. Just to see how *WordPerfect* does by itself on hyphenation, let Automatic hyphenation stand. Click on OK, or press Return.

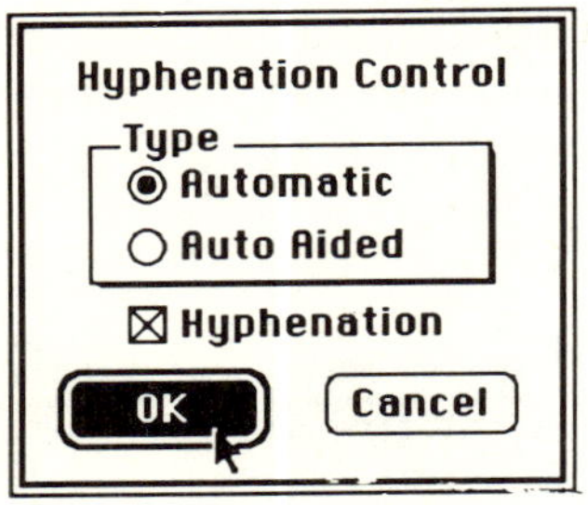

Figure 6-42. The Hyphenation Control dialog box with Hyphenation on and Automatic Hyphenation selected.

Step 20. Before you take this step, look at the series of codes you have entered into this macro (see Figure 6-43). Then choose Hide Codes from the Edit menu.

Figure 6-43. The series of codes that make up the three-column format macro.

Step 21. End definition of the macro by choosing Define Macro from the Macro submenu of the Special menu.

That's the three-column format macro. Give it a block of text to work on and see what happens:

Open a new file. Don't execute the three-column format macro yet. Copy the following block of text, purloined from an 18th-century periodical called *The Spectator.* The author is Richard Steele, and the essay from which this passage is taken appeared on Friday, March 2, 1771:

> The first of our Society is a Gentleman of Worcestershire, of antient Descent, a Baronet, his Name Sir Roger de Coverly. His great Grandfather was Inventor of the Famous Country-Dance which is call'd after him. All who know that Shire, are very well acquainted with the Parts and Merits of Sir Roger. He is a Gentleman that is very singular in his Behaviour, but his Singularities

proceed from his good Sense, and are Contradictions to the Manners of the World, only as he thinks the World is in the wrong. However, this Humour creates him no Enemies, for he does nothing with Sowrness or Obstinacy; and his being unconfined to Modes and Forms, makes him but the readier and more capable to please and oblige all who know him. When he is in Town he lives in Soho-Square. It is said he keeps himself a Batchelour by reason he was crossed in Love, by a perverse beautiful Widow of the next County to him. Before this Disappointment, Sir Roger was what you call a fine Gentleman, had often supped with my Lord Rochester and Sir George Etherege, fought a Duel upon his first coming to Town, and kick'd Bully Dawson in a publick Coffee-house for calling him Youngster. But being ill used by the above-mentioned Widow, he was very serious for a Year and a half; and tho' his Temper being naturally jovial, he at last got over it, he grew careless of himself and never dressed afterwards; he continues to wear a Coat and Doublet of the same Cut that were in Fashion at the Time of his Repulse, which, in his merry Humours, he tells us, has been in and out twelve Times since he first wore it. 'Tis said Sir Roger grew humble in his Desires after he had forgot this cruel Beauty, insomuch that it is reported he has frequently offended in Point of Chastity with Beggars and Gypsies; But this is look'd upon by his Friends rather as Matter of Raillery than Truth. He is now in his Fifty sixth Year, cheerful, gay, and hearty, keeps a good House both in Town and Country; a great Lover of Mankind; but there is such a mirthful Cast in his Behaviour, that he is rather beloved than esteemed. His Tenants grow rich, his Servants look satisfied, all the young Women profess Love to him, and the young Men are glad of his Company. When he comes into a House he calls the Servants by their Names, and talks all the way up Stairs to a Visit. I must not omit that Sir Roger is a Justice of the Quorum; that he fills the Chair at a Quarter-Session with great Abilities, and three Months ago gain'd universal Applause by explaining a Passage in the Game-Act.

What you have here is a batch of unformatted text.

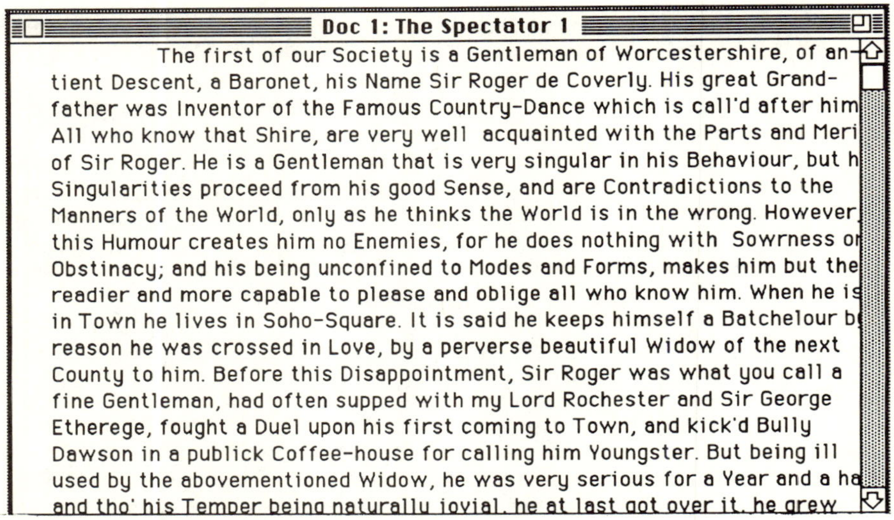
Doc 1: The Spectator 1

The first of our Society is a Gentleman of Worcestershire, of antient Descent, a Baronet, his Name Sir Roger de Coverly. His great Grandfather was Inventor of the Famous Country-Dance which is call'd after him All who know that Shire, are very well acquainted with the Parts and Meri of Sir Roger. He is a Gentleman that is very singular in his Behaviour, but h Singularities proceed from his good Sense, and are Contradictions to the Manners of the World, only as he thinks the World is in the wrong. However this Humour creates him no Enemies, for he does nothing with Sowrness o Obstinacy; and his being unconfined to Modes and Forms, makes him but the readier and more capable to please and oblige all who know him. When he i in Town he lives in Soho-Square. It is said he keeps himself a Batchelour b reason he was crossed in Love, by a perverse beautiful Widow of the next County to him. Before this Disappointment, Sir Roger was what you call a fine Gentleman, had often supped with my Lord Rochester and Sir George Etherege, fought a Duel upon his first coming to Town, and kick'd Bully Dawson in a publick Coffee-house for calling him Youngster. But being ill used by the abovementioned Widow, he was very serious for a Year and a h and tho' his Temper being naturally jovial, he at last got over it, he grew

Figure 6-44. First screen of unformatted text.

Next comes a test of the three-column format macro you just created. Move the cursor to the top of the file by pressing Enter, Enter, Enter, Up Arrow (Enter is on the numeric keypad). This shortcut may not work on your Macintosh. In that case, use the scroll bar and then press the Left-Arrow key repeatedly. That positions the cursor in front of all codes.

Now execute the macro.

Step 1. Choose Execute Macro from the Macro submenu of the Special menu.
Step 2. Select *3-column format* in the dialog box.
Step 3. Click on Execute or press Return.
Step 4. If you created the macro correctly, the *Spectator* page will now be reformatted into three columns. But it's still in Geneva font rather than Venice. What went wrong?

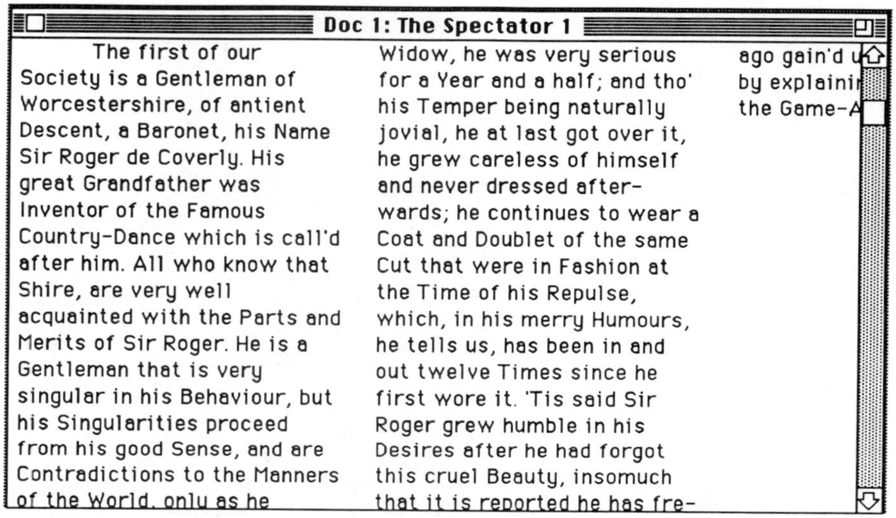

Figure 6-45. The reformatted first screen of *The Spectator* in Geneva font.

This is another good opportunity for troubleshooting with the Revealed Codes. If you bring up the codes by choosing Show Codes from the Edit menu, you will see the problem immediately. The culprit is the Geneva font code sitting right behind the cursor.

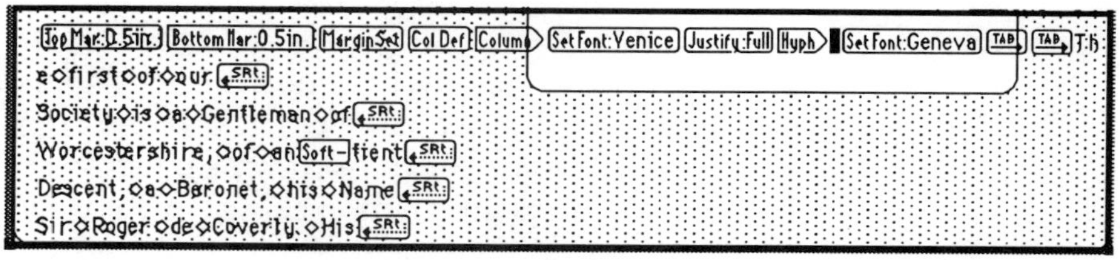

Figure 6-46. With the Codes revealed, the Geneva Font code is discovered lurking right behind the cursor.

This is exactly as it should be. When you insert something in front of work you have already written, *WordPerfect* protects the original font until you instruct it otherwise. In this case, you inserted a macro full of formatting instructions; *WordPerfect* throws up a Geneva Font code to preserve the typeface already in the document. To remove it, you only have to press a Right Arrow to move the cursor behind (or to the right of) the Geneva font code; then press Delete (Backspace) to remove it.

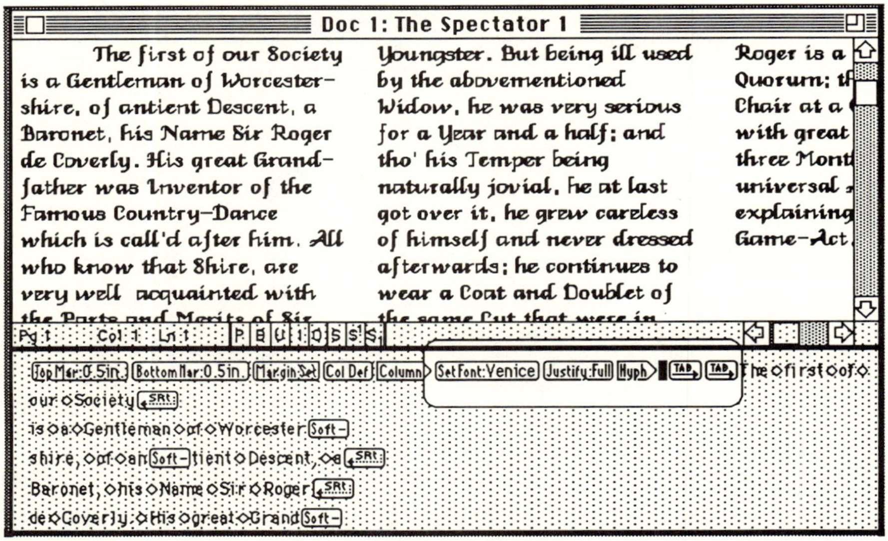

Figure 6-47. With the Geneva font removed, the document is reformatted in the Venice font.

You will notice also in Figure 6-47 that the document text is not right-justified, even though the Full Justification icon appears in the Codes part of the Screen. This is a manifestation of the bug mentioned earlier. Until *WordPerfect* gets it straightened out you can correct the problem by choosing Show Ruler from the Format menu, then clicking on the Full Justification icon.

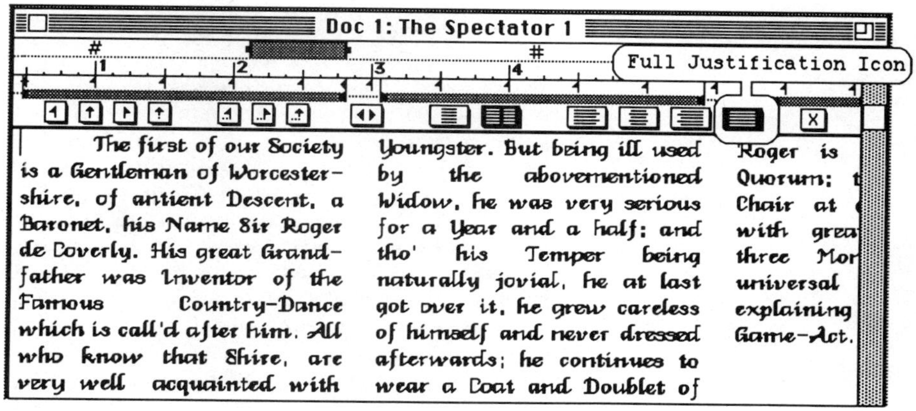

Figure 6-48. The text after selecting the Full Justification icon.

- Now that the 18th-century newsletter is in the three-column format, you can play around with this format in all kinds of ways, manipulating headlines, rules between the columns, graphics within the columns, and so on. One thing to remember is that once the columns are defined, you can easily move in and out of the column format simply by clicking the appropriate icon on the ruler.
- Suppose, for example, you want to start the story with text that goes all the way across the page, and then switch into the column format after two or three lines. Here's what you do.

Beginning the Columns Within the Body of the Text

Step 1. Reveal the codes by choosing Show Codes from the Edit menu.

Step 2. Move the cursor to the top of the text by hitting Enter, Enter, Up Arrow (or use the scroll bar, if this key combination doesn't work on your Macintosh). Check the position of the cursor among the codes, and move it to the right with the Right-Arrow key until it's at the end of all the formatting codes, just in front of the tabs that begin the text.

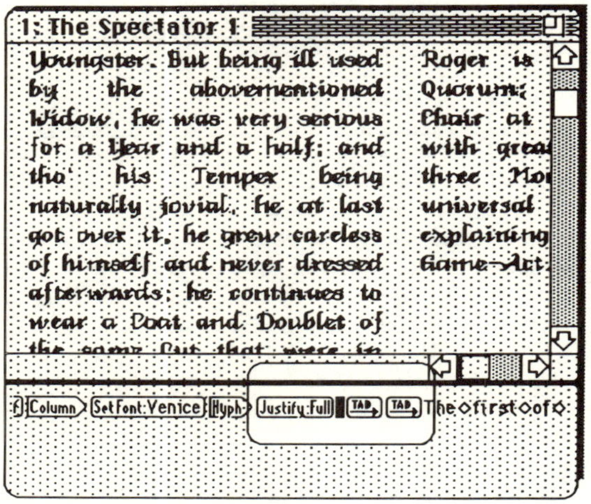

Figure 6-49. The cursor positioned just before the tabs.

Step 3. Choose Show Ruler from the Format menu.

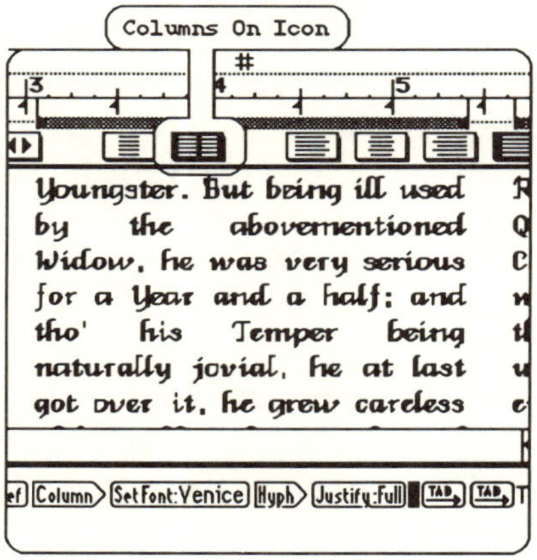

Figure 6-50. The ruler with the Columns On icon highlighted.

Step 4. Click on the Columns Off icon.

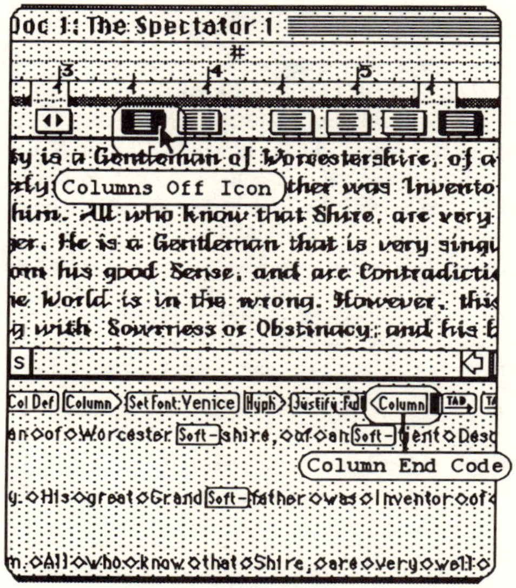

Figure 6-51. The ruler with the Columns Off icon selected. Note that an End Columns Code has appeared before the cursor in the Show Codes section of the screen, and that the text has been reformatted without columns.

Step 5. The text is now reformatted without columns. Move to the end of the fourth line of the text and position the cursor at the right end of the line by pressing Enter, Enter, Right Arrow, or by pressing the Right-Arrow key repeatedly.

Step 6. Press two Returns to create a space after the fourth line. Click on the Columns On icon again. The text is reformatted into the same three columns, and you see that a Begin Column Code has appeared before the cursor.

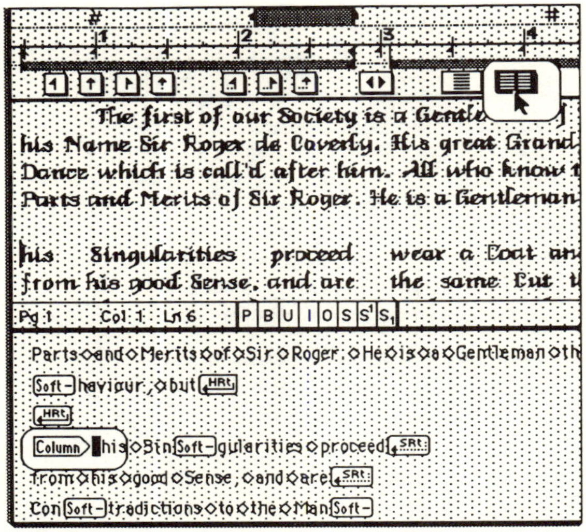

Figure 6-52. With the Columns On icon selected again, the text following the cursor is reformatted into the same three columns. Note the Column Begin code in front of the cursor.

Choose Hide Codes from the Edit menu and Hide Ruler from the Format menu to see a full screen of text.

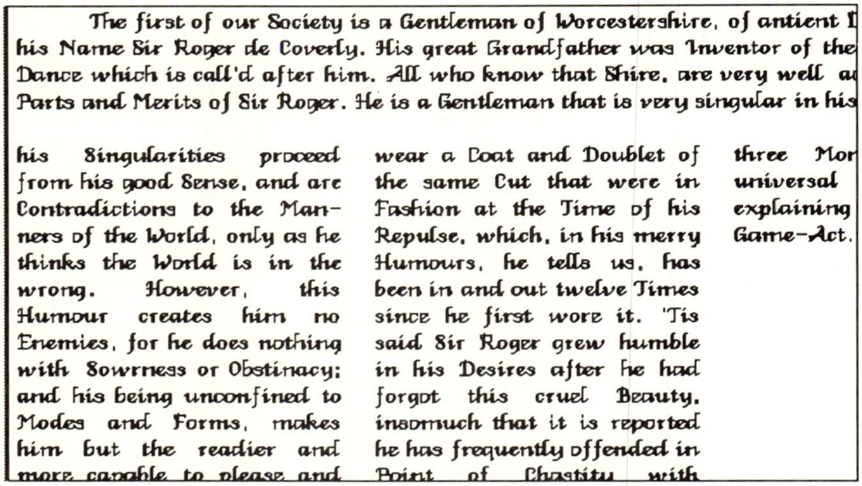

Figure 6-53. A full screen of the formatted text.

You can switch back and forth between this Columns On and Columns Off format as often as you wish. The column definitions stand until you change them. Save this file as *Spectator 3* by choosing Save As . . . from the File menu and typing in *Spectator 3* when the dialog box appears. You'll use this file again.

Parallel Columns

Parallel columns are read left to right. A quarterly earnings report is a good example, and you're going to set up a macro for creating one right now. This is an enormous macro (it has over 100 steps). It gets a big, complicated job done easily.

You may want to add additional lines or other kinds of data. It will be easy if you follow this model.

The Quarterly Financials Macro

This macro creates the whole setup for a summary of a company's quarterly income and earnings report: the kind you would find in a quarterly report to shareholders. The macro is long and contains some new tricks, so be careful to do exactly what the Mac tells you to do, step by step.

Step 1. Choose Define Macro from the Macro submenu of the Special menu.
Step 2. Type *Quarterly Financials.*
Step 3. Open a new file by choosing New from the File menu.
Step 4. Choose Show Codes from the Edit menu.
Step 5. Choose Center from the Line submenu of the Format menu.
Step 6. Select the font you want to use for your company's name (for this example select Venice, if it is available).
Step 7. Select the font size you want (for this example, select 18). Check the codes on the lower part of the screen to see whether there are any font or size codes behind the cursor. If there are, erase them by moving the cursor to the right with the Right Arrow, then deleting with the Delete or Backspace key.
Step 8. Choose Macro Input from the Macro submenu of the Special menu.
Step 9. Type *Enter company name.*
Step 10. Click on OK.
Step 11. Press two Returns.

Step 12. Choose Center as before.

Step 13. Select the font for the subheading (I selected New York). Use the Right Arrow and Delete to get rid of the previous font.

Step 14. Select the font size for the subheading (for this example, choose 14).

Step 15. Turn on Bold.

Step 16. Type *Financial Highlights.*

Step 17. Press two Returns.

Step 18. Press five Tabs.

Step 19. Select font size for the third line (choose 12). Use Right Arrow and Delete to remove any previous font size codes.

Step 20. Choose Macro Input from the Macro submenu of the Special menu.

Step 21. Type *Enter quarter (First, Second, etc.).*

Step 22. Click on OK.

Step 23. Type *Quarter Ended* (precede this entry with a space to make the printout format correctly).

Step 24. Press Return.

Using Parallel Columns

Step 25. Choose Column Options . . . from the Columns submenu of the Format menu. From this point on, the procedure is different from that used with newspaper columns.

Step 26. Click on Parallel Columns.

Step 27. Enter 4 as the number of columns.

Step 28. Press Tab twice to take you down to the Column Margin table.

Step 29. You'll note that 0.25 inches was left as the space between columns. This seems to work well. The other measurements will be determined by the length of words, the number of digits in the figures to go into the columns, and so on. There will be a certain amount of trial and error as you set up the column margins.

In this case, you need four columns of the following dimensions:

Column	**Left**	**Right**
Column 1	1.0 inch	2.75 inches
Column 2	3.0 inches	4.25 inches
Column 3	4.5 inches	5.75 inches
Column 4	6.0 inches	6.75 inches

That makes a total of 5.0 inches in the four columns, and adding the three column dividers of 0.25 inches each should give you a total width of 5.75 inches. This will fit neatly on a Macintosh SE or Macintosh Plus screen.

After that exhaustive explanation, enter 1 for the left margin of column 1.

Step 30. Press Tab.
Step 31. Enter 2.75.
Step 32. Press Tab.
Step 33. Enter 3.
Step 34. Press Tab.
Step 35. Enter 4.25.
Step 36. Press Tab.
Step 37. Enter 4.5.
Step 38. Press Tab.
Step 39. Enter 5.75.
Step 40. Press Tab.
Step 41. Enter 6.
Step 42. Press Tab.
Step 43. Enter 6.75.
Step 44. Press Tab. At this point, your screen should look like Figure 6.54.

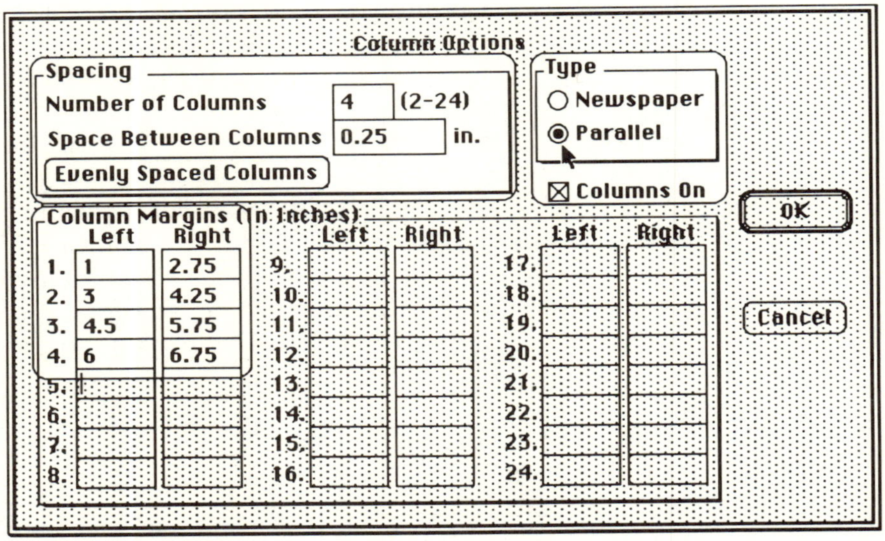

Figure 6-54. The Column Options dialog box, with four columns selected, parallel type, and the left and right margins indicated.

Step 45. Click on OK.
Step 46. You are now in the parallel column mode (note the Column Define and Column Begin codes).

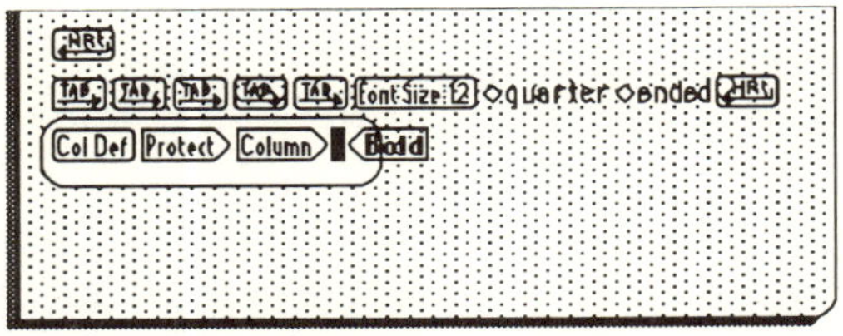

Figure 6-55. The Column Define and Column Begin Codes preceding the cursor.

Moving from One Parallel Column to the Next

Move from one column to another by hitting Command-Return, which inserts a Hard Page code. Since you don't want anything in Column 1, Row 1, press Command-Return. The location indicator at the left end of the status line now gives a column number as well as a page number and line number.

Step 47. Choose Macro Input from the Macro submenu of the Special menu.
Step 48. In the Input dialog box, type *Quarter ending date.*

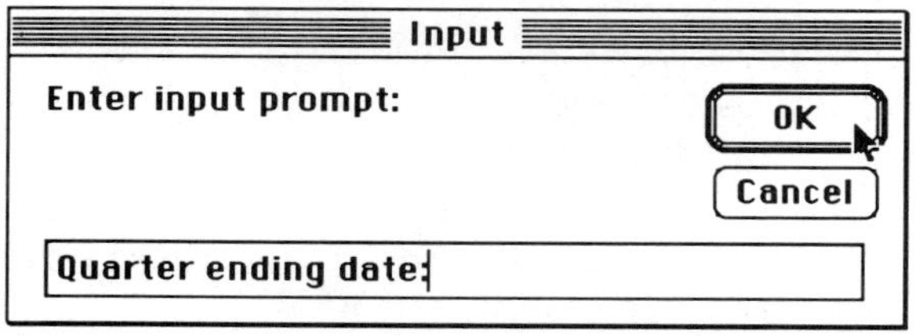

Figure 6-56. The Input dialog box, with the prompt for entering the date of the quarter ending.

Step 49. Click on OK.
Step 50. Press Command-Return.
Step 51. Choose Macro Input from the Macro submenu of the Special menu.
Step 52. In the Input dialog box, type *Year-ago quarter ending date.*
Step 53. Click on OK.
Step 54. Press Command-Return to move to column 4.
Step 55. Type *Change.*
Step 56. Press Command-Return to move to column 1 in the next row.

Now you are going to install some special tabs that will make it easy to line up figures:

Step 57. Choose Tabs from the Line submenu of the Format menu. The ruler will appear, with the shaded bars showing the sizes and dimensions of the four columns.
Step 58. Begin by clearing all tabs. Click on Delete.

Using Decimal Tabs

Step 59. For this financial summary you're going to use the type of tab called a *decimal tab,* which permits you to line up all numbers along their decimal points. Click on Decimal as the type of tab.
Step 60. Since you have text in column 1, you won't be needing any tabs. If you look at the shaded bar representing column width and location for column 2, you see that in order to leave plenty of room for large numbers to the left of the dec-

imal, the tab should be located at about the 4-inch mark. Enter 4 for the New Tab position.

Step 61. Click on Set.

Step 62. To locate the tab in column 3 at 5.5 inches, enter 5.5 for the New Tab position.

Step 63. Click on Set.

Step 64. To locate the tab in column 4 at 6.5 inches, enter 6.5 for the New Tab position.

Step 65. Click on Set.

Step 66. That's all the tab settings you will need for this financial table. Click on OK.

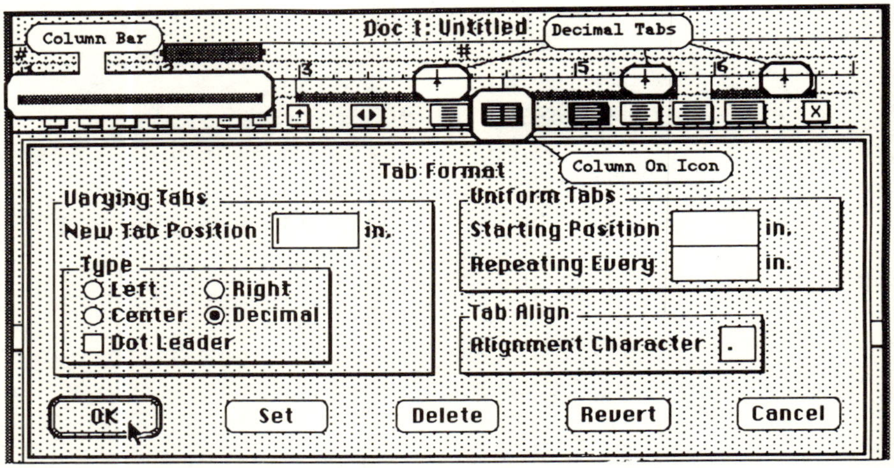

Figure 6-57. The Tab Format dialog box, with decimal tabs, shaded bars denoting column width and location, and the highlighted Columns icon.

Step 67. Type *Revenues*.

Step 68. Turn off Bold by clicking on the *B* in the status line.

Step 69. Press Command-Return to move to column 2.

Step 70. Press Tab.

Step 71. Choose Macro Input from the Macro submenu of the Special menu.

Step 72. Type *Quarterly revenues in thousands.*

Step 73. Click on OK.

Step 74. Press Command-Return to move to column 3.

Step 75. Press Tab.

Step 76. Choose Macro Input from the Macro submenu of the Special menu.
Step 77. Type *Year-ago quarterly revenues in thousands.*
Step 78. Click on OK.
Step 79. Press Command-Return.
Step 80. Press Tab.
Step 81. Choose Macro Input from the Macro submenu of the Special menu.
Step 82. Type *Year-ago quarterly revenues in thousands.*
Step 83. Click on OK.
Step 84. Press Tab.
Step 85. Choose Macro Input from the Macro submenu of the Special menu.
Step 86. Type *Percent revenue change from year ago.*
Step 87. Click on OK.
Step 88. Type %.
Step 89. Press Command-Return.
Step 90. Turn on Bold.
Step 91. Type *Net Income.*
Step 92. Turn Bold off.
Step 93. Press Command-Return.
Step 94. Press Tab.
Step 95. Choose Macro Input from the Macro submenu of the Special menu.
Step 96. Type *Quarterly net income in thousands.*
Step 97. Click on OK.
Step 98. Press Command-Return.
Step 99. Press Tab.
Step 100. Choose Macro Input from the Macro submenu of the Special menu.
Step 101. Type *Year-ago quarterly net income in thousands.*
Step 102. Click on OK.
Step 103. Press Command-Return.
Step 104. Press Tab.
Step 105. Choose Macro Input from the Macro submenu of the Special menu.
Step 106. Type *Percent net income change from year ago.*
Step 107. Click on OK.
Step 108. Type %.
Step 109. Press Command-Return.
Step 110. Turn Bold on.

Step 111. Type *Earnings per share.*
Step 112. Turn Bold off.
Step 113. Press Command-Return.
Step 114. Press Tab.
Step 115. Choose Macro Input from the Macro submenu of the Special menu.
Step 116. Type *Quarterly earnings per share.*
Step 117. Click on OK.
Step 118. Press Command-Return.
Step 119. Press Tab.
Step 120. Choose Macro Input from the Macro submenu of the Special menu.
Step 121. Type *Year-ago quarterly earnings per share.*
Step 122. Click on OK.
Step 123. Press Command-Return.
Step 124. Press Tab.
Step 125. Choose Macro Input from the Macro submenu of the Special menu.
Step 126. Type *Percent EPS change from year ago.*
Step 127. Click on OK.
Step 128. Type *%.*
Step 129. Press Command-Return.
Step 130. Turn Bold on.
Step 131. Type *Backlog.*
Step 132. Turn Bold off.
Step 133. Press Command-Return.
Step 134. Press Tab.
Step 135. Choose Macro Input from the Macro submenu of the Special menu.
Step 136. Type *Quarterly backlog in thousands.*
Step 137. Click on OK.
Step 138. Press Command-Return.
Step 139. Press Tab.
Step 140. Choose Macro Input from the Macro submenu of the Special menu.
Step 141. Type *Year ago quarterly backlog in thousands.*
Step 142. Click on OK.
Step 143. Press Command-Return.
Step 144. Press Tab.
Step 145. Choose Macro Input from the Macro submenu of the Special menu.

Step 146. Type *Percent change in backlog from year ago.*
Step 147. Click on OK.
Step 148. Type %.
Step 149. Choose Show Ruler from Format menu.
Step 150. Click on the Columns Off icon.
Step 151. Press Return.
Step 152. Type *(Dollar amounts in thousands except for earnings per share.).*
Step 153. Press Return.
Step 154. Hide the ruler by choosing Hide Ruler from the Format menu.
Step 155. Hide the Codes by choosing Hide Codes from the Edit menu.
Step 156. End the macro creation by choosing Define Macro from the Macro submenu of the Special menu.

Check your screen against the one in Figure 6-58 to see whether you have executed all the steps correctly.

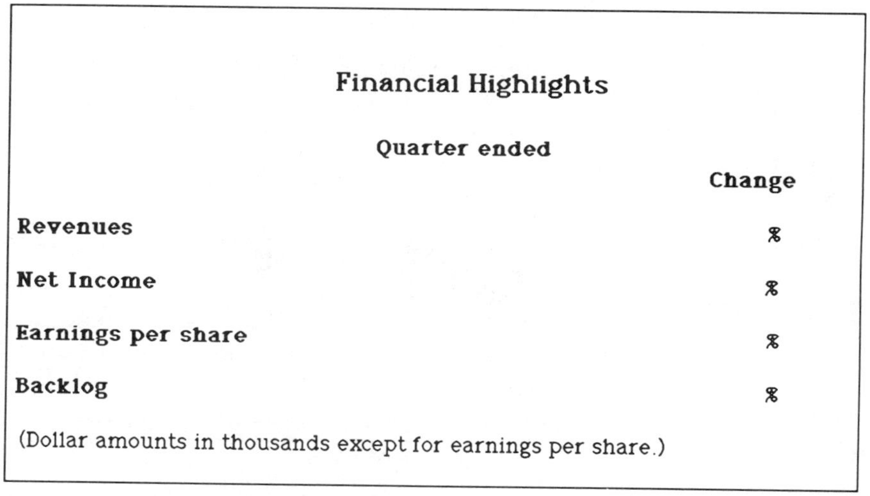
Financial Highlights

Quarter ended

	Change
Revenues	%
Net Income	%
Earnings per share	%
Backlog	%

(Dollar amounts in thousands except for earnings per share.)

Figure 6-58. The appearance of the screen when creation of the macro is completed.

A better way to find out whether this macro really works is

to plug in some numbers and see what happens. You can use any numbers in the example.

Step 1. Choose Execute Macro from the Macro submenu of the Special menu.
Step 2. Select *Quarterly Financials* from the dialog box.

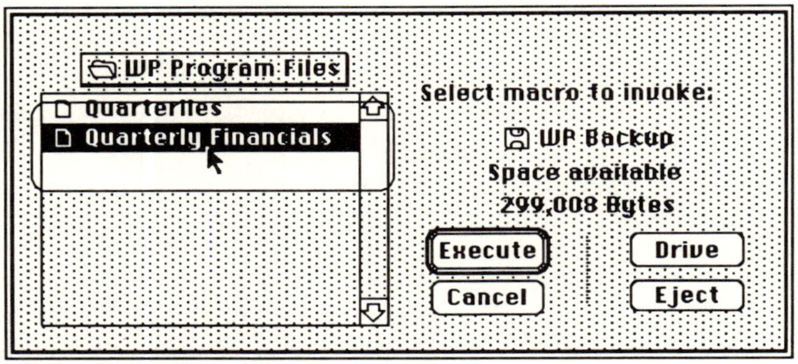

Figure 6-59. Select *Quarterly Financials* from the dialog box.

Step 3. Your first input prompt should be *Enter company name.* Type in your own company name, or enter *Wanton Widgets, Inc.*

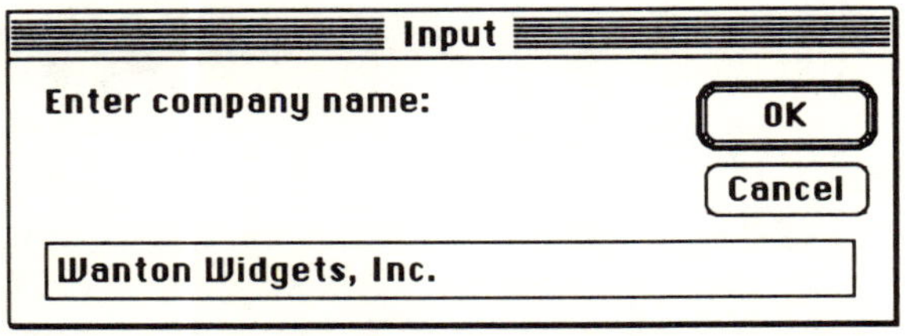

Figure 6-60. The Input Prompt asking for company name.

Step 4. Click on OK.
Step 5. The next input prompt asks you to enter the quarter. Type *First.*

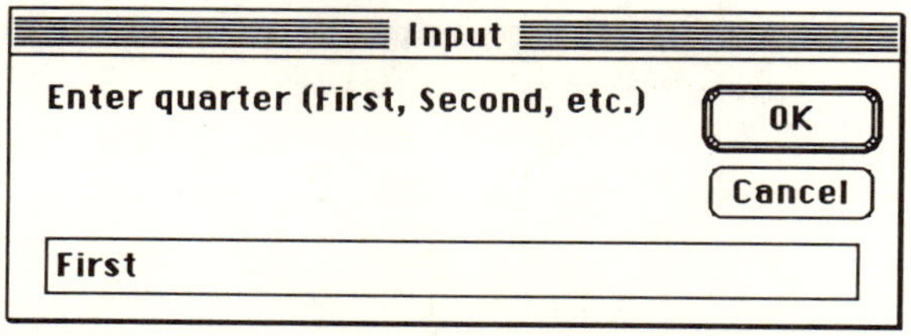

Figure 6-61. The Input Prompt asking which quarter.

Step 6. Click on OK.
Step 7. When you are prompted to enter the quarter ending date, type *March 31, 1988*.

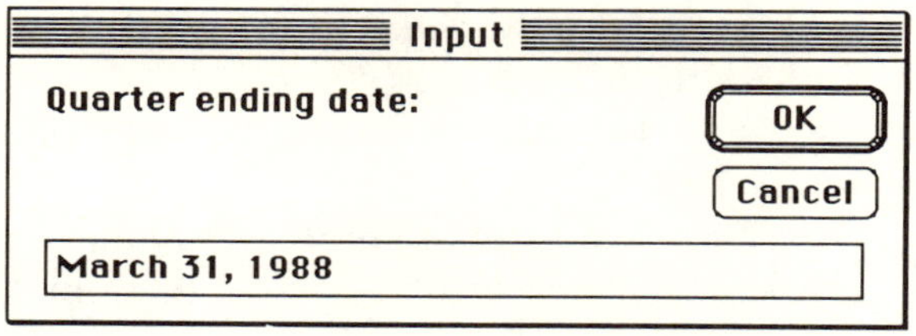

Figure 6-62. Enter the Quarter ending date.

Step 8. Click on OK.
Step 9. The next prompt should ask for the Year-ago quarter ending date. Type in *March 31, 1987*.

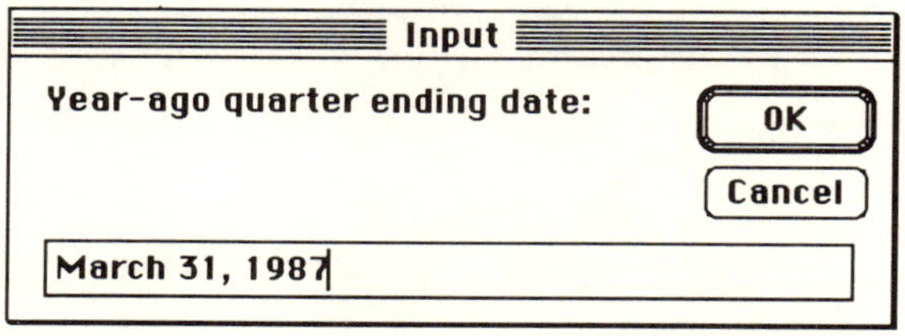

Figure 6-63. Enter the Year-ago quarter ending date.

Step 10. Click on OK.
Step 11. When prompted for quarterly revenues in thousands, type $19,054.

Step 12. At the prompt for year-ago quarterly revenues, type $16,601.
Step 13. For percent revenue change from year ago, type +15.
Step 14. For quarterly net income, type $1,940.
Step 15. For year-ago quarterly net income, type $1,657.
Step 16. For percent net income change, type +17.
Step 17. For quarterly earnings per share, type $.29.
Step 18. For year-ago quarterly earnings per share, type $.25.
Step 19. For percent EPS change from year ago, type +16.
Step 20. For quarterly backlog in thousands, type $119,000.
Step 21. For year-ago quarterly backlog, type $105,000.
Step 22. For percent change in backlog, type +13.

That should do it. After your disk drives run for a few seconds, you should see a quarterly financial statement formatted and ready for printing.

With this macro you can plug in any company, any figures you wish.

You should also be able, by following this macro through its creation very carefully, to add or delete rows from this table.

You may think you've seen everything there is to know about macros. Actually, you've only scratched the surface.

Chapter 7

More Powerful Macro Recipes

Chapter 7

More Powerful Macro Recipes

The macro is probably the most important tool in the word processing toolbox for increasing your personal productivity. As you have seen, macros are the devices by which the computer remembers long, frequently repeated tasks, and reduces them to a much smaller number of keystrokes.

In this chapter, you are going to create a series of handy macros. You should follow the directions step by step to understand how they are constructed and how they work. You should then modify them so they best suit your own work, and file them in your own growing macro library.

In the process of setting up these workhorse macros, you will pick up a number of new *WordPerfect* features and learn new applications for already familiar features. You will

- Format a special stationery size.
- Get better acquainted with Pause Macro and Input Macro.
- Learn multiple macro nesting.
- Chain macros together.
- Make macros repeat as many times as you want.
- Put together a Search and Change macro.

Start by creating a macro that will format a letter on Monarch-size stationery. Monarch stationery is 7.25 × 10.5 inches. It's a stationery size that is effective for elegant, personal messages.

Monarch Form Letter Macro

Step 1. Begin by opening a document by selecting New on the File menu. Then select Define Macro . . . from the Macro submenu of the Special menu.
Step 2. Type *Monarch format* as the name of the macro.
Step 3. Click on Save.

Step 4. Choose Page Layout . . . from the Page submenu of the Format menu.

Step 5. Press Tab, 1.625, Tab, 1.5, Tab, 1.625 to enter these values into the margin-setting boxes at the top of the dialog box.

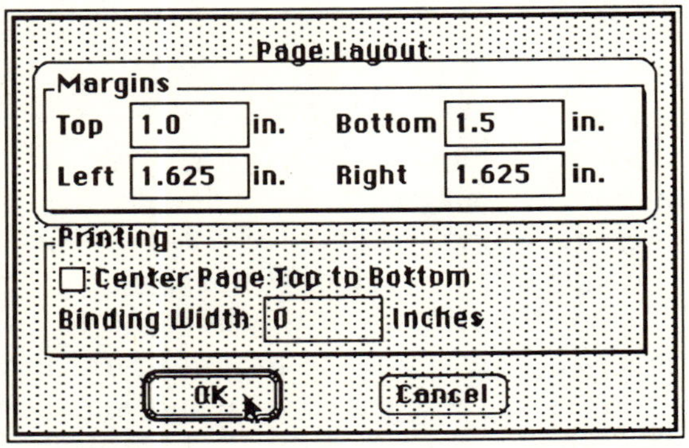

Figure 7-1. The margin settings for Monarch stationery.

Step 6. Click on OK or hit Return.

Step 7. Select New York font from Font menu.

Step 8. Select 10 from Font menu.

Step 9. Press Return five times.

Step 10. Choose Tabs from the Line submenu of the Format menu.

Step 11. In the Tabs Dialog Box, click on Delete.

Step 12. Type 2.25 and click on Set. Type 2.88 and click on Set. Type 4.25 and click on Set.

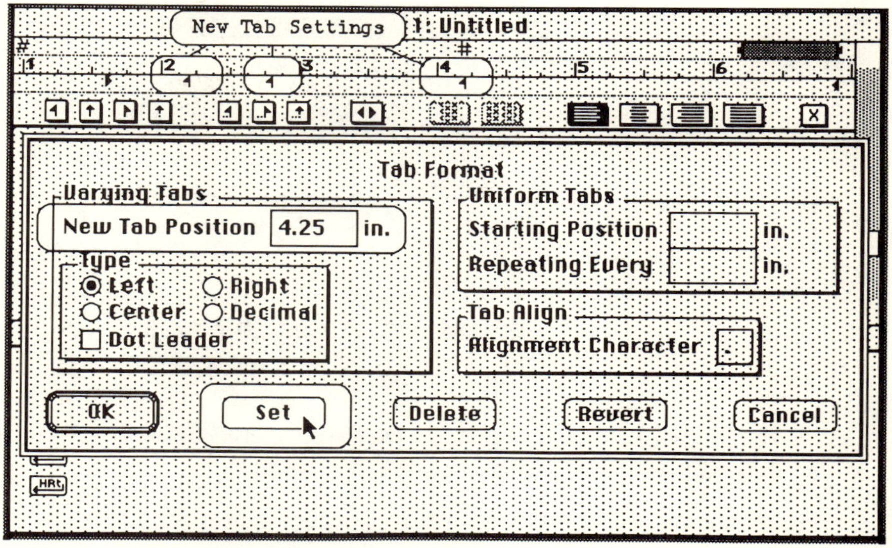

Figure 7-2. Tab settings for the Monarch letter.

Step 13. Click on OK or hit Return.
Step 14. Press the Tab key three times.
Step 15. Choose Insert Function from the Date submenu of the Special menu. Now the correct date will be entered whenever you activate this macro.
Step 16. Press Return three times.
Step 17. Choose Define Macro . . . from the Macro submenu of the Special menu.

That completes the Monarch format macro. Let's give it a dry run to see if everything was entered correctly.

Run Monarch Format Macro

Step 1. Choose Execute Macro . . . from the Macro submenu of the Special menu.
Step 2. Select Monarch Format as the macro to execute.
Step 3. Click on Execute or hit Return.
Step 4. Choose Show Codes from the Edit menu. This is what the sequence of codes should look like on your screen if you created the macro properly.

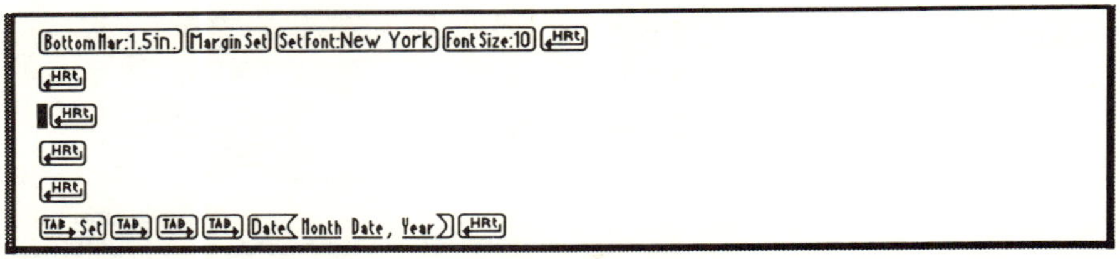

Figure 7-3. The codes for the Monarch format macro.

Address and Salutation Macro

Importing Information with a Macro

Step 1. If you don't have a file open, open one. Choose Define Macro . . . from the Macro submenu of the Special menu.

Step 2. Type *Address and Salute* as the name of this macro.

Step 3. Click on Save.

Step 4. Choose Open . . . from the File menu.

Step 5. Select Phone Book.

Step 6. Click on Open or press Return.

Step 7. Choose Pause Macro from the Macro submenu of the Special menu. At this point you have to stop the macro while you select the address to insert into this letter.

Step 8. Select the address to be inserted into the letter.

Step 9. Choose Resume Macro from the Macro submenu of the Special menu.

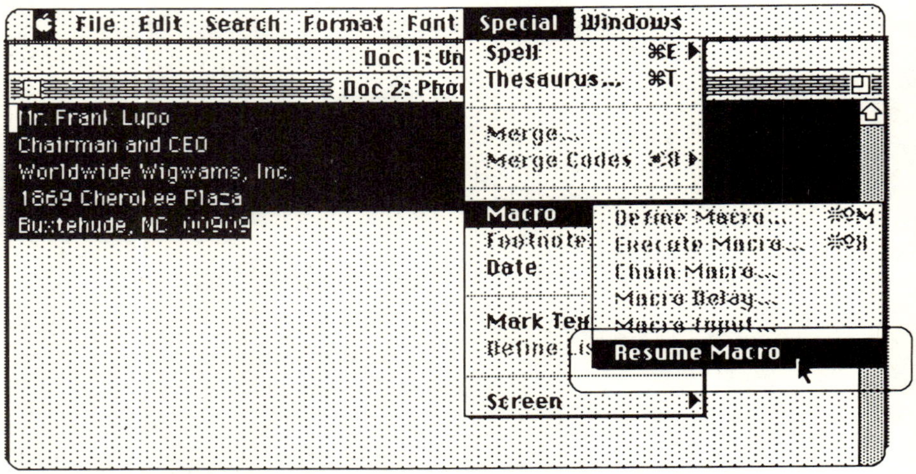

Figure 7-4. Choosing Resume Macro after selecting the address to be inserted into the letter.

Step 10. Choose Copy from the Edit menu to copy the address so it can be transferred to the letter.

Step 11. Choose Doc 1. Untitled from the Windows menu. Since there are only two documents open, you could also accomplish the same thing by pressing Command-W to Cycle Windows.

Figure 7-5. Choosing Doc 1 from the Windows menu.

Step 12. Choose Paste from the Edit menu to Paste the address into the letter.

Step 13. Press Return twice. Select Phone Book on the Windows menu and select Close from the File menu to close the Phone Book file.

Step 14. At this point you want to enter the salutation for the letter. Choose Macro Input . . . from the Macro submenu of the Special menu.

Step 15. Type *Enter salutation.* You might want to add an example like *(Dear Sam)* if others who will be using the macro aren't familiar with salutations.

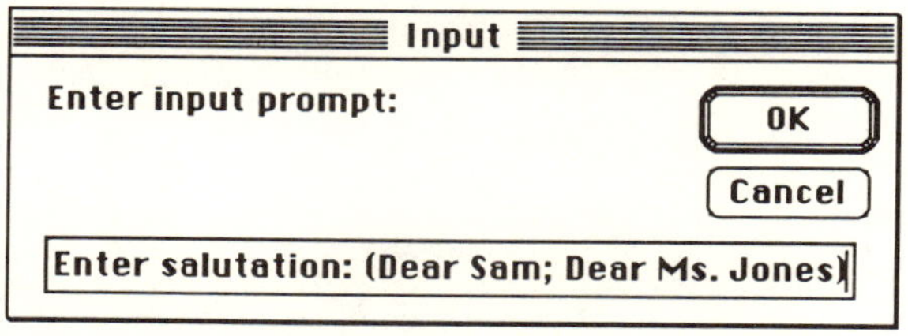

Figure 7-6. Entering the input prompt for the salutation.

Step 16. Click on OK or hit Return.
Step 17. Press Return twice.
Step 18. Choose Define Macro . . . from the Macro submenu of the Special menu.

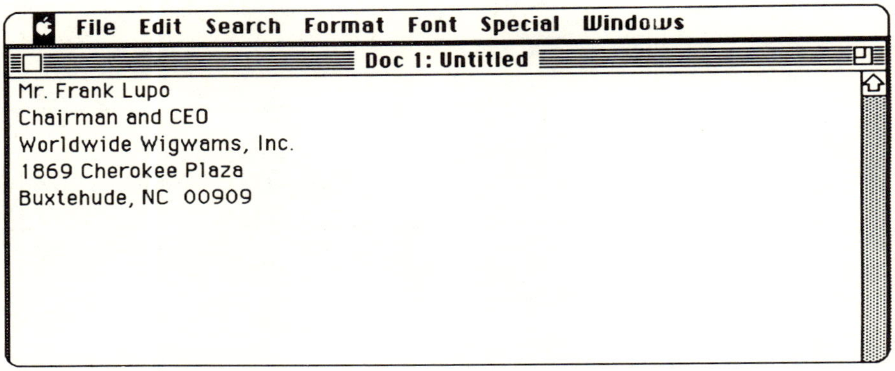

Figure 7-7. Here's what the screen should look like when you end defining the Address and Salute macro.

That should finish the Address and Salutation Macro. Here's a run-through.

Run Address and Salutation Macro

Step 1. Choose Execute Macro . . . from the Macro submenu of the Special menu.
Step 2. Select Address and Salute from the macro list.
Step 3. Click on Execute or hit Return.
Step 4. Select the address you want to use on the letter.
Step 5. Choose Resume Macro from the Macro submenu of the Special menu.

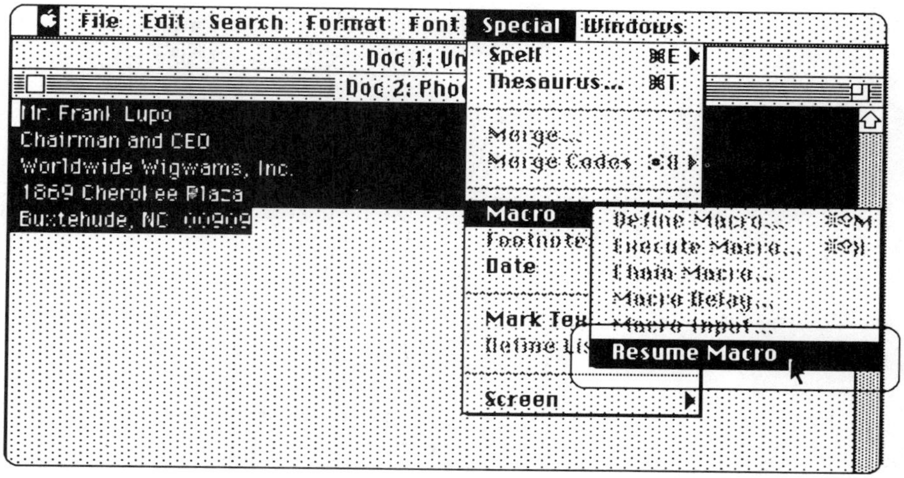

Figure 7-8. Choosing Resume Macro after selecting the Lupo address to be inserted into the letter.

Step 6. Type *Dear Mr. Lupo.*

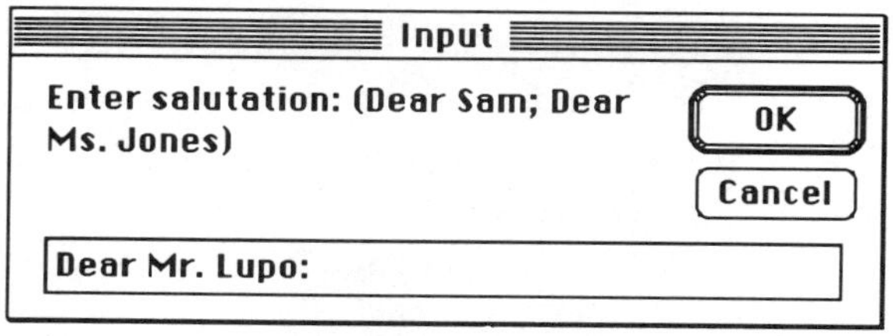

Figure 7-9. The Input Dialog Box with the salutation entered for Frank Lupo.

Step 7. Click on OK or hit Return.

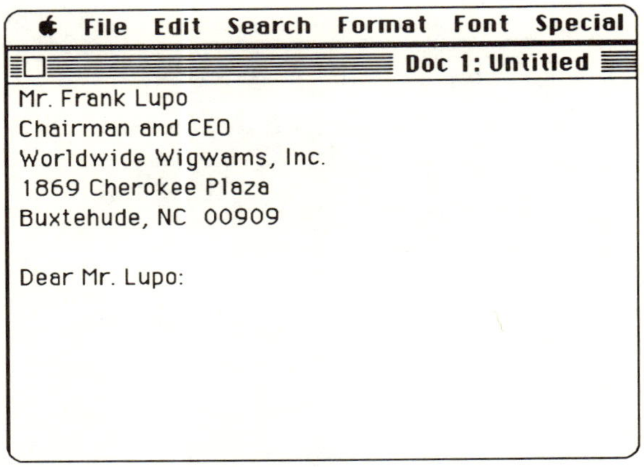

Figure 7-10. The screen at the completion of the macro.

Boilerplate Macros

If you're like most people in business, there are certain letters or documents or pieces of documents that you write over and over again.

Such oft-repeated material is called *boilerplate.* When you were dependent on a typewriter, you had to knock out dreary boilerplate passages over and over again, with different errors and corrections every time. Those days are gone forever. Now that you are unleashing the power of *WordPerfect,* boilerplate can be instantaneously and perfectly reproduced at the press of a few keys. Simply create a macro for each boilerplate passage you use. You can even allow for slight variations in the boilerplate passages by inserting Input Macros.

In the pages following, you're going to create a form letter that uses three boilerplate paragraphs. The paragraphs are supplied for you to copy as exercises, but if you want to follow this model to create some boilerplate macros of your own, all the better.

Paragraph 1 Macro

Automating Boilerplate

Step 1. Open a new document and choose Define Macro from the Macro submenu of the Special menu.

Step 2. For the name of the macro, type *Paragraph 1.*

Step 3. Press Tab.
Step 4. Type

> Thank you so much for your willingness to contribute to our 1988 Goods and Services Auction, which will be held in the Lifetime Suite, Tower Building, on November 31, 1989. Your kind donation of

At this point you insert an Input Macro which will prompt you to insert a description of the donation.

Step 5. Choose Macro Input . . . from the Macro submenu of the Special menu.
Step 6. Type *Enter donation: (A Ming vase, the Hope Diamond, etc.)*

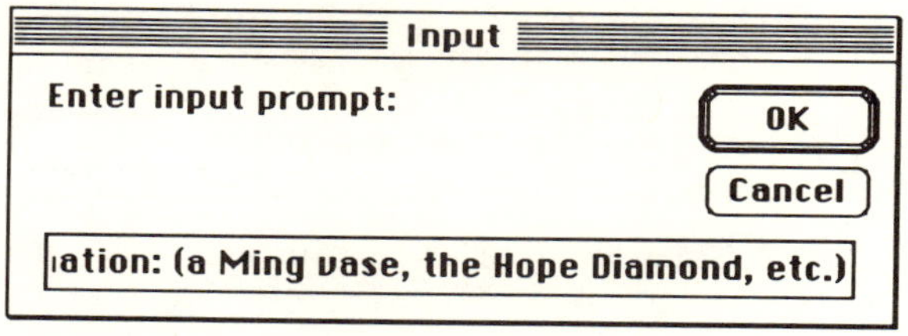

Figure 7-11. The donation input prompt.

Step 7. Click on OK.
Step 8. Type *will truly add panache to our event.*
Step 9. Choose Define Macro . . . from the Macro submenu of the Special menu.

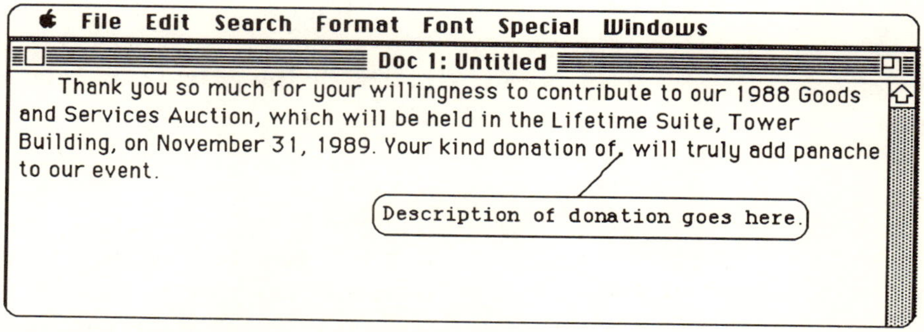

Figure 7-12. The Mac screen at the end of defining the macro.

Paragraph 2 Macro

Like the Paragraph 1 Macro, Paragraph 2 has a built-in Input prompt.

Step 1. Choose Define Macro . . . from the Macro submenu of the Special menu. Name the macro Paragraph 2.
Step 2. Press Tab.
Step 3. Type *As* and leave a space after the word.
Step 4. Choose Macro Input . . . from the Macro submenu of the Special menu.
Step 5. Type *Enter name of contact person.*

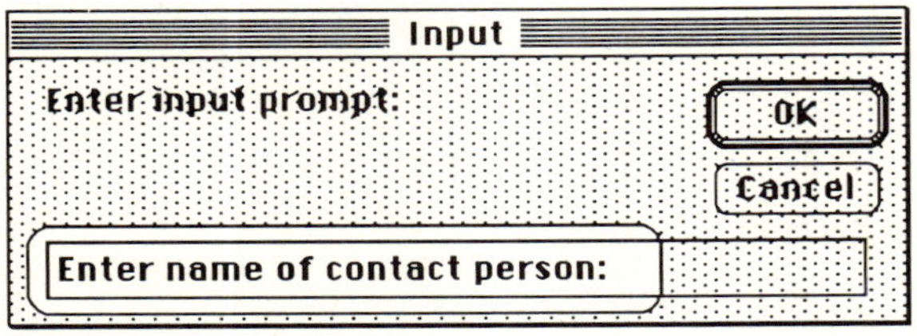

Figure 7-13. The Input prompt for the contact person.

Step 6. Click on OK.
Step 7. Type

> doubtless told you, monies raised through our Auction directly support Helping Hands for Health Food Addicts, including services such as free Twinkies distribution, pork fat injections, and tofu withdrawal therapy. Your support and other contributions from such fine establishments as Louie's Gooeycakes and Jim Bob's Roadside Footlongs help us provide quality programs for hundreds of desperate people each year.

Step 8. Choose Define Macro . . . from the Macro submenu of the Special menu.

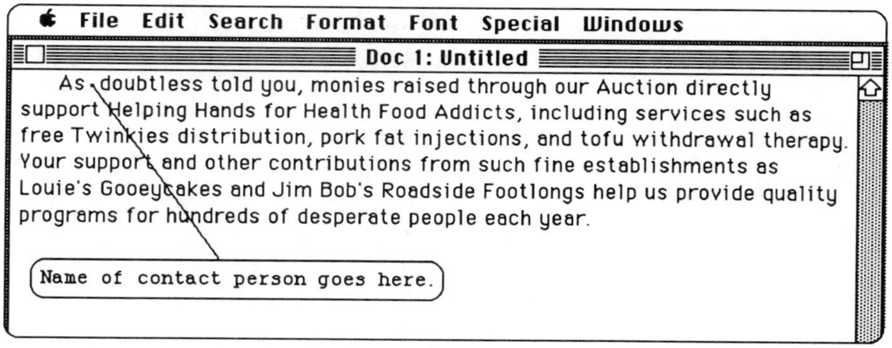

Figure 7-14. The screen after definition of the macro is completed.

Paragraph 3 Macro

Paragraph 3 is straight boilerplate with no inputs and no pauses. It will be the same every time.

Step 1. Choose Define Macro . . . from the Macro submenu of the Special menu and name the macro Paragraph 3.
Step 2. Press Tab.
Step 3. Type *I thank you on behalf of the Auction Committee and the many men and women who will benefit from your generosity.*
Step 4. Choose Define Macro . . . from the Macro submenu of the Special menu.

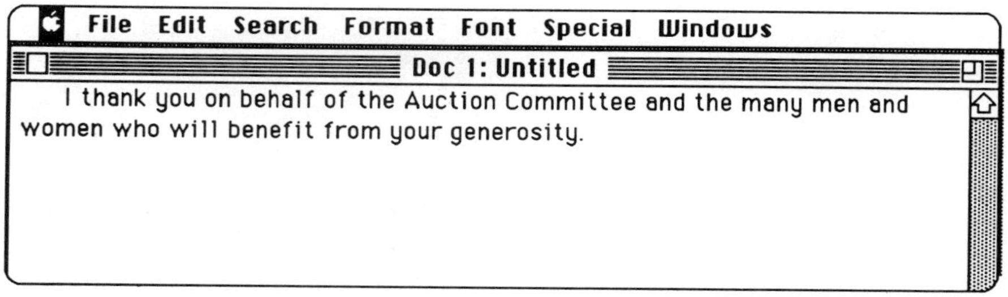

Figure 7-15. The screen after defining the Paragraph 3 macro.

Closing Macro

This is another straightforward text macro.

Step 1. Choose Define Macro . . . from the Macro submenu of the Special menu.
Step 2. Type *HHHFA Closing* as the name of this macro.
Step 3. Press Tab three times.
Step 4. Type *Sincerely yours,*.
Step 5. Press Return four times.
Step 6. Press Tab three times.
Step 7. Type *Priscilla T. J. Bonservice*.
Step 8. Press Return.
Step 9. Press the Tab key three times.
Step 10. Type *Executive Director*.
Step 11. Choose Define Macro . . . from the Macro submenu of the Special menu.

Figure 7-16. The screen after defining the closing macro.

The Total HHHFA Letter Macro

This macro will combine the Monarch format, Address and Salute, Paragraph 1, Paragraph 2, Paragraph 3, and HHHFA Closing into a single process.

Letters, contracts, and other documents are often constructed from different combinations of frequently-used components. Here you will put together a letter composed of a series of macros. You should find this model valuable in your own work.

Step 1. Choose Define Macro . . . from the Macro submenu of the Special menu.
Step 2. Type *HHHFA Letter* as the name of the total macro. (*HHHFA*, of course, stands for *Helping Hands for Health Food Addicts*.)
Step 3. Hit Return or click on Save.
Step 4. Choose Execute Macro . . . from the Macro submenu of the Special menu.
Step 5. Select Monarch format as the macro to invoke.
Step 6. Hit Return or Click on Execute.

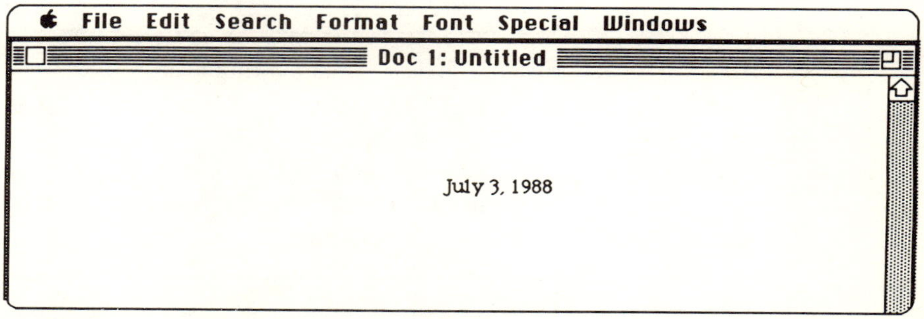

Figure 7-17. The screen as it should look after executing the Monarch Format Macro.

Step 7. Choose Execute Macro . . . from the Macro submenu of the Special menu.
Step 8. Select Address and Salute as the macro to invoke.

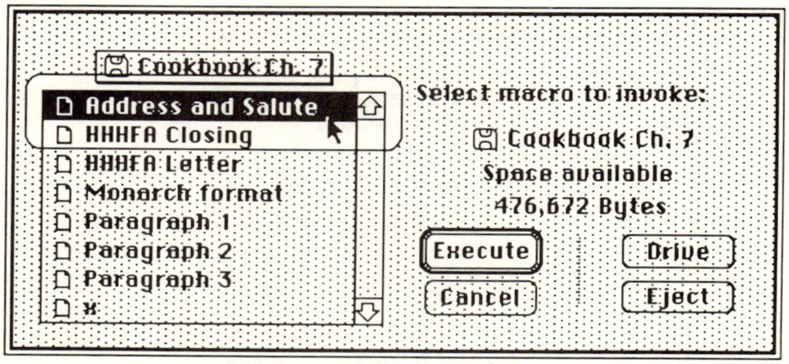

Figure 7-18. Selecting Address and Salute as the second macro to invoke.

Step 9. Hit Return or click on Execute.
Step 10. Choose Resume Macro from the Macro submenu of the Special menu.
Step 11. Click on OK or hit Return when the salutation Input Dialog Box appears.

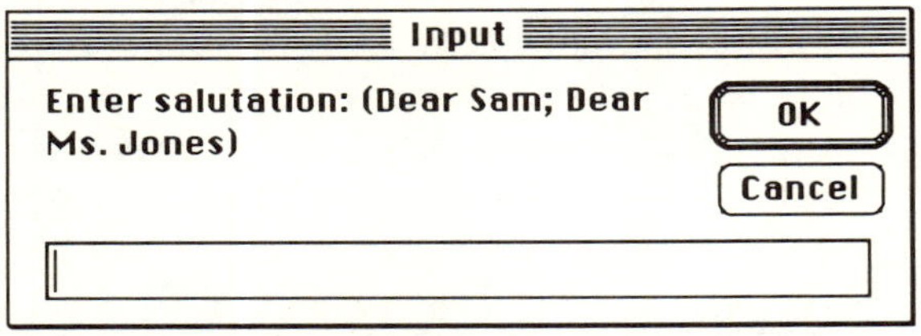

Figure 7-19. The salutation input dialog box.

Step 12. Hit two Returns.
Step 13. Choose Execute Macro . . . from the Macro submenu of the Special menu.
Step 14. Select Paragraph 1 from the list of macros to invoke.
Step 15. Click on Execute or hit Return.
Step 16. Click on OK or hit Return when the donation input box appears.

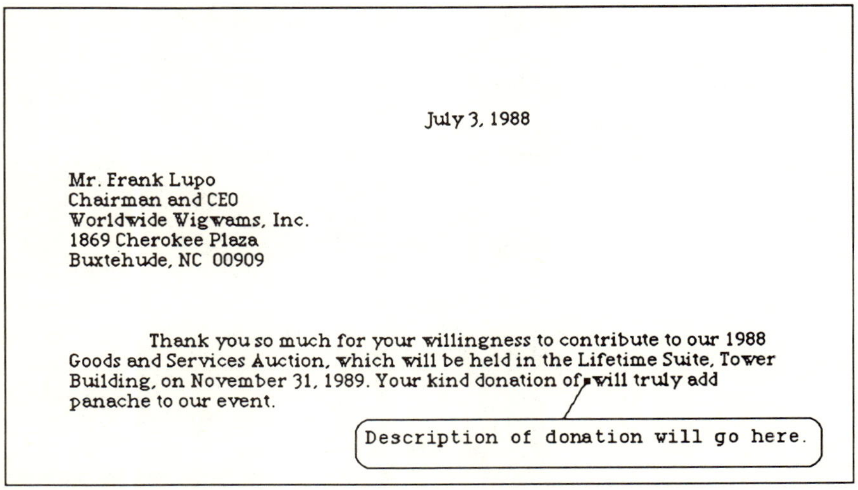

Figure 7-20. Here's the screen after the Paragraph 1 macro has been executed.

Step 17. Hit two Returns.
Step 18. Choose Execute Macro . . . from the Macro submenu of the Special menu.
Step 19. Select Paragraph 2 from the list of macros to invoke.
Step 20. Click on Execute or hit Return.
Step 21. Click on OK or hit Return when the contact person Input Dialog Box appears.
Step 22. Press Return twice.
Step 23. Choose Execute Macro . . . from the Macro submenu of the Special menu.
Step 24. Select Paragraph 3 from the list of macros to invoke.
Step 25. Click on Execute or hit Return.
Step 26. Press Return twice.
Step 27. Choose Execute Macro . . . from the Macro submenu of the Special menu.
Step 28. Select HHHFA Closing from the list of macros to invoke.
Step 29. Click on Execute or hit Return.
Step 30. Choose Define Macro . . . from the Macro submenu of the Special menu.

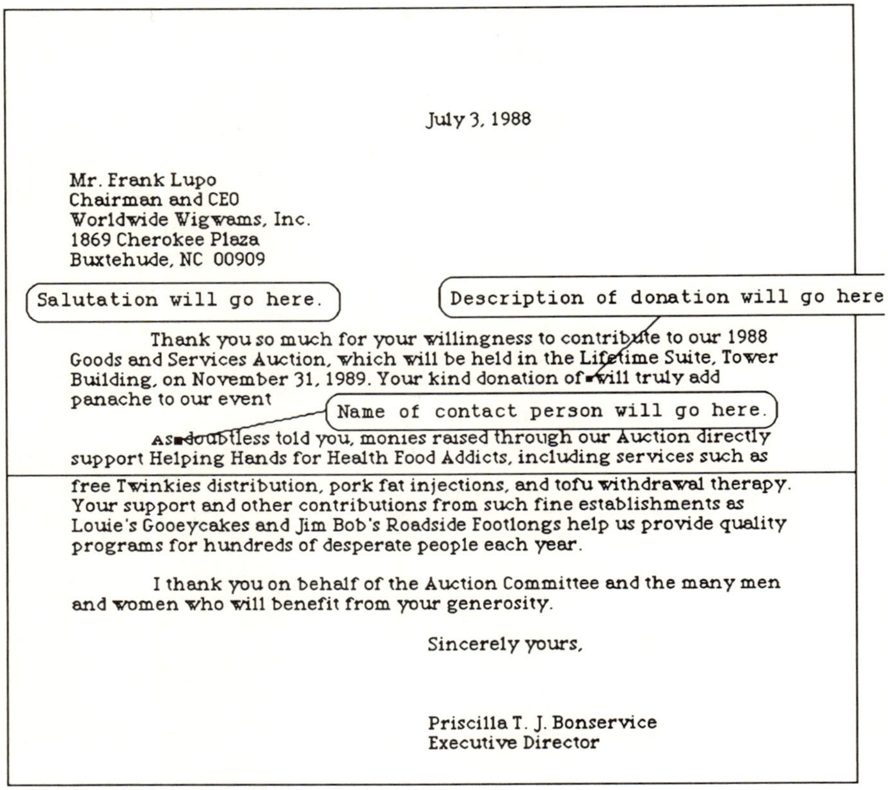
July 3, 1988

Mr. Frank Lupo
Chairman and CEO
Worldwide Wigwams, Inc.
1869 Cherokee Plaza
Buxtehude, NC 00909

Salutation will go here.

Description of donation will go here

Thank you so much for your willingness to contribute to our 1988 Goods and Services Auction, which will be held in the Lifetime Suite, Tower Building, on November 31, 1989. Your kind donation of will truly add panache to our event

Name of contact person will go here.

As doubtless told you, monies raised through our Auction directly support Helping Hands for Health Food Addicts, including services such as free Twinkies distribution, pork fat injections, and tofu withdrawal therapy. Your support and other contributions from such fine establishments as Louie's Gooeycakes and Jim Bob's Roadside Footlongs help us provide quality programs for hundreds of desperate people each year.

I thank you on behalf of the Auction Committee and the many men and women who will benefit from your generosity.

Sincerely yours,

Priscilla T. J. Bonservice
Executive Director

Figure 7-21. The Mac screen (actually two screens combined in this figure) after definition of the HHHFA Letter macro has been completed.

Let's see if it runs. Run the total HHHFA Letter macro

Step 1. Open a new file by choosing New from the File menu.
Step 2. Choose Execute Macro . . . from the Macro submenu of the Special menu.
Step 3. Select HHHFA Letter from the list of macros to invoke.

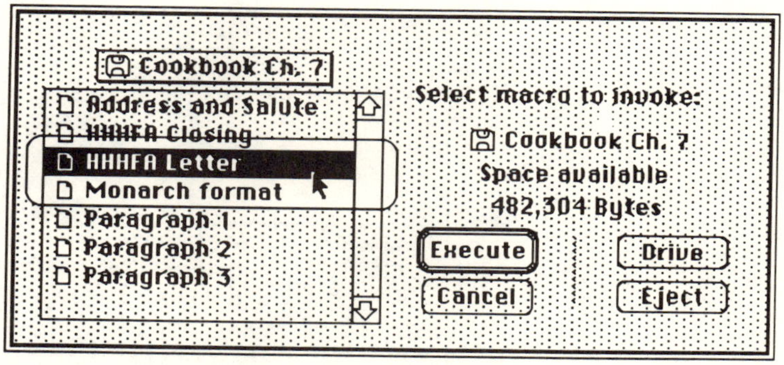

Figure 7-22. Selecting HHHFA Letter as the macro to invoke.

Step 4. Click on Execute or hit Return.
Step 5. Select the Lupo address by pressing Command-Shift-A.

Figure 7-23. The Lupo address selected for copying into the letter.

Step 6. Choose Resume Macro from the Macro submenu of the Special menu.

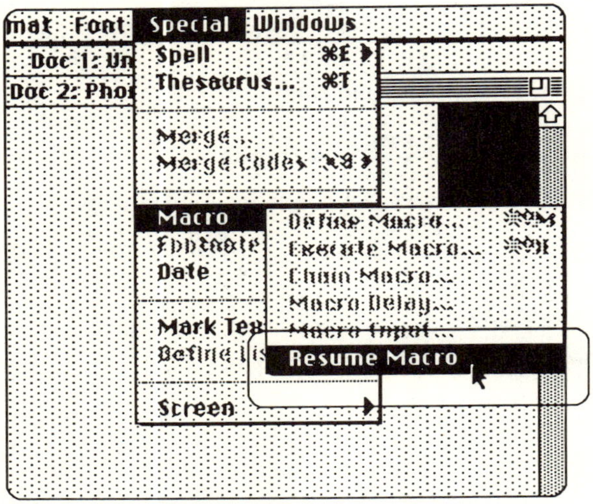

Figure 7-24. Selecting Resume Macro.

Step 7. Type in the salutation *Dear Mr. Lupo.*
Step 8. Click on OK or hit Return.
Step 9. Type in the description of the donation: *a six-foot hero sandwich.*
Step 10. Click on OK or hit Return.
Step 11. Type in the name of the contact person: *Greenberry Swango.*

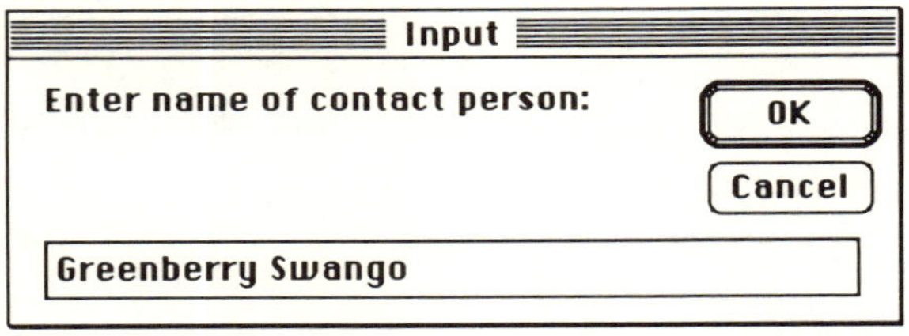

Figure 7-25. The contact person input dialog box with *Greenberry Swango* typed in.

Step 12. Click on OK or hit Return.

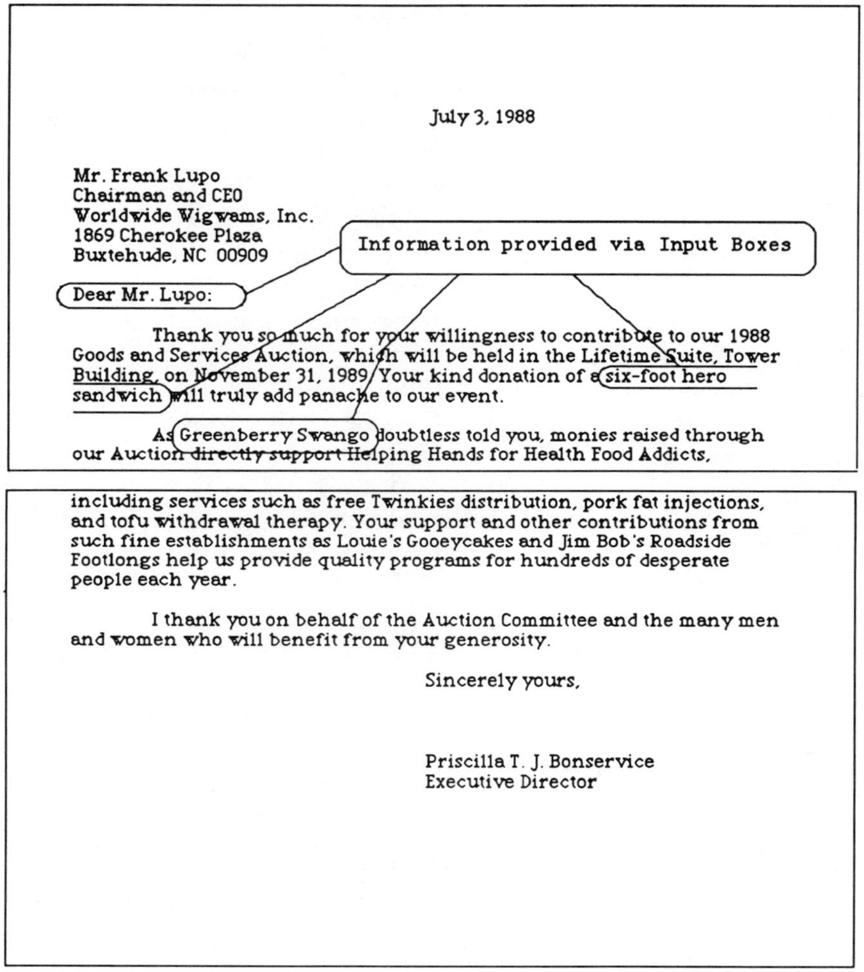

July 3, 1988

Mr. Frank Lupo
Chairman and CEO
Worldwide Wigwams, Inc.
1869 Cherokee Plaza
Buxtehude, NC 00909

Information provided via Input Boxes

Dear Mr. Lupo:

Thank you so much for your willingness to contribute to our 1988 Goods and Services Auction, which will be held in the Lifetime Suite, Tower Building, on November 31, 1989. Your kind donation of a six-foot hero sandwich will truly add panache to our event.

As Greenberry Swango doubtless told you, monies raised through our Auction directly support Helping Hands for Health Food Addicts, including services such as free Twinkies distribution, pork fat injections, and tofu withdrawal therapy. Your support and other contributions from such fine establishments as Louie's Gooeycakes and Jim Bob's Roadside Footlongs help us provide quality programs for hundreds of desperate people each year.

I thank you on behalf of the Auction Committee and the many men and women who will benefit from your generosity.

Sincerely yours,

Priscilla T. J. Bonservice
Executive Director

Figure 7-26. The screen display after running the HHHFA Letter Macro. This is two screens.

It takes some doing to create the individual pieces and then nail them all together. However, if you're sending a letter to a long list of people and the letter differs only in small details from one person to the next, this kind of document-assembly macro can save you huge amounts of toil and grief.

Fast File Macro

We've been sending all sorts of things to Frank Lupo simply because he's been the only name on our Phone Book file. The truth is that our contact file is one of the most important elements in our business and private lives. You can continually add to it and otherwise modify it.

There's no reason why the job of building our contact file shouldn't be made easier just like other jobs.

The Fast File macro will prompt you for each entry in order and insert the entries into the file in a consistent way.

Step 1. Open the Phone Book file.
Step 2. Choose Define Macro . . . from the Macro submenu of the Special menu.
Step 3. Type *Fast File* as the macro name.
Step 4. Click on Save or press Return.
Step 5. Choose Macro Input from the Macro submenu of the Special menu.
Step 6. Type *Enter complete name. (Include Mr., Ms., etc.)*

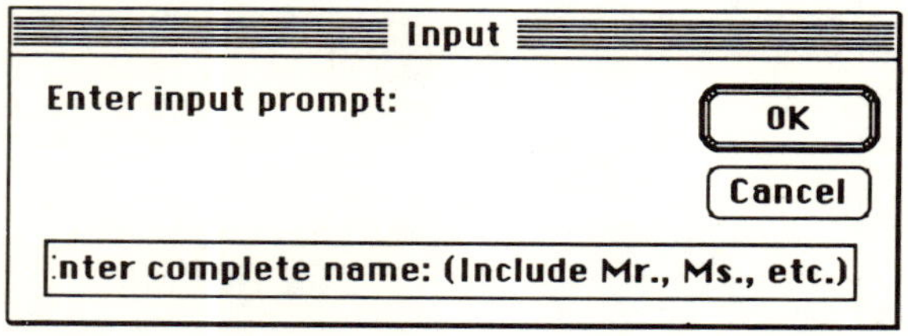

Figure 7-27. The Input prompt for entering the name.

Step 7. Click on OK or hit Return.
Step 8. Return.
Step 9. Choose Macro Input from the Macro submenu of the Special menu.
Step 10. Type *Enter title.*

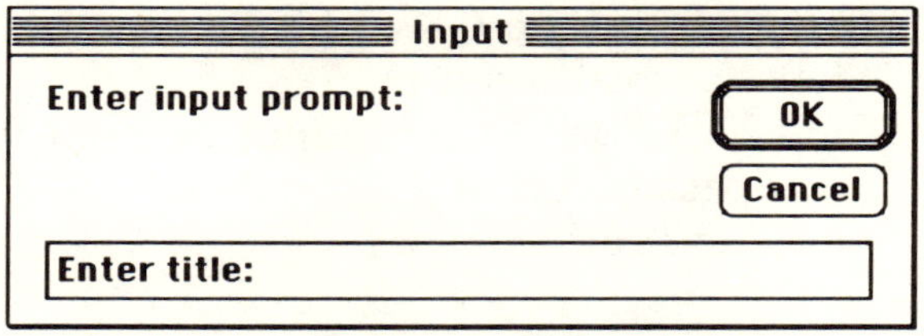

Figure 7-28. The Input prompt for entering the title.

Step 11. Click on OK or hit Return.
Step 12. Return.
Step 13. Choose Macro Input from the Macro submenu of the Special menu.
Step 14. Type *Enter company or organization.*

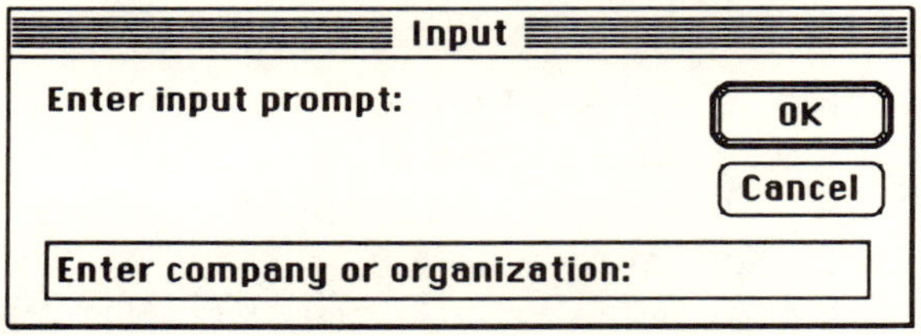

Figure 7-29. The company or organization Input prompt.

Step 15. Click on OK or hit Return.
Step 16. Press Return.
Step 17. Choose Macro Input from the Macro submenu of the Special menu.
Step 18. Type *Enter street address or P.O. box.*

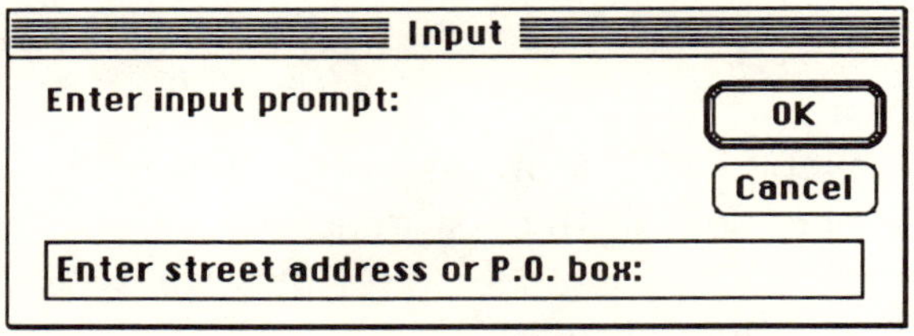

Figure 7-30. The street address prompt.

Step 19. Click on OK or hit Return.
Step 20. Press Return
Step 21. Choose Macro Input from the Macro submenu of the Special menu.
Step 22. Type *Enter city.*

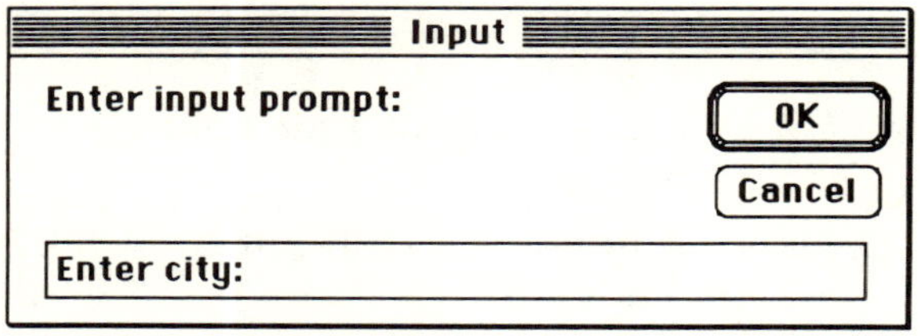

Figure 7-31. The city prompt.

Step 23. Click on OK or hit Return.
Step 24. Enter a comma and press the space bar.
Step 25. Choose Macro Input from the Macro submenu of the Special menu.
Step 26. Type *Enter 2-letter state abbreviation.*

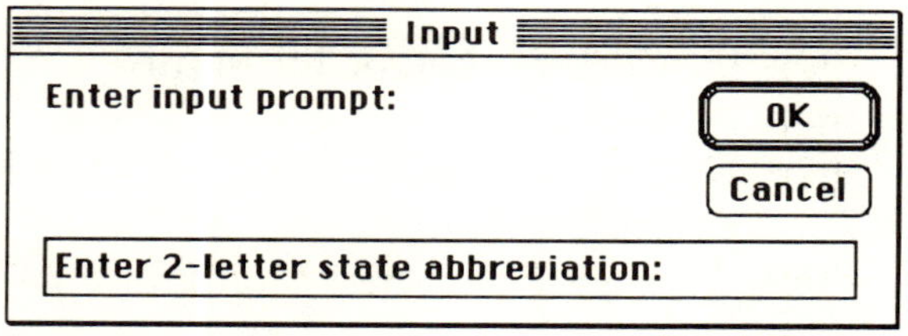

Figure 7-32. State abbreviation prompt.

Step 27. Click on OK or hit Return.
Step 28. Hit the space bar twice.
Step 29. Choose Macro Input from the Macro submenu of the Special menu.
Step 30. Type *Enter zip code.*

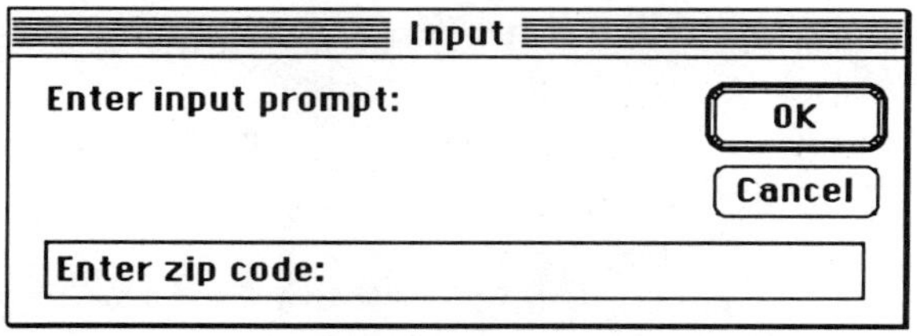

Figure 7-33. Zip code prompt.

Step 31. Click on OK or hit Return.
Step 32. Return.
Step 33. Choose Macro Input from the Macro submenu of the Special menu.
Step 34. Type *Enter salutation. (Dear Sam; Dear Ms. Jones).*

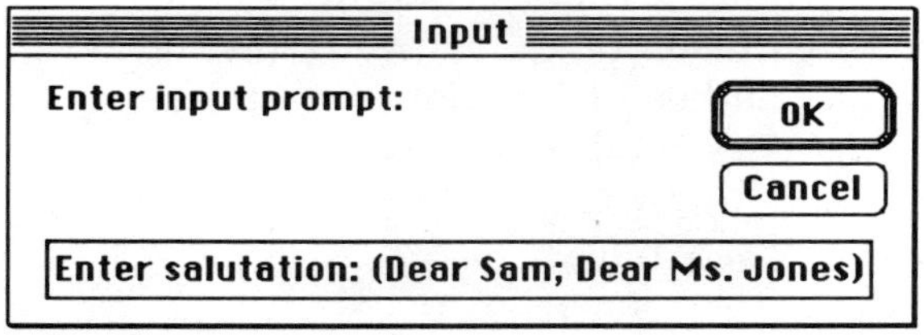

Figure 7-34. Salutation prompt.

Step 35. Click on OK or hit Return.
Step 36. Return
Step 37. Choose Macro Input from the Macro submenu of the Special menu.
Step 38. Type *Enter telephone number, including area code.*

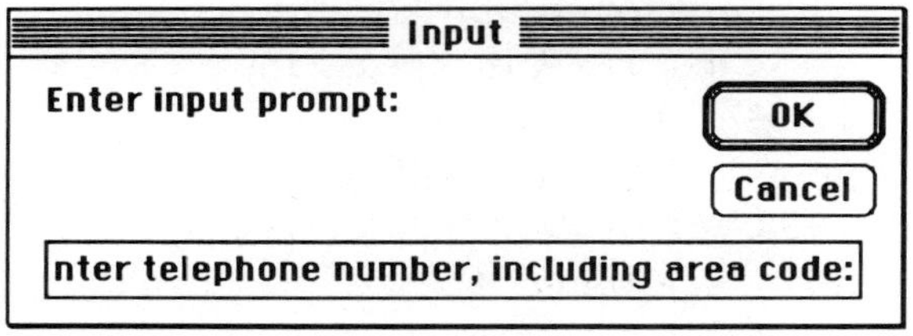

Figure 7-35. Telephone number prompt.

Step 39. Click on OK or hit Return.
Step 40. Press Return twice.
Step 41. Choose Define Macro from the Macro submenu of the Special menu.

That completes definition of the Fast File macro. Before you run it, here's something new you'll want to know about entering macros. With the Fast File macro, as with others you will create, you're likely to want to run it several times in a row. You will often have several new names and addresses to add to your Phone Book file, for example. Is there an easy way to run the macro several times at once? It is possible, and after a quick run-through to make sure the Fast File macro runs correctly, you'll see how it's done.

Here are four names to use for practice.

Ms. Longfred Lilliput Langtry
President
Ladies of the Confederate Renaissance
1860 Lollipop Lane
Languor, LA 79979
Dear Lilli:
(876) 209-2909

Dr. Parkinson P. Proudfeather
Vice President and Chief Financial Officer
Skedaddle Skateboards Ltd.
One Platitude Plaza
Nearmiss, NE 76667
Dear Dr. Proudfeather:
(493) 222-4466

Mr. J. Justinian Joyboy
Director—Public Affairs
Cherokee Chickpeas, Inc.
47 Chevy Chase
Oblong, OK 00703
Dear Justin:
(979) 640-3232

Dr. Phyllis P. Phicklephoot, Ph.D.
Pharmacist
St. Hoipolloi Hospital
33 Billybob Bypass
Alabaster, AR 76567
Dear Dr. Phicklephoot:
(229) 929-2929.

Here's how to use the Fast File macro with a single entry:

Step 1. Close the Phone Book file by clicking on the Close Box.
Step 2. In response to the dialog box asking if you want to save the changes you made to Phone Book, click on No.
Step 3. Open the Phone Book file again by choosing Open from the File menu, selecting Phone Book, and clicking on Open.
Step 4. Choose Execute Macro . . . from the Macro submenu of the Special menu.
Step 5. Select Fast File as the macro to invoke.
Step 6. Click on Execute or hit Return.
Step 7. Type *Ms. Longfred Lilliput Langtry*.

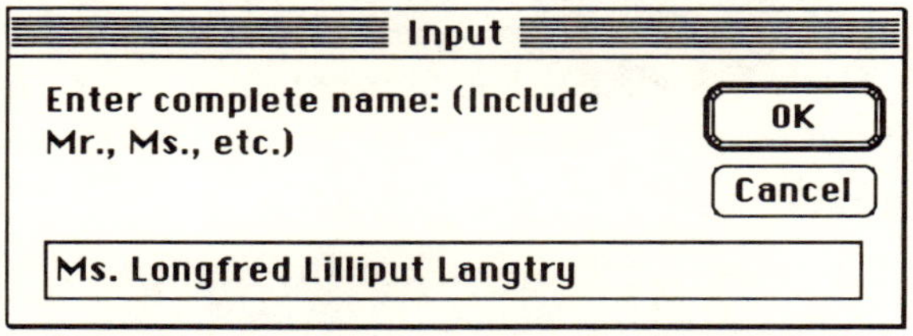

Figure 7-36 Responding to the Name Input prompt.

Step 8. Click on OK or hit Return.
Step 9. Type *President*.

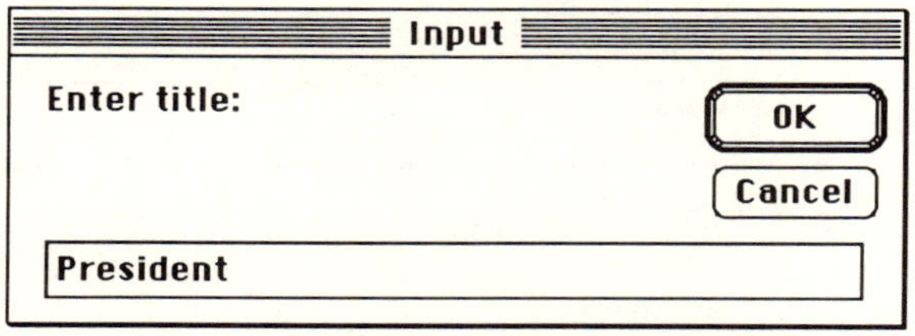

Figure 7-37. Responding to the Title prompt.

Step 10. Click on OK or hit Return.
Step 11. Type *Ladies of the Confederate Renaissance*.

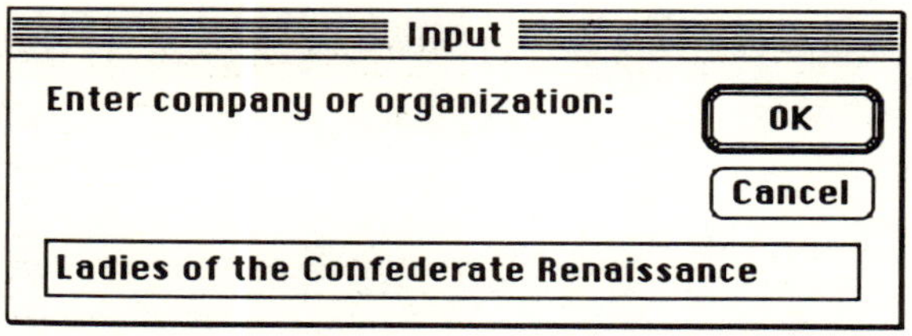

Figure 7-38. Responding to the Company or Organization prompt.

Step 12. Click on OK or hit Return.
Step 13. Type *1861 Lollipop Lane*.

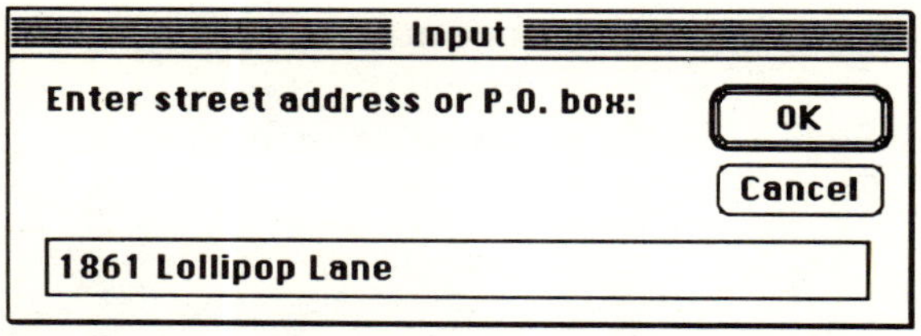

Figure 7-39. Responding to the Street Address prompt.

Step 14. Click on OK or hit Return.
Step 15. Type *Languor*.

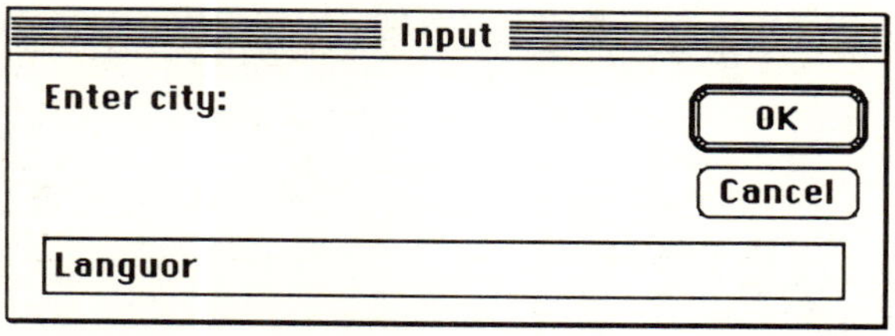

Figure 7-40. Responding to the City prompt.

Step 16. Click on OK or hit Return.
Step 17. Type *LA*.

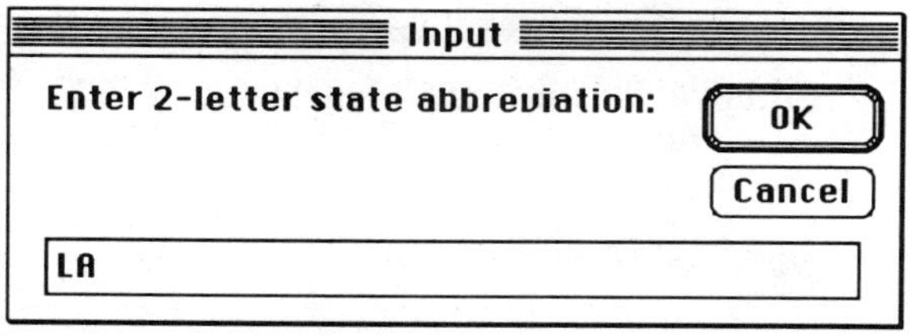

Figure 7-41. Responding to the State prompt.

Step 18. Click on OK or hit Return.
Step 19. Type 79979.

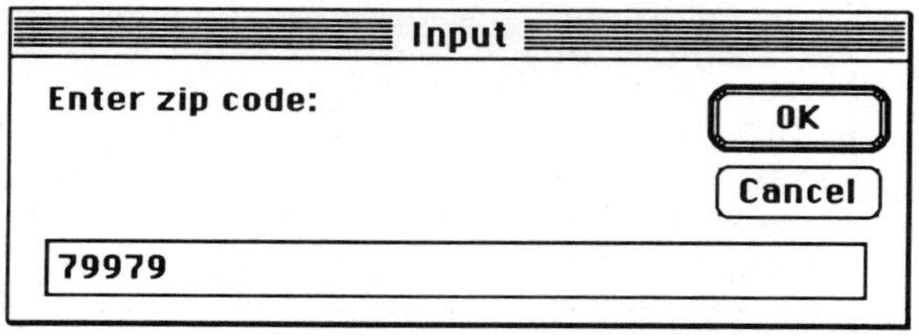

Figure 7-42. Responding to the Zip Code prompt.

Step 20. Click on OK or hit Return.
Step 21. Type *Dear Lilli:*.

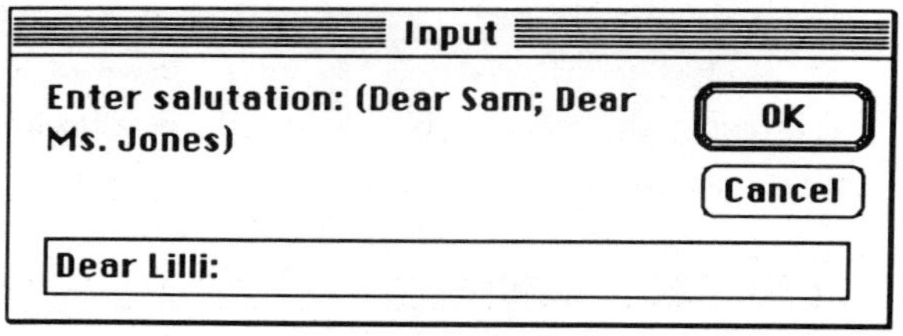

Figure 7-43. Responding to the Salutation prompt.

Step 22. Click on OK or hit Return.
Step 23. Type (876) 209-2909.

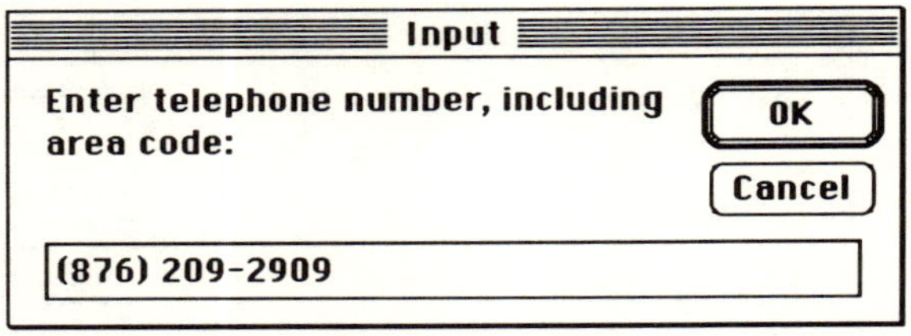

Figure 7-44. Responding to the Telephone Number prompt.

Step 24. Click on OK or hit Return.

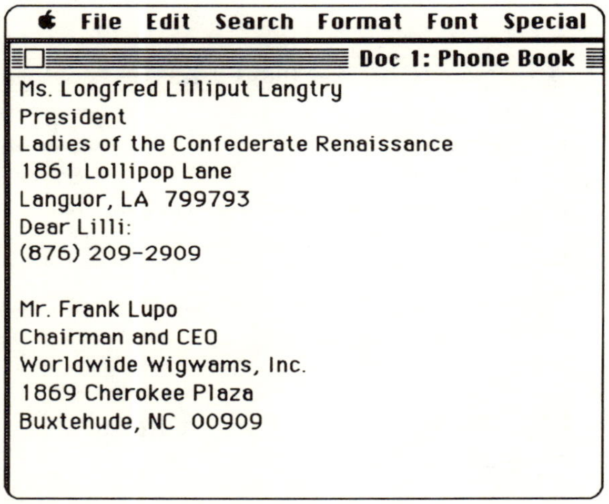

Figure 7-45. Here's the screen after running the Fast File macro one time.

That should take care of one Fast File entry. Now you have three more to do.

Repeating a Macro

I'm going to start you out on this one, then leave you on your own to finish.

Running Macros Repeatedly

Step 1. Press Esc.
Step 2. Type 3 for the number of repetitions.

Figure 7-46. The Repeat Count dialog box with the number of repetitions set at 3.

Step 3. First point to remember: Don't click on OK or hit Return. If you click on OK or press Return, the program won't execute. Instead, give the Execute Macro . . . command. However (this is the second point to remember), you aren't going to give the command with the mouse by pulling down the Special menu. Instead, give the command from the keyboard by pressing Command-Shift-X. That's the only way it works. Try running the macro with the mouse and it won't be executed.

Step 4. Select Fast File from the list of macros to invoke.

Step 5. Click on Execute or press Return. Now you're on your own. Just respond to the dialog boxes and fill in the information from the other three people listed above. Dr. Proudfeather, Mr. Joyboy, and Dr. Phicklephoot. (Be sure to go through with this exercise. It's good practice and it will give you a better feeling for how the program runs. You'll need the data in the next chapter.)

The dialog boxes keep coming around until you've entered the information for all three. When you click on OK or hit Return for the last time, the screen clears to reveal that your Phone Book file now has five residents and looks like Figure 7-47.

```
Ms. Longfred Lilliput Langtry
President
Ladies of the Confederate Renaissance
1861 Lollipop Lane
Languor, LA  799793
Dear Lilli:
(876) 209-2909

Dr. Parkinson P. Proudfeather
Vice President and Chief Financial Officer
Skedaddle Skateboards Ltd.
One Platitude Plaza
Nearmiss, NE  76667
Dear Dr. Proudfeather:
(493) 222-4466

Mr. J. Justinian Joyboy
```

```
Director--Public Affairs
Cherokee Chickpeas, Inc.
47 Chevy Chase
Oblong, OK  00703
Dear Justin:
(979) 640-3232

Dr. Phyllis P. Phicklephoot, Ph. D.
Pharmacist
St. Hoipolloi Hospital
33 Billybob Bypass
Alabaster, AR  76567
Dear Dr. Phicklephoot:
(229) 929-2929

Mr. Frank Lupo
Chairman and CEO
Worldwide Wigwams, Inc.
```

Figure 7-47. The contents of the Phone Book after running the Fast File Macro three more times.

Press Release Macro

Does your business issue press releases and announcements? Do you have your own business and worry about not putting out enough press releases, but hate the time it takes to set one up? From now on press releases are going to be a snap.

Create Press Release Macro

Step 1. Open a new file by choosing New from the File menu.
Step 2. Choose Define Macro . . . from the Macro submenu of the Special menu.
Step 3. Type *Press Release* as the name of the macro.

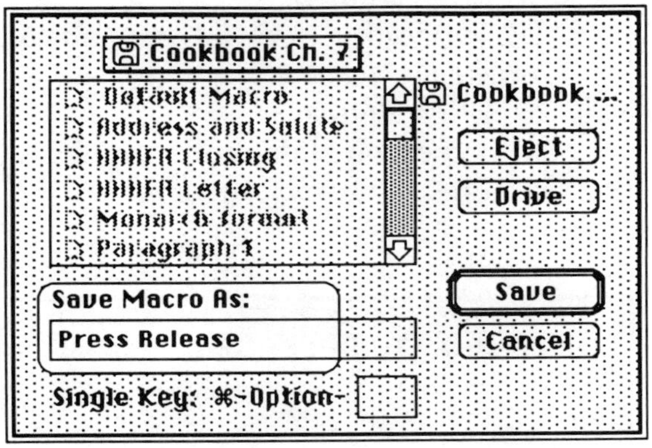

Figure 7-48. Naming this macro *Press Release*.

Step 4. Click on Save or press Return.
Step 5. Choose Show Codes from the Edit menu.
Step 6. Select Helvetica from the Font menu.
Step 7. Select 14-point from the Font menu.
Step 8. Click on *B* for boldface type.
Step 9. Type *FOR IMMEDIATE RELEASE FOR IMMEDIATE RELEASE FOR IMME* . . . until you get to h = 7.5 inches or less.
Step 10. Press Return.
Step 11. Select Times from the Font menu.
Step 12. Select 12-point from the Font menu.
Step 13. Press Return four times.
Step 14. Type *Contact:*
Step 15. Click on *P* to return to plain text.
Step 16. Press Return.
Step 17. Type your name, or *D. Drummond Dullard*.
Step 18. Press Return.

Step 19. Type your title, or Director—Corporate Communications.
Step 20. Press Return.
Step 21. Type the name of your company or organization, or *Worldwide Wigwams, Inc.*
Step 22. Press Return.
Step 23. Type your street address, or *1869 Cherokee Plaza.*
Step 24. Press Return.
Step 25. Type your city and state address, plus zip code, or type *Buxtehude, NC 00909.*
Step 26. Press Return.
Step 27. Type your telephone number, or (024) 104-1040.
Step 28. Press Return four times.

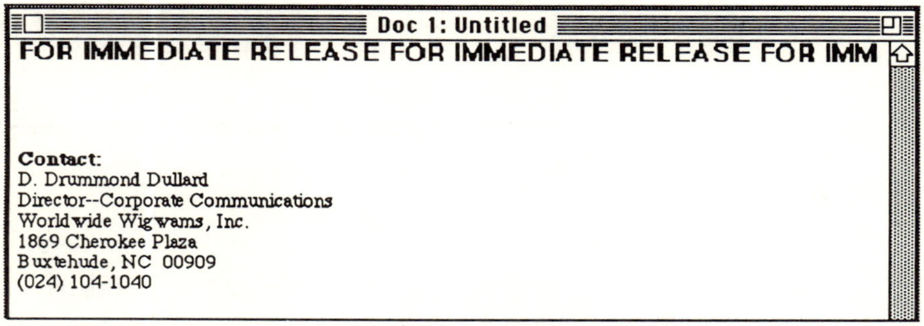

Figure 7-49. After Step 28, the screen should look like this.

Step 29. Select Helvetica from the Font menu.
Step 30. Select 14-point from the Font menu.
Step 31. Click on *B* to turn on boldface.
Step 32. Type *Headline:.*
Step 33. Press the space bar.
Step 34. Click on *P* to return to plain type.
Step 35. Select Times from the Font menu.
Step 36. Choose Pause Macro from the Macro submenu of the Special menu. This is where your headline will go.
Step 37. Choose Resume Macro from the Macro submenu of the Special menu.
Step 38. Enter three Returns.
Step 39. Select 12-point from the Font menu.
Step 40. Press Tab.

Step 41. Type the name of the city where your business or organization is located, or *Buxtehude.*

Step 42. Type a comma and press the space bar.

Step 43. Choose Insert Function from the Date submenu of the Special menu.

Step 44. Type a dash.

Step 45. Choose Spacing . . . from the Line submenu of the Format menu.

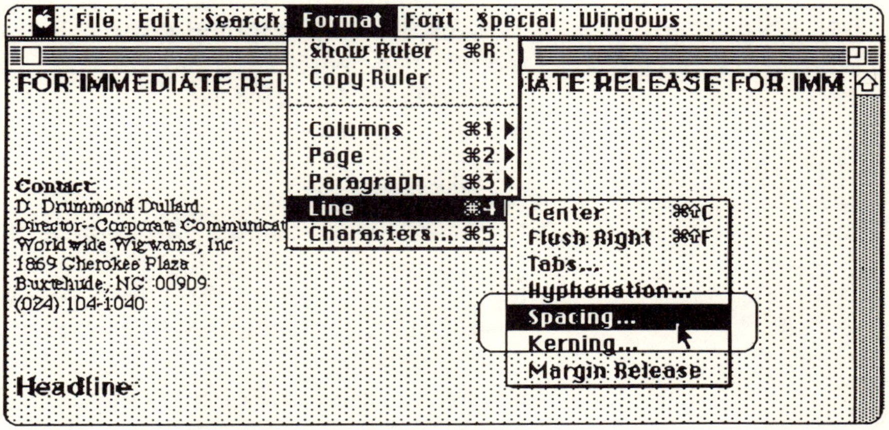

Figure 7-50. Choosing Spacing . . . from the Line submenu of the Format menu.

Step 46. Click twice on the Up Arrow under Line Spacing in the Spacing dialog box to change spacing to 2.0 lines (double spacing).

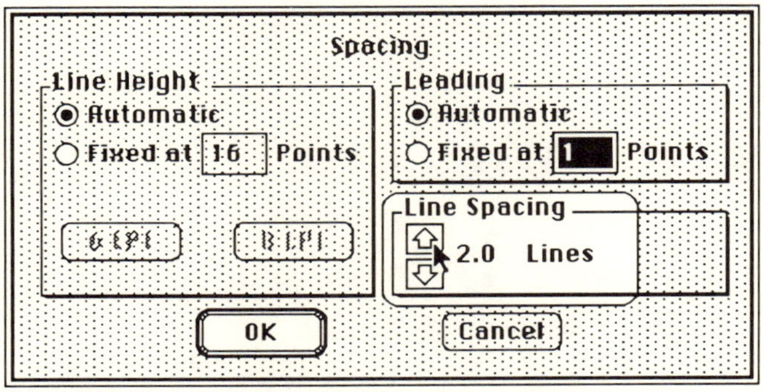

Figure 7-51. Changing line spacing to 2.0 lines (double spacing) by clicking on the Up Arrow under Line Spacing.

Step 47. Click on OK or hit Return.
Step 48. Choose Pause Macro from the Macro submenu of the Special menu. This is where you will enter the body of the press release.
Step 49. Choose Resume Macro from the Macro submenu of the Special menu.
Step 50. Press Return.
Step 51. Press Command-Shift-C to center the Cursor. (This is just to put some variety into your life. You could have accomplished the same thing, of course, by choosing Center from the Line submenu of the Format menu.)
Step 52. Type *-end-*.
Step 53. Press Return.
Step 54. Center the Cursor by pressing Command-Shift-C.
Step 55. Type five asterisks separated by spaces.
Step 56. Press Return.
Step 57. Choose Spacing . . . from the Line submenu of the Format menu.
Step 58. Click twice on the Down Arrow under Line Spacing in the Spacing dialog box to change spacing back to 1.0 lines (single spacing).
Step 59. Click on OK or hit Return.
Step 60. Click on *B* to switch to boldface type.
Step 61. Type *For further information, please contact.*
Step 62. Press the space bar.
Step 63. Click on *P* to return to plain type.

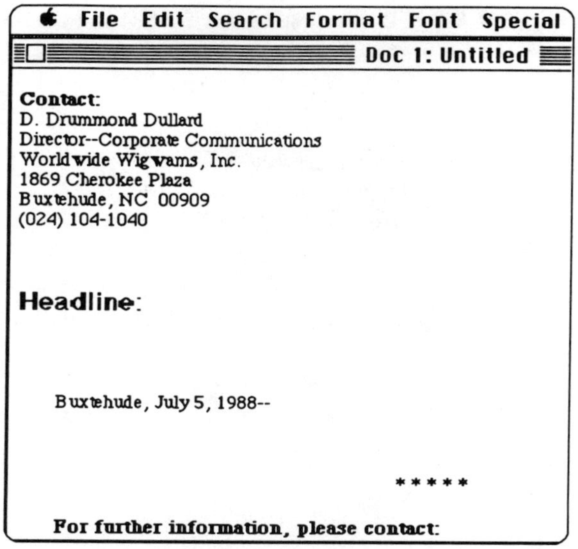

Figure 7-52. The appearance of the screen after Step 63.

Step 64. Type your name, title, company or organization, street or P.O. box address, city, 2-letter state abbreviation, zip code, and phone number. Or type: *D. Drummond Dullard, Director—Corporate Communications, Worldwide Wigwams, Inc., 1869 Cherokee Plaza, Buxtehude, NC 00909, (024) 104-1040.*

Step 65. Choose Hide Codes from the Edit menu.

Step 66. End definition of the macro by choosing Define Macro . . . from the Macro submenu of the Special menu.

FOR IMMEDIATE RELEASE FOR IMMEDIATE RELEASE FOR IM

Contact:
D. Drummond Dullard
Director--Corporate Communications
Worldwide Wigwams, Inc.
1869 Cherokee Plaza
Buxtehude, NC 00909
(024) 104-1040

Headline:

Buxtehude, July 5, 1988--

-end-

*****

For further information, please contact: D. Drummond Dullard, Director--Corporate Communications, Worldwide Wigwams, Inc., 1869 Cherokee Plaza, Buxtehude, NC 00909, (024) 104-1040.

Figure 7-53. The screen display when you finish defining the Press Release macro.

That completes the Press Release macro. It took 66 steps and many more keystrokes. When you run the macro now, it will take only a tiny part of that effort.

Running the Press Release Macro

Got some hot news to send out into the world? Why don't you try putting this new Press Release macro through its paces. Otherwise, practice on the Worldwide Wigwams announcement.

Step 1. Open a new file.
Step 2. Choose Execute Macro . . . from the Macro submenu of the Special menu.
Step 3. Select Press Release from the list of macros.

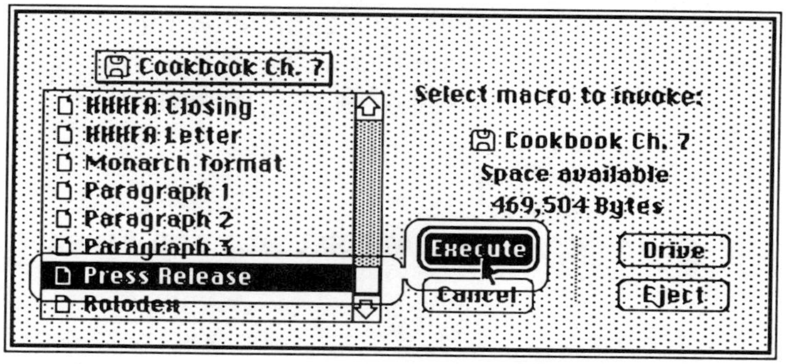

Figure 7-54. Executing the Press Release macro.

Step 4. Click on Execute or hit Return.

Step 5. When the macro pauses for the headline, type Worldwide Wigwams Defies Consumer Complaints, Doubles Chocolate Ration

Step 6. Choose Resume Macro from the Macro submenu of the Special menu.

Step 7. When the macro pauses again for the text of the press release, type the following.

> Frank Lupo, Chairman and Chief Executive Officer of Worldwide Wigwams, Inc., announced today his response to the reports of consumer complaints about WW's widely-imitated Evening-Turndown-and-After-Dinner-Mint Program. Rumors circulating in the media mention irate customer letters about showing up at critical business meetings with ears full of melted chocolate. "Horse biscuits!" says Lupo. "They're just a bunch of disgruntled slide-rule salesmen, blackguards and slugabeds. The sensible guests feel just as I do about the ETADM program. I like it—we'll all have some more!"
>
> Lupo announced that, effective immediately, Worldwide Wigwam guests would be greeted in the evenings by four after-dinner mints instead of the usual two.
>
> WW's new policy is not expected to have an immediate effect on occupancy rates, but since major competitors are likely to follow suit, Hershey Foods reacted enthusiastically to the announcement.

Step 8. Choose Resume Macro from the Macro submenu of the Special menu.

Step 9. Print the completed memo by choosing Print . . . from the File menu.
Step 10. Click on OK or hit Return.

FOR IMMEDIATE RELEASE FOR IMMEDIATE RELEASE FOR IM

Contact:
D. Drummond Dullard
Director--Corporate Communications
Worldwide Wigwams, Inc.
1869 Cherokee Plaza
Buxtehude, NC 00909
(024) 104-1040

Headline: Worldwide Wigwams Defies Consumer Complaints, Doubles Chocolate Ration

Buxtehude, July 6, 1988--Frank Lupo, Chairman and Chief Executive Officer of Worldwide Wigwams, Inc., announced today his response to the reports of consumer complaints about WW's widely-imitated Evening-Turndown-and-After-Dinner-Mint Program. Rumors circulating in the media mention irate customer letters about showing up at critical business meetings with ears full of melted chocolate.

"Horse biscuits!" says Lupo. "They're just a bunch of disgruntled slide-rule salesmen, blackguards and slugabeds. The sensible guests feel just as I do about the ETADM program. I like it--we'll all have some more!"

Lupo announced that, effective immediately, Worldwide Wigwam guests would be greeted in the evenings by four after-dinner mints instead of the usual two.

WW's new policy is not expected to have an immediate effect on occupancy rates, but since major competitors are likely to follow suit, Hershey Foods reacted enthusiastically to the announcement.

-end-

* * * * *

For further information, please contact: D. Drummond Dullard, Director--Corporate Communications, Worldwide Wigwams, Inc., 1869 Cherokee Plaza, Buxtehude, NC 00909, (024) 104-1040.

Figure 7-55. The printed version of the completed press release.

Repeating Search and Change Macro

You must have had this experience: After finishing a document or letter and printing it out, you realize you would like it much more if you had put all the names in boldface, or all the headings in italics, or all the numbers in parentheses. Nevertheless, you let it stand because it was too much trouble to make all the changes.

A repeating macro, that searches for a certain kind of character group, makes a change, then searches for the next occurrence of the group, can take care of such a job in short order. In this section you'll create such a search and change macro.

The secret is to create a macro that does the job one time; then *chain* the macro to itself so it will repeat the macro until it finds no more jobs to do. Creating the macro can be a bit tricky because you have to be sure the computer understands exactly what you want it to do and what you don't want it do to. We'll go through one problem together. That will help you create future macros that solve particular problems.

Type the first four steps of the previous Press Release macro, but don't insert any boldface or italic commands.

Step 1. Open a new file.
Step 2. Choose Execute Macro . . . from the Macro submenu of the Special menu.
Step 3. Select *Press Release* from the list of macros.
Step 4. Click on Execute or hit Return.

Here's a Macro for putting all of those steps into boldface. This should help you think through the writing of a macro for doing repetitive jobs.

Step 1. Move the cursor to the beginning of the text by placing the mouse pointer there and clicking. Choose Define Macro . . . from the Macro submenu of the Special menu.
Step 2. Type *Search and Change* as the name of the macro.

Using Search and Replace

Step 3. Click on Save or press Return.
Step 4. Choose Forward . . . from the Search menu.

Figure 7-56. Choosing Forward . . . from the Search menu.

Step 5. Type Step as the word or string of characters to look for.

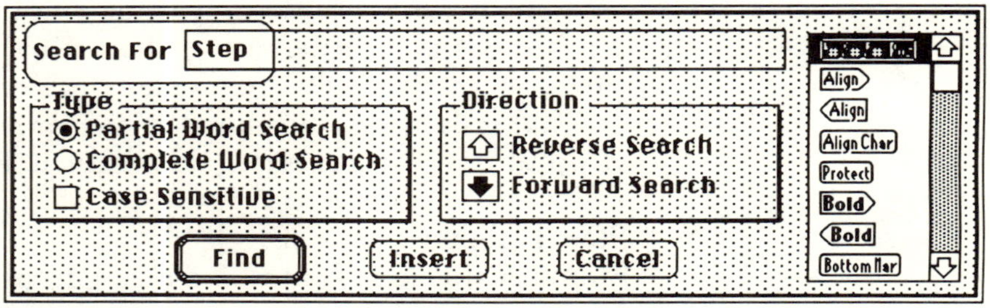

Figure 7-57. Instructing *WordPerfect* to search for the word *Step*.

Step 6. Click on Find or hit Return. The first occurrence of Step will be Selected or highlighted.

That's straightforward enough. The next step is to change the type from plain to boldface. That involves selecting or highlighting the word *step* and the following number. Since the word step is already selected, it's necessary only to hold down the Shift key and select a few characters to the right.

Step 7. Hold down the Shift key while hitting the Right Arrow key until all of Step 1. is highlighted.

Step 8. Click on *B* to change the Selected characters to boldface. Then choose Select Off on the Select submenu of the Edit menu.

Here a new trick comes into play. You have just created a macro that searches for a specific string of characters and makes a change. You could sit at the keyboard and execute the macro over and over until all of the desired strings were changed or you could instruct the macro to repeat itself a specific number of times. Instead, you are going to chain the macro to itself, so it will repeat the requested action until it can find no more occurrences of *step* and cancels itself.

Chaining a Macro to Itself

Step 9. Choose Chain Macro . . . from the Macro submenu of the Special menu.

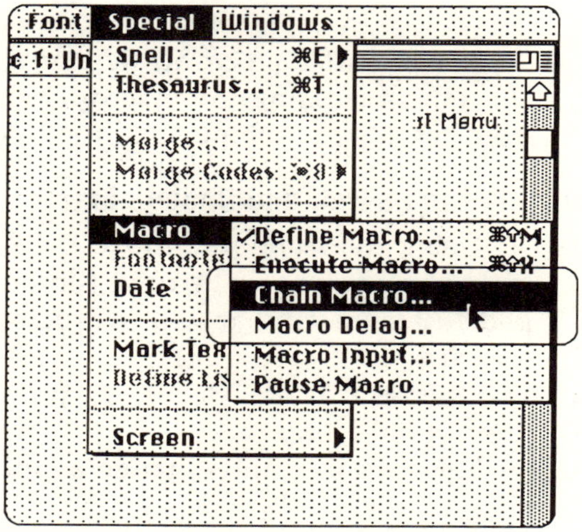

Figure 7-58. Choosing Chain Macro . . . from the Macro submenu of the Special menu.

Step 10. Select Search and Change as the macro to chain. In other words, you are chaining the macro to itself.

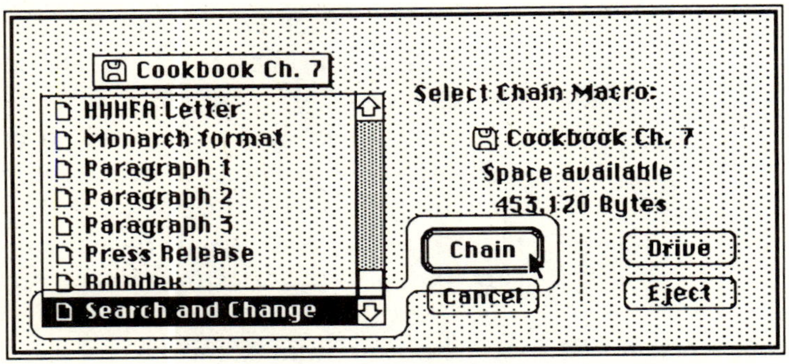

Figure 7-59. Choosing Search and Change as the macro to Chain to the Search and Change Macro.

Step 11. Click on Chain or hit Return.

Step 12. Finish creating the macro by choosing Define Macro . . . from the Macro submenu of the Special menu.

Running the Search and Change Macro

Step 1. Using the same file, move the Cursor to the top by pressing Enter, Enter, Up Arrow. (Enter is on the numeric keypad.) Remember that you instructed the program to search forward.

Step 2. Choose Execute Macro . . . from the Macro submenu of the Special menu.

Step 3. Select Search and Change as the macro to Execute.

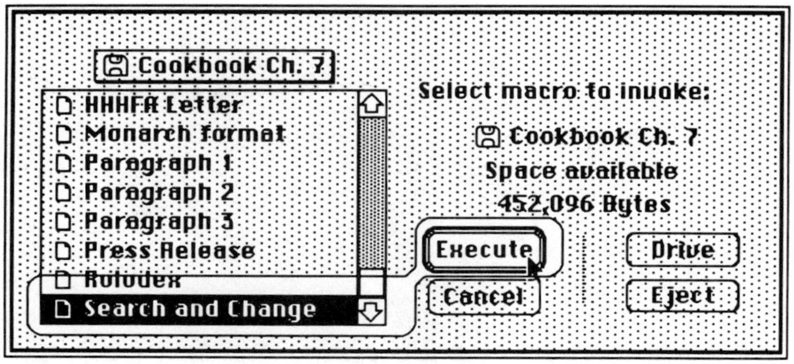

Figure 7-60. Selecting Search and Change as the macro to Execute.

Step 4. Click on Execute or press Return. You can see Step 1, Step 2, and so on, flashing as the macro repeats its operation on each one. When it has finished, the Mac beeps and very briefly flashes *Not found* at the bottom of the screen. This terminates the macro.

Chapter 8

How to Create Databases with *WordPerfect*

Chapter 8

How to Create Databases with *WordPerfect*

We work with databases all the time. They organize and store information for us—information we expect to need in the future and want to be able to extract with a minimum of effort. They can be simple, like a grocery list, or they can be tremendously complex and detailed, like the U.S. Census files or the commercial mailing lists that professional list brokers acquire and sell.

In the discussion of databases, you will read jargon from the database racket: files, records, fields, retrieve fields, end of record, and so on. We will have names or symbols for each. Don't be intimidated. The terms will be defined as the concepts are introduced. You'll quickly recognize the simple logic behind the whole process. In general, the jargon will be kept to a bare minimum.

Database Terms Defined

The terms *file* and *database* generally can be used interchangeably. A file is one collection of data, organized into *records* and *fields*.

A record is one unit of a file or database, determined by the primary purpose of the database. For example, a telephone list could have the primary purpose of organizing all the people you call. It could also be designed to identify and organize the companies you do business with.

In the case of the people phone list, a record (the smallest unit on the list) would consist of the data or information about a single person on the list: his or her title, company, address, phone number, and so on. In the case of the company phone list, a record would consist of the data or information about each individual company on the list. Those individual records might well contain the names of several different people.

A grocery list is a simple form of database. In one sense, a grocery list could consist of a single record with a number of individual bits of data. The record could be defined by the date:

The grocery list of July 8 would be one record, the list of July 15 another record, and so on.

Let's get away from this abstract discussion and look at a concrete example. *WordPerfect,* like any word processor, is limited in the area of database management. *WordPerfect* isn't meant to be the *ne plus ultra* of database manipulation. If you're working with batches of information that will require hundreds or thousands of records, with dozens of fields per record, and you want to be able to manipulate and display that data in all kinds of different formats, you should buy a professional database management package such as *dBase Mac.* You won't want to try to manage that data with a word processor. *WordPerfect* can't yet sort data, a function very important to database management, but the good people in Utah promise that sorting capacity is on the way, so maybe you'll see it in an upgrade.

If your database is of modest size, and you want to use it primarily for preparing lists and doing automated mailings, *WordPerfect* will do a fine job for you.

Here's a grocery list from July 8:

tomatoes	soda
bell peppers	cheese
sweet basil (fresh)	skim milk
linguini	oregano (dried)
tomato sauce	peppercorns
beer	soup

The list can be seen as a simple database consisting of a single record with 12 pieces of data. On the other hand, if you're going to pick up those items at a familiar supermarket, you probably subdivide the list into fields as soon as you walk in the door. The fields might be called Aisle 1, Aisle 2, and so on, or you might divide up the list this way:

Produce	**Condiments**	**Canned goods**
tomatoes	oregano	tomato sauce
bell peppers	peppercorns	soup
sweet basil		

Beverages	**Dairy**	**Pasta**
beer	cheese	linguini
soda	skimmed milk	

That gives you a database or file with six fields:

produce	dairy
beverages	canned goods
condiments	pasta

Some fields have three items, some fields have two, and some have one. Now, if you add the grocery list of July 15, you'll have two records, each containing at least six fields. Some fields may be empty, though. You may buy no pasta next week, for example.

Let's look back at the list we were working with in Chapter 7. Here it is:

Ms. Longfred Lilliput Langtry
President
Ladies of the Confederate Renaissance
1860 Lollipop Lane
Languor, LA 79979
Dear Lilli:
(876) 209-2909

Dr. Parkinson P. Proudfeather
Vice President and Chief Financial Officer
Skedaddle Skateboards Ltd.
One Platitude Plaza
Nearmiss, NE 76667
Dear Dr. Proudfeather:
(493) 222-4466

Mr. J. Justinian Joyboy
Director—Public Affairs
Cherokee Chickpeas, Inc.
47 Chevy Chase
Oblong, OK 00703
Dear Justin:
(979) 640-3232

Dr. Phyllis P. Phicklephoot, Ph. D.
Pharmacist
St. Hoipolloi Hospital
33 Billybob Bypass
Alabaster, AR 76567
Dear Dr. Phicklephoot:
(229) 929-2929.

Remember from the letter you were working on in Chapter 7 that all of these people were donors to a benefit auction run by an organization called Helping Hands for Health Food Addicts. You will also remember that reference was made to their donations and also to their contact person. Let's add those donations and contact people to our list; it will now look like this:

1. Ms. Longfred Lilliput Langtry
President
Ladies of the Confederate Renaissance
1860 Lollipop Lane
Languor, LA 79979
Dear Lilli:
(876) 209-2909
Donation: a six-foot hero sandwich
Contact: Deirdre Dunbar-Dinwiddy

2. Dr. Parkinson P. Proudfeather
Vice President and Chief Financial Officer
Skedaddle Skateboards Ltd.
One Platitude Plaza
Nearmiss, NE 76667
Dear Dr. Proudfeather:
(493) 222-4466
Donation: the Hope Diamond
Contact: F. Farnsworth Fignewton

3. Mr. J. Justinian Joyboy
Director—Public Affairs
Cherokee Chickpeas, Inc.
47 Chevy Chase
Oblong, OK 00703
Dear Justin:
(979) 640-3232
Donation: a Ming vase
Contact: Quigley McQ. Quark

4. Dr. Phyllis P. Phicklephoot, Ph. D.
Pharmacist
St. Hoipolloi Hospital
33 Billybob Bypass
Alabaster, AR 76567
Dear Dr. Phicklephoot:
(229) 929-2929.

Donation: a lifetime membership in the Elvis Presley Resurrection and Reconstruction Society.
Contact: Roustabout "Rusty" Relique

There are four records. Each record contains a number of potential fields. I say "potential" because to some extent, it's up to you to decide what constitutes a field. The potential fields I see are:

Field 1: Name
Field 2: Title
Field 3: Company or organization
Field 4: Street or post office address
Field 5: City
Field 6: State
Field 7: ZIP code
Field 8: Salutation
Field 9: Telephone number
Field 10: Donation
Field 11: Contact person
Field 12: First name
Field 13: Last name
Field 14: Sex

You can probably think of others. When you're deciding how to set up your database, concentrate on the specific functions you want it to perform and the ways you are going to be extracting information from it. Then make it no more complicated than it absolutely has to be. If you can get along with eight fields, don't set up thirteen fields just to show that you know how to do it.

For the purposes of the HHHFA, Fields 1 through 11 will suffice. In fact, they could probably get along with a single address field combining street address, city, state, and ZIP code, but in this example they will be separate in order to illustrate some points.

To make the Mac understand what you're doing and to keep your data neatly organized until you are ready for it, insert some codes that will identify the various records, fields, and so on. You'll have to tell the Mac when a record begins and ends, when a field begins and ends, how to know which field to extract, where to put information on printouts, and so forth. Here are the first *WordPerfect* database codes you will use. They're called *merge codes*. The apparent reason for the name is that the expected major use for databases in a word processing program is for creating mail-merge letters.

Merge Code*	**Meaning**
^R	End of field
^E	End of record
^F	Retrieve field.

* These codes consist of a control character followed by an uppercase letter. Holding the Control key down and pressing *R*, *E*, or *F* will have the same apparent effect, but these codes will not work. You must insert the codes using the Merge Codes menu.

Start with Lilli. Let's enter her record with the correct control codes:

Step 1. Open a new File by choosing New from the File Menu.
Step 2. Type *Ms. Longfred Lilliput Langtry.*

Entering End of Field Code

Step 3. Choose End of Field from the Merge Codes submenu of the Special menu. (You may prefer to use the keyboard and enter the End of Field code by pressing Command-Shift-R.)

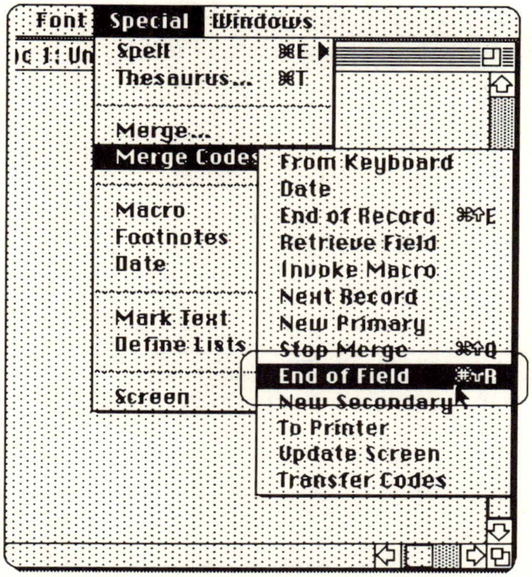

Figure 8-1. Choosing End of Field from the Merge Codes submenu of the Special menu.

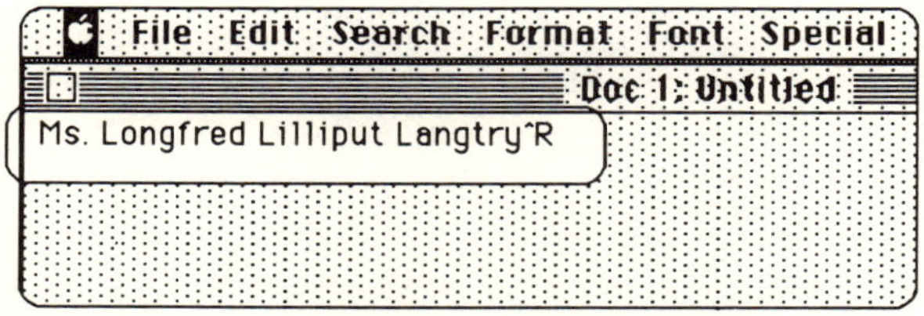

Figure 8-2. The first line of the address with an End of Field code.

Step 4. Type *President*.
Step 5. Choose End of Field from the Merge Codes submenu of the Special menu.
Step 6. Choose Show Codes from the Edit menu. Notice that when you enter the End of Field code, the program also inserts a Hard Return (HRt) that moves you down to the next line.

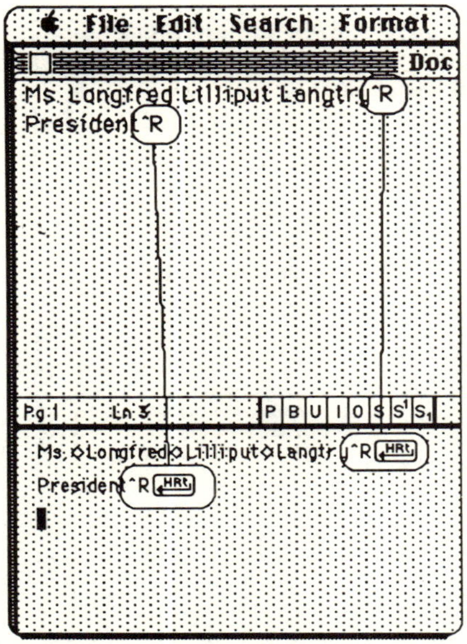

Figure 8-3. Show Codes reveals that the End of Field code consists of a ˆR plus a HRt (hard right or carriage return).

Step 7. Type *Ladies of the Confederate Renaissance.*
Step 8. Choose End of Field from the Merge Codes submenu of the Special menu, or press Command-Shift-R.
Step 9. Type *1860 Lollipop Lane.*
Step 10. Enter End of Field code as above.
Step 11. Type *Languor* and enter End of Field code as above.
Step 12. Type *LA* and enter End of Field code.
Step 13. Type 79979 and enter End of Field code.
Step 14. Type *Lilli* and enter End of Field code.
Step 15. Type (876) 209-2909 and enter End of Field code.
Step 16. Type *a six-foot hero sandwich* and enter End of Field code.
Step 17. Type *Deirdre Dunbar-Dinwiddy* and enter End of Field code.

That completes the entry for record 1. You should now tell the Mac that this is the End of Record 1:
Step 18. Choose End of Record from the Merge Codes submenu of the Special menu, or press Command-Shift-E.

Entering End of Record Code

Take a look at your screen now. There are eleven fields that you listed above—name, title, company or organization, street or

P.O. address, city, two-letter state abbreviation, ZIP code, salutation, telephone number, donation, and contact person. Although they're not numbered (and this is a disadvantage of a word processor database), the program assigns numbers to them. The one that comes first is called Field 1, the second Field 2, and so on.

A crucial point to remember: You must have 11 fields in every record you enter from now on. If you don't have the data on any field—if you're missing a phone number or contact person, for example—you must enter an End of Field code in the empty line. The computer must see 11 End of Field codes, whether the fields actually have any content or not.

Now let's get the rest of the Phone Book entries into database or Merger format. Along the way, you're going to pick up a couple of new tricks.

Move the Cursor to the bottom of the Langtry record and press Return to create a blank line.

Open the Phone Book file if you haven't done so already. Place the Cursor in front of Dr. Parkinson P. Proudfeather.

Step 1. Press Command-Shift-N to turn Select On.
Step 2. Hit Enter, Enter, Down Arrow to Select through the end of the Phone Book file.
Step 3. Choose Copy from the Edit menu.
Step 4. Cycle back to your original document with the Langtry database entry by clicking on the document or choosing Doc 1 from the Windows menu.
Step 5. Insert the Phone Book material you just copied into Doc 1 by choosing Paste from the Edit menu.
Step 6. Return the cursor to the beginning of the Proudfeather entry.

The goal is to use search and replace techniques to put the remaining Phone Book data into database or Merger form without having to retype every entry.

Let's think it through. First of all, in the current Phone Book format, you have a lot of lines (most of which will become fields) that end in a hard return (HRt).

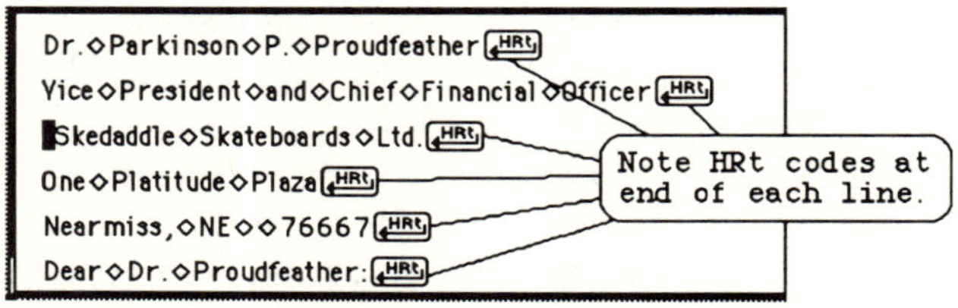

Figure 8-4. The HRt codes at the each of each Phone Book line.

To turn these lines into fields that will be recognized by *WordPerfect,* these lines should end with ^R-HRt. Let's tell the Mac to look for HRt's, and every time it finds one, replace it with a ^R-HRt.

Step 1. Choose Replace from the Search menu.

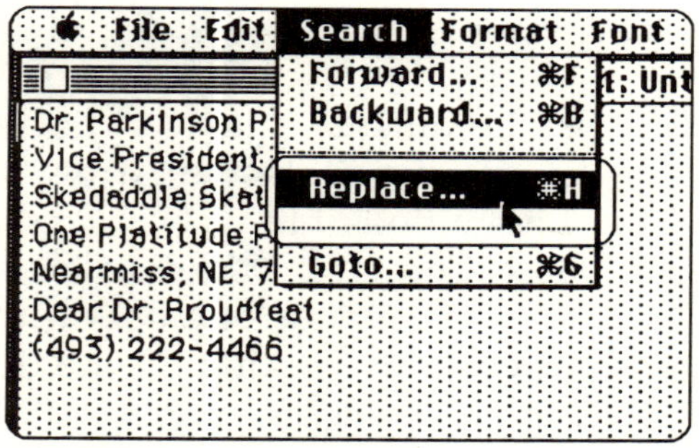

Figure 8-5. Choosing Replace from the Search menu.

Searching and Replacing Formatting Codes

Step 2. How do you tell the Mac to look for a HRt? There is a list of codes at the right-hand side of the Search/Replace dialog box. Use the scroll bar to scroll the directory until you locate the code for HRt.

Step 3. Select the HRt code by clicking on it.

Figure 8-6. The Code Directory in the Search/Replace dialog box with the HRt code selected.

Step 4. Insert the HRt code into the Search box by clicking on Insert.

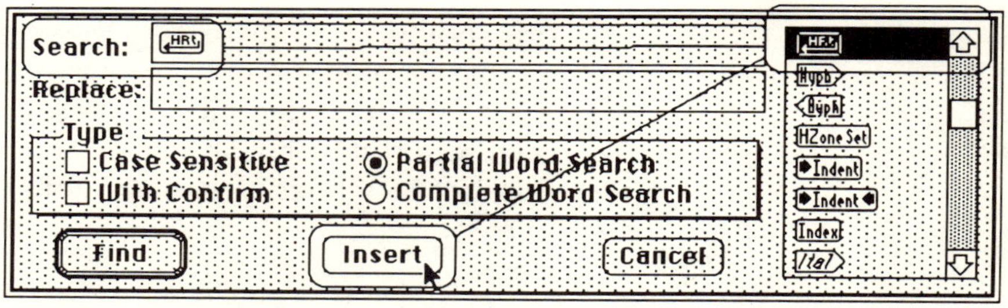

Figure 8-7. The HRt code inserted into the Search box.

Step 5. Press Tab to move the cursor into the Replace box. Remember that you aren't replacing a HRt with a ˆR. You're replacing the HRt with a ˆR-HRt. So don't forget to insert the HRt again.

Step 6. Locate and Select ˆR in the Code Directory.

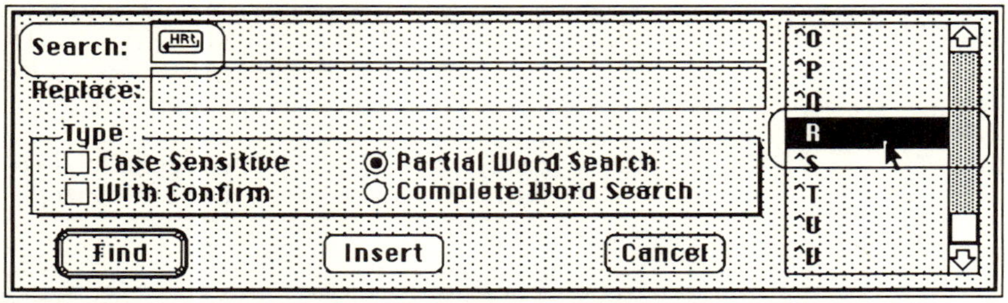

Figure 8-8. ^R selected in the Code Directory.

Step 7. Click on Insert to insert the ^R code into the Replace box.
Step 8. Locate and Select HRt in the Code Directory.
Step 9. Click on Insert to insert the HRt code into the Replace box.

You should be almost ready to go. The Search and Replace dialog box says you're going to search for HRt codes and replace them with ^R-HRt codes. Just to be careful, ask the Mac to confirm each action it's about to take. This will slow down the process a bit, but it will let you see how the program works from step to step.

Step 10. Click on With Confirm.

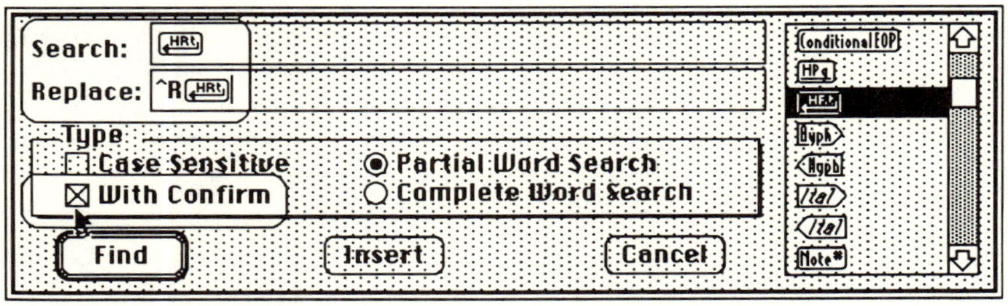

Figure 8-9. The Search and Replace dialog box ready to roll, with Confirm activated.

Now you're ready to go.

Step 11. Click on Find, or hit Return. The program pauses at the first HRt for your confirmation, with a small dialog box that asks whether you want to Replace, Skip this one, or Cancel the Search and Replace routine.

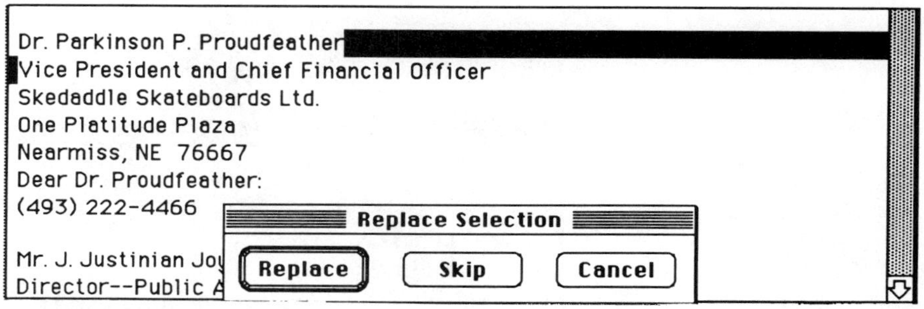

Figure 8-10. The Confirmation dialog box, asking if you want to replace the first occurrence of HRt, at the end of the Proudfeather name, with ^R-HRt.

Step 12. Click on Replace, or hit Return. The program moves on to the next HRt and pauses with the dialog box.
You can see the new End of Field code at the end of the Proudfeather line.

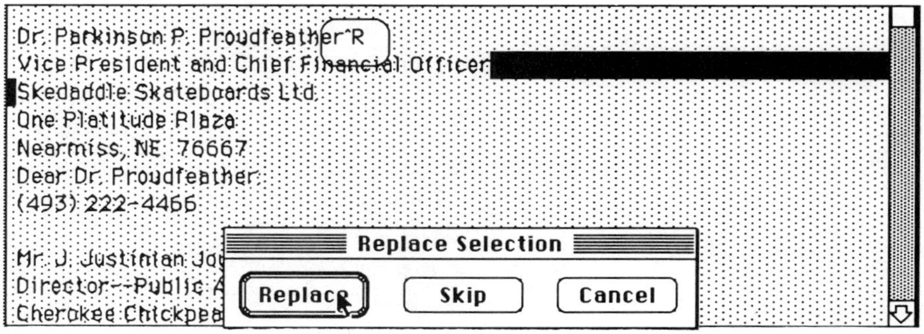

Figure 8-11. A ^R code has been inserted at the end of the first line of the Proudfeather record, and the program is now paused for your next confirmation.

Step 13. When the program stops at the HRt that creates a blank line between records, click on Skip so the program will move on. You want to keep that blank line.
Step 14. Continue to click on Replace or hit Return for each instance.

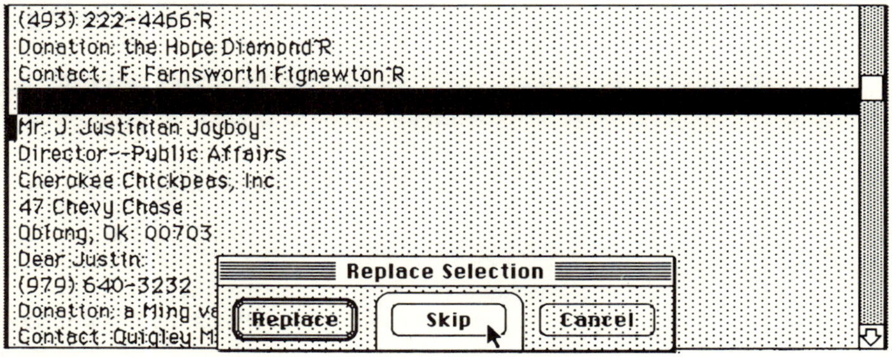

Figure 8-12. Clicking on Skip to command the program to ignore the HRt between records.

Go through the rest of the file in this fashion, entering ˆRs at the end of each line and leaving the blank lines between records. When you're finished, move the cursor back to the top of the file.

When you entered the record for Lilli Langtry, you made separate fields for city, state, and zip code. You'll have to do that for the rest of the records. How do you do it easily?

Well, the name of the city is always followed by a comma and a space. Simply tell the Mac to search for the comma-space combinations and replace them with ˆR-HRts.

Step 1. Choose Replace . . . from the Search menu.
Step 2. When the Search and Replace dialog box appears, type a comma and then a space for the Search box.
Step 3. Now you already have a ˆR-HRt in the Replace box, so click on With Confirm.

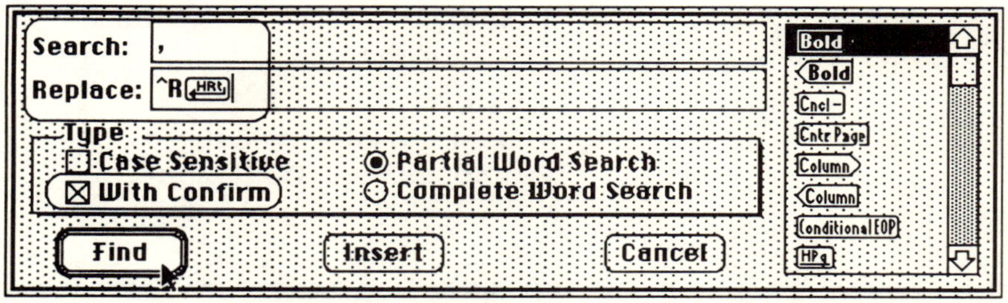

Figure 8-13. The Search/Replace box ready to replace a comma-space with a ^R-HRt.

This search is ready to go.

Step 4. Click on Find or hit Return.
The first stop is at the comma following Nearmiss, the city in Nebraska where Skedaddle Skateboards Ltd. is located. The Replace Selection dialog box asks if you want to replace the comma. You do.

Step 5. Click on Replace or hit Return.
The program now stops after Cherokee Chickpeas, the company that Justin Joyboy works for. This comma simply separates the company name from Inc., so you don't want a HRt here.

Step 6. Click on Skip. The program stops after Oblong.

Step 7. Click on Replace or hit Return.

Step 8. Stop after Phyllis PhicklePhoot, where the comma separates her name from her degree. Click on Skip.

Step 9. Stop after Alabaster, the city in Arkansas where St. Hoipolloi Hospital is located. Click on Replace, or hit Return.

Step 10. Stop between Wigwams and Inc. Click on Skip.

Step 11. The final stop is between Buxtehude and NC. Click on Replace or hit Return.

Return the cursor to the top of the file. You still have to separate the state and zip code into separate fields. The two-letter state abbreviation is followed by two spaces, so let's replace those two spaces with ^R-HRts.

Step 1. Choose Replace . . . from the Search menu.
Step 2. When the dialog box appears, type two spaces in the Search Box.
Step 3. You already have the ˆR HRt combination in the Replace box, so click on With Confirm.

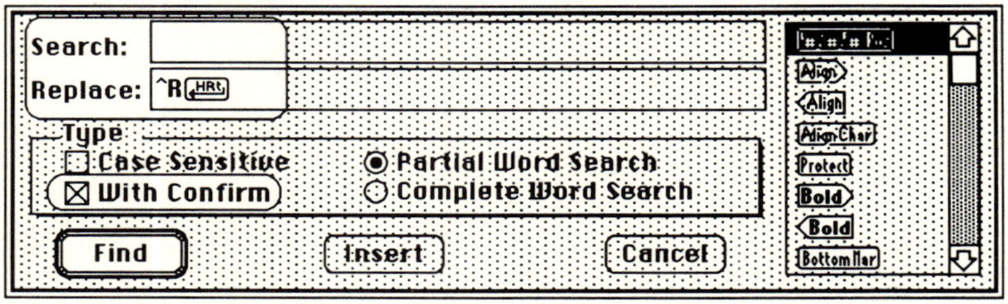

Figure 8-14. The Search and Replace box ready to search for a space-space combination and replace it with the ˆR-HRt codes.

Step 4. Click on Find or press Return.
Step 5. The first stop is between NE and the zip code. Click on Replace or hit Return. Finish this on your own, replacing between the states and zip codes, skipping otherwise.
Return the cursor to the top of the file. You now need to remove all the extraneous information so nothing remains in each record but the data pertaining to that record. The words *Dear, Donation,* and *Contact,* for example, are really general field characteristics, not data unique to the individual records. *Dear* means you're in the Salutation field; and *Donation* and *Contact* are the field names themselves. If this isn't quite clear to you, hang on. It will be clear soon. For now, get rid of those three words.

Using Search and Replace to Delete Data

Step 1. Choose Replace . . . from the Search menu.
Step 2. Type *Dear* followed by a space in the Search box. Don't forget the space.
Step 3. Press Tab to move to the Replace box.
Step 4. Click the Mouse with the Pointer in the Replace box anywhere after the HRt code.

Step 5. Hit the Delete key twice to erase the ^R and HRt codes. The Search and Replace box should look as it does in Figure 8-15, with the word *Dear* followed by a space in the Search box and nothing in the Replace box.

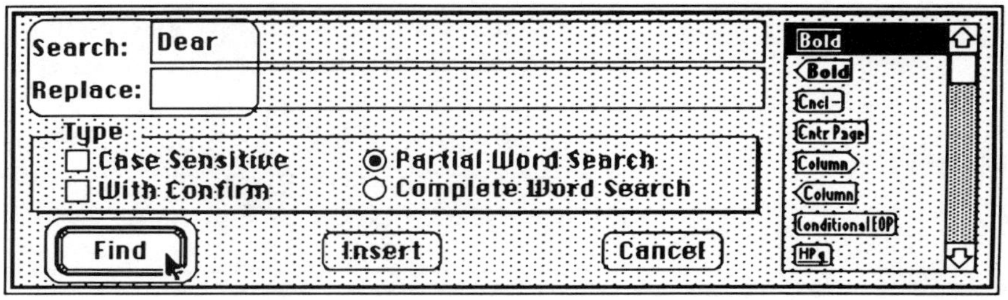

Figure 8-15. The Search and Replace box set up to erase the word *Dear* wherever it occurs.

This means you're going to find all occurrences of *Dear* followed by a space and replace it with nothing. You are instructing the computer to erase the word *Dear*.

Step 6. Click on With Confirm so you can watch the program move through its paces.

Step 7. Click on Find or press Return. The dialog box appears next, warning you that if you go ahead, you'll erase the search string wherever it occurs. This is exactly what you want to happen.

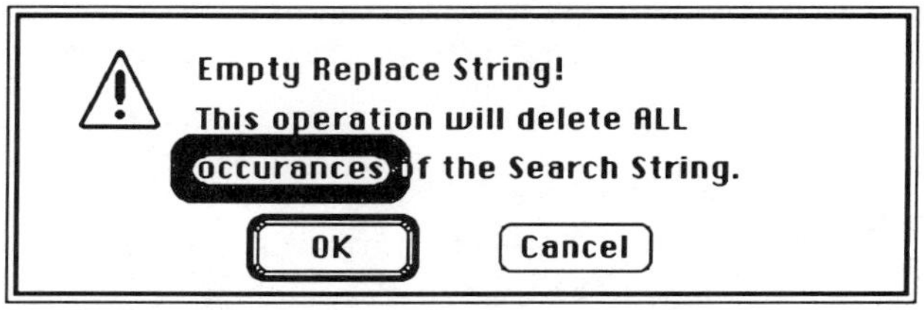

Figure 8-16. The Empty Replace String warning box, alerting that you are about to erase *Dear* wherever it appears (note the spelling of *occurrences*).

Step 8. Click on OK or hit Return.

Now that you know how it's done, go through this procedure on your own to remove the words *Donation* and *Contact*. Be sure to include the colon and space after each word.

Next, insert an End of Record code (ˆE) at the end of each record.

Finally, notice that some fields are missing in the record of our old friend Frank Lupo. His record is missing a salutation; type in *Mr. Lupo,* followed by an End of Field code. He is also missing a telephone number, a donation, and a contact person. Leave all three blank, but put in End of Field codes for them so *WordPerfect* can account for all fields. When you finish, the Lupo record should look like Figure 8-17.

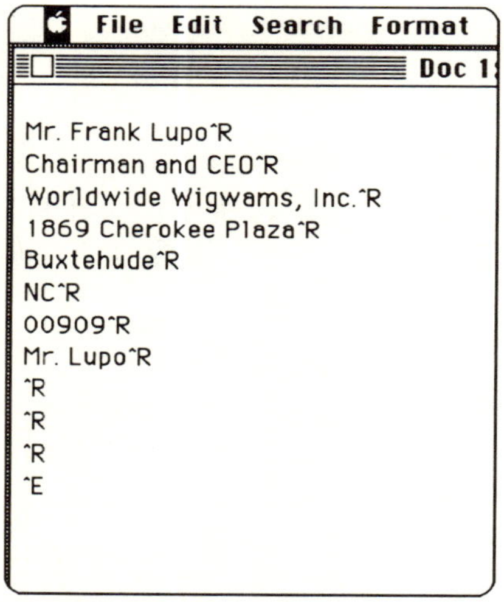

Figure 8-17. The Frank Lupo record. The three ˆRs standing alone indicate data missing in three fields—telephone number, donation, and contact.

With those last touches, the Phone Book has become more than a mere list. It is now a database, which means you can access it quickly, logically, selectively, and in customized formats that suit your own particular needs.

The uses to which you put database information need not be complicated. They can be as simple as the office phone directory. Suppose, for example, that the Phone Book file were your own company's list of clients, and you wanted to make up a phone directory to distribute to your fellow workers. In its simplest form, the phone directory might contain no more than a name and a telephone number. Let's give that a try.

Extracting Information from a Database

The Phone Book file you have just created is what *WordPerfect* calls a *secondary file*. In order to extract information from that secondary file, you have to create a primary file that contains formatting instructions and command codes.

In the upcoming pages, you're going to open a New File, put in some command codes for extracting data from the Phone Book, and give the new file a title and a format.

Using Dot Leader in a Telephone Listing

Step 1. Open a new file by choosing New from the File menu.
Step 2. Choose Tabs from the Line submenu of the Format menu.
Step 3. Click on Delete to remove all Tab stops.
Step 4. Click on Dot Leader in the Type section of the Tab Format dialog box. This will put a row of dots leading up to whatever is located at the next tab stop.

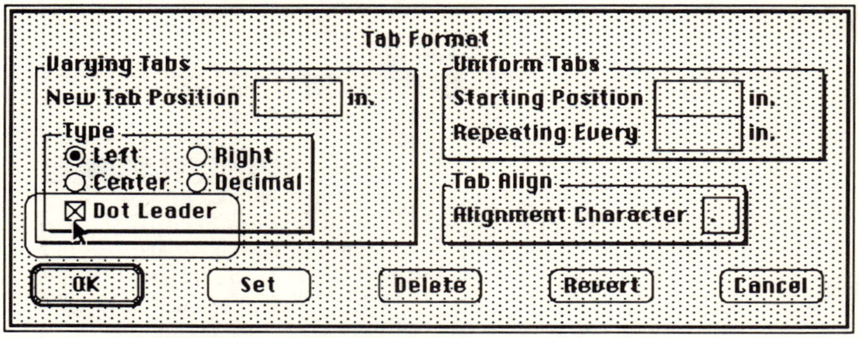

Figure 8-18. Clicking on Dot Leader in the Tab Format dialog box.

Step 5. Type 6 to put a Dot Leader Tab at six inches.
Step 6. Click on Set to set the new Tab.

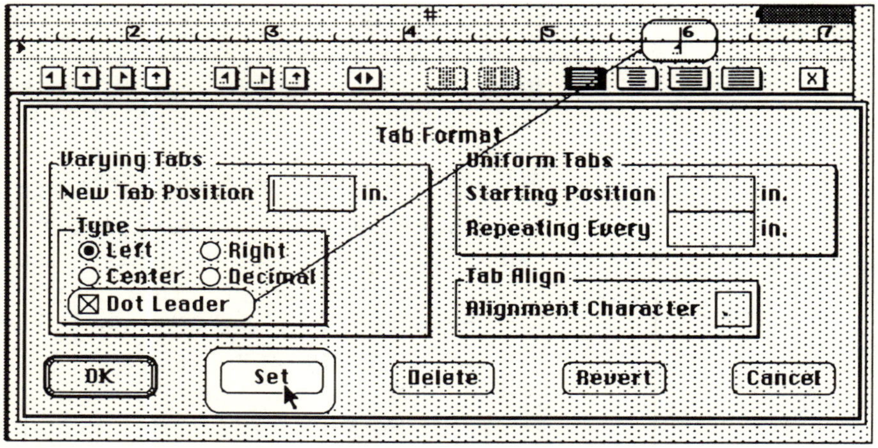

Figure 8-19. The tab setting for our Client Phone Directory file: one dot leader tab at six inches.

Step 7. Click on OK or hit Return.
Step 8. At the left margin, choose Retrieve Field from the Merge Codes submenu of the Special menu.

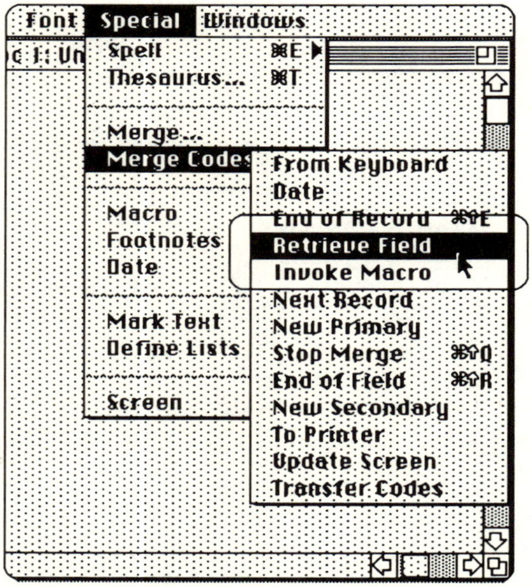

Figure 8-20. Choosing Retrieve Field from the Merge Codes submenu of the Special menu.

Step 9. The next thing you see is a dialog box asking for the Merge Field Number.

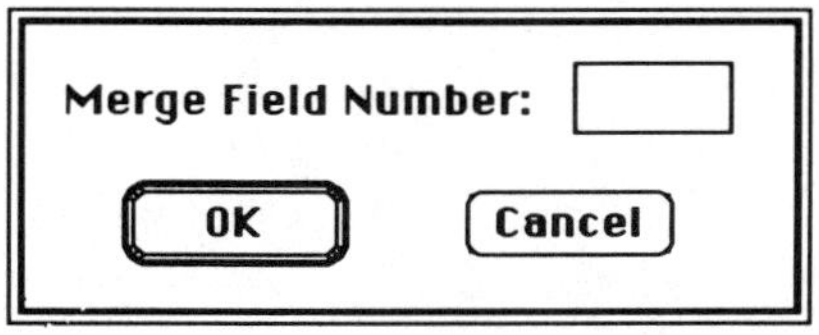

Figure 8-21. The Merge Field Number dialog box.

Step 10. Type 1 into the Merge Field Number dialog box. This means you're asking *WordPerfect* to Retrieve Field 1, the Name field.

Step 11. Click on OK or hit Return. On your left margin you'll see the characters ˆF1ˆ. When you Merge this file with a database file or secondary file, the data from Field 1 (the Name field) will be placed in this location. In other words, this is where you'll find the names.

Step 12. Press the Tab key. A line of dots will appear between ˆF1ˆ and the current cursor location.

Step 13. Choose Retrieve Field from the Merge Codes submenu of the Special menu.

Step 14. Type 9 into the Merge Field Number dialog box. This means you are asking *WordPerfect* to retrieve Field 9, the Telephone Number field.

Step 15. Click on OK or hit Return.

You will see the characters ˆF1ˆ at the left side of the screen and ˆF9ˆ at the right side of screen, connected by a line of dots.

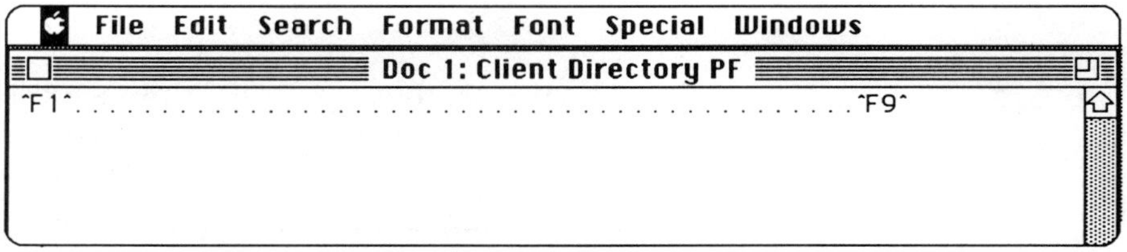

Figure 8-22. The screen of the Primary File, almost ready to run. Client names will appear at the ˆF1ˆ location and their telephone numbers at the ˆF9ˆ location.

The last step is to put in some commands that tell *WordPerfect* to continue to the next record, and not create a separate page for each record. These commands are new.

Merge Codes	**Meaning**
^N	Next Record
^P	New Primary

The N P P combination is a special command that tells *WordPerfect* to keep moving to the next record, and not to put a page break between records. With this new information, let's go on. Pressing Control-N and Control-P will insert the same symbol into the text, but it will not work when it comes time to run the mail-merge. You must enter these control symbols using the Merge Codes menu.

Step 16. Press Return.
Step 17. Choose Next Record from the Merge Codes submenu of the Special menu.
Step 18. Choose New Primary from the Merge Codes submenu of the Special menu.
Step 19. Once again, choose New Primary.

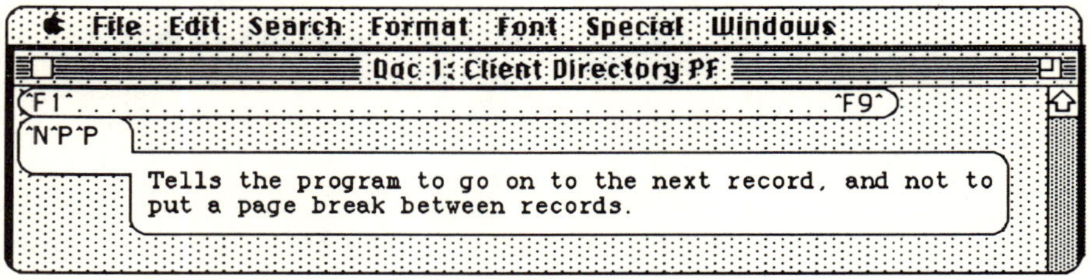

Figure 8-23. The completed Primary File.

That's all there is to it. Now save this file as Client Directory PF (for *Primary File*).

Step 20. Click on the close box.
Step 21. When the Save changes to . . . dialog box appears, click on Yes or press Return.

Step 22. When the Save Document As dialog box appears, type *Client Directory PF.*

Step 23. Click on Save or press Return.

How to Merge Two Files

Merging Secondary (Data) File and Primary (Template) File

Step 1. Open a new file by choosing New from the File menu.

Step 2. Choose Merge . . . from the Special menu.

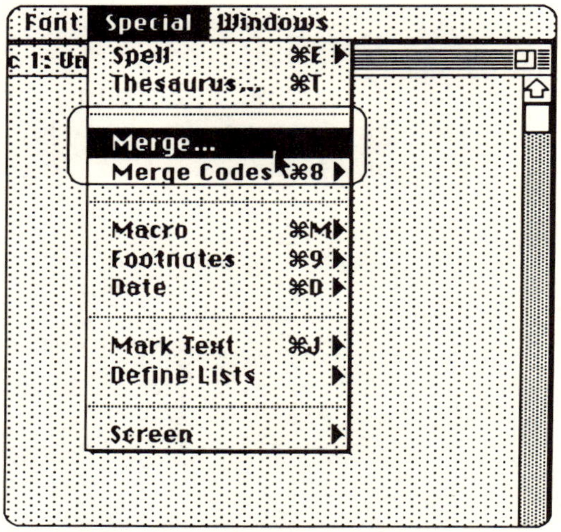

Figure 8-24. Choosing Merge . . . from the Special menu.

Step 3. When the Primary File dialog box appears, select Client Directory PF as the primary file for the Merge.

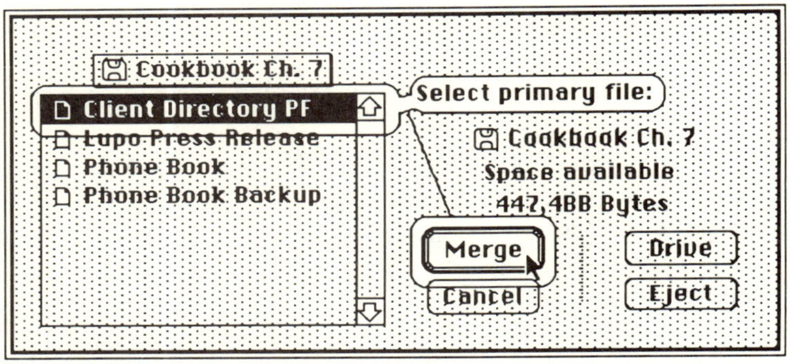

Figure 8-25. Selecting Client Directory PF as the primary file for the merge.

Step 4. Click on Merge or hit Return.
Step 5. When the Secondary File dialog box appears, select Phone Book as the secondary file for the merge.

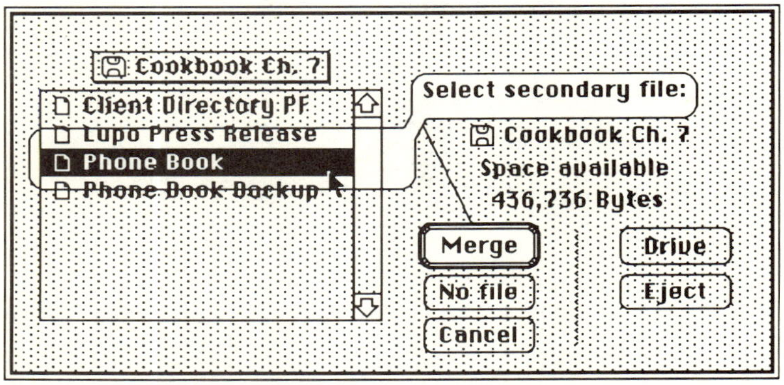

Figure 8-26. Selecting Phone Book as the secondary file for the merge.

Step 6. Click on Merge or hit Return.

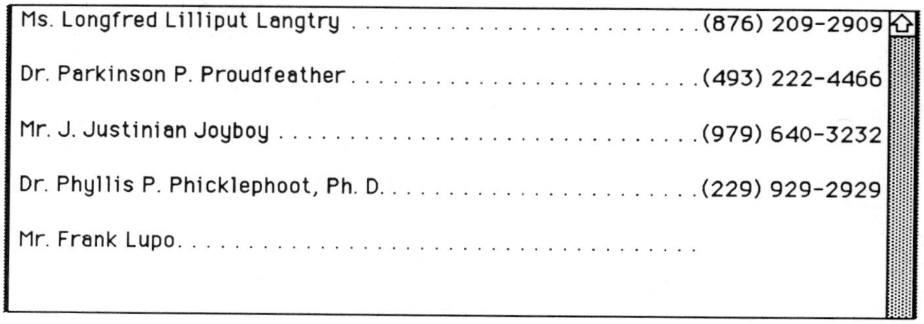

Ms. Longfred Lilliput Langtry	(876) 209-2909
Dr. Parkinson P. Proudfeather	(493) 222-4466
Mr. J. Justinian Joyboy	(979) 640-3232
Dr. Phyllis P. Phicklephoot, Ph. D.	(229) 929-2929
Mr. Frank Lupo	

Figure 8-27. The phone directory generated by merging the Client Directory PF file and the Phone Book file.

And what about Frank Lupo? You'll recall that you left a blank field where his phone number should be because you didn't have the number. It's probably unlisted to escape irate customers with chocolate in their ears.

You may now give this directory a title and a date, select a new font, or whatever you want. Like this:

Step 1. Move the cursor to the top of the file by pressing Enter, Enter, Enter, Up Arrow.
Step 2. Choose Monaco (or whatever font you prefer) from the Font menu.
Step 3. Choose 14 from the Font menu as the Font size for the file heading.
Step 4. Click on B to put the heading in boldface type.
Step 5. Center the heading by choosing Center from the Line submenu of the Format menu.
Step 6. Type Client Telephone Directory.
Step 7. Press Return twice.
Step 8. Choose Show Codes from the Edit menu.
Step 9. Move the cursor to the right with Right Arrow until it's positioned after the Set Font Geneva code.
Step 10. Press Delete to remove the Geneva Font code.
Step 11. Choose Hide Codes from the Edit menu.

And there is your telephone directory.

```
                    Client Telephone Directory

Ms. Longfred Lilliput Langtry .......................(876) 209-2909

Dr. Parkinson P. Proudfeather .......................(493) 222-4466

Mr. J. Justinian Joyboy..............................(979) 640-3232

Dr. Phyllis P. Phicklephoot, Ph. D. .................(229) 929-2929

Mr. Frank Lupo ......................................
```

Figure 8-28. The finished Client Telephone Directory.

If you are overwhelmed by the amount of work you did to turn out this five-line directory, just remember you were creating a quick model here. This directory could have had many names. It could have been dozens of pages long and it would have taken the same amount of work to create.

There are any number of reports and information formats you could create, using the 11 fields in the Client Directory PF file. For example, you might want a report that lists the companies or organizations, the donations they made, and the person responsible for contacting them. Since company or organization is Field 3, donations are entered in Field 10, and contact persons are found in Field 11, you might want to create a primary file that looks something like Figure 8-29.

```
Doc 1: Company Donations PF
Company: ^F3^
Donation: ^F10^
Contact Person: ^F11^

^N^P^P
```

Figure 8-29. The primary file for a report listing companies, their donations, and the persons who contacted them.

When you merge this primary file with the Phone Book, you'll receive a report that looks like Figure 8-30.

Doc 1: Co/Org Donations

Company: Ladies of the Confederate Renaissance
Donation: a six-foot hero sandwich
Contact Person: Deirdre Dunbar-Dinwiddy

Company: Skedaddle Skateboards Ltd.
Donation: the Hope Diamond
Contact Person: F. Farnsworth Fignewton

Company: Cherokee Chickpeas, Inc.
Donation: a Ming vase
Contact Person: Quigley McQ. Quark

Company: St. Hoipolloi Hospital
Donation: a lifetime membership in the Elvis Presley Resurrection and Reconstruction Society.
Contact Person: Roustabout "Rusty" Relique

Company: Worldwide Wigwams, Inc.

Figure 8-30. The Company Donation report.

Of all the forms and reports you might extract from a database, the most popular among users of word processor software is the personalized mass mail letter or mail-merge, covered in Chapter 9.

Chapter 9

How to Do a Mail-Merge

Chapter 9

How to Do a Mail-Merge

In the past, one of the most costly and labor-intensive tasks of large organizations was mass mailing. Mass mailing is the dissemination of a form letter to a list of constituents, customers, vendors, employees, or others.

The typical mass-mailing letter carried essentially the same message to everyone on the list. In the early days of the form letter, the senders tried to compose a message that could be identical for all recipients because customization and personalization of the form letter even for a small number of individuals was very expensive.

If the letters weren't actually typed by hand, they had uniform content, but no inside addresses and generalized salutations such as *Dear Homeowner*, *Dear Customer*, or *Dear Chevrolet owner*.

As the printing firms and letter shops acquired computerized equipment to handle the job, greater personalization and customization became possible. Mass mailings could be sent out to millions of customers and prospective customers, each with individual inside addresses and salutations.

As the technology became more sophisticated and high-speed computerized ink-jet printers were developed, mass mailers could incorporate all kinds of electronic tricks to give their letters personal touches. One of the most familiar manifestations of this form is the letter that arrives from the giant magazine subscription and sweepstakes houses. On the outside of the envelope, printed in large bold letters, is a message informing you that you have almost certainly won an enormous amount of cash. Inside the envelope is a bogus check with your name printed on it, and perhaps a dozen other pieces of personalized promotional material.

You don't have to be in the giant sweepstakes racket or be able to tap a huge advertising budget to perform all kinds of mail-merge magic. With the advent of the microcomputer and sophisticated word processing software such as *WordPerfect*, the necessary horsepower is right on your desk. It's cheap and easy.

Using Mail-Merge

In Chapter 7 you used macros to assemble a letter from Helping Hands for Health Food Addicts to send to a few notables who made donations to the HHHFA Goods and Services Auction. That letter-assembly macro represented a great advance in productivity, analogous to hitching a team of mules to the plow after tilling the soil by hand. With the mail-merge technique we're going to put the mules out to pasture and buy a tractor. You'll see the productivity curve shoot straight up.

When you look at that letter, you'll see that many elements of the letter are now fields in the Phone Book database. In the address, the name is Field 1, the title is Field 2, the salutation is Field 8, the description of the donation is Field 10, and so on. Because of this, you should replace the elements in the letter with the merge codes that represent the appropriate fields.

The basic letter itself will become a computer program. If you aren't a computer programmer, don't let that statement frighten you. A computer program is simply a series of commands that tell a computer what to do and when to do it. It's no different from giving a new colleague directions to the washroom. You tell him or her where to turn, what to look for, where to find things. After you are done with your list of instructions, your colleague runs the program through his or her head and finds the washroom.

You've already written one computer program: The primary file you wrote in the previous chapter is a program. Within that document, codes direct the Mac to retrieve particular fields from a database called a secondary file. The codes may also direct the Mac to wait for input from the keyboard, to execute a macro, or to shift to a different secondary file.

At the end of the program command file or primary file there are commands directing the Mac to go to the next record, to send data to the printer, to put no page breaks between files, or other instructions.

Let's walk through the steps for turning the HHHFA letter into a primary file for a mail-merge, and discuss the commands as we go.

Step 1. Open a new file. Choose Retrieve Field from the Merge

Codes submenu of the Special menu, or press Command-8, then *F* from the keyboard.

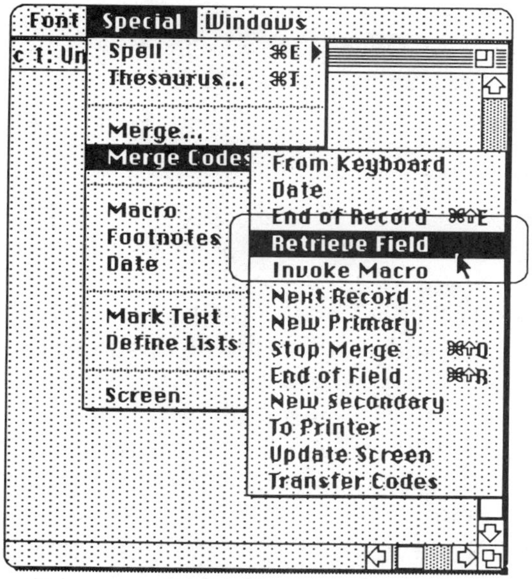

Figure 9-1. Choosing Retrieve Field from the Merge Codes submenu of the Special menu.

Step 2. Type 1 as the field to retrieve.

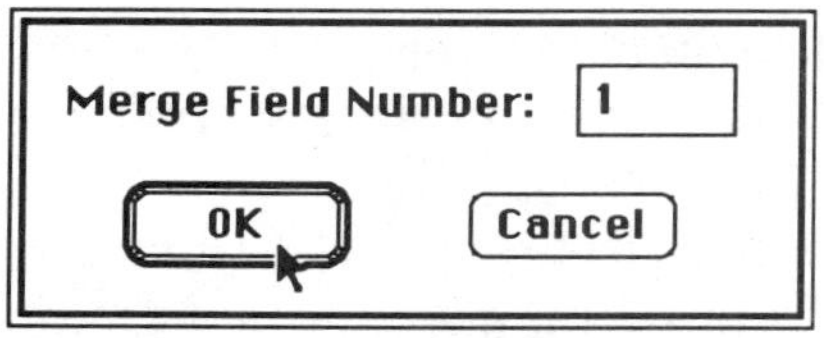

Figure 9-2. The Field Number dialog box, with 1 entered as the field to retrieve.

The command will put the addressee's name at this location.

Step 3. Click on OK or hit Return.
Step 4. Press Return.

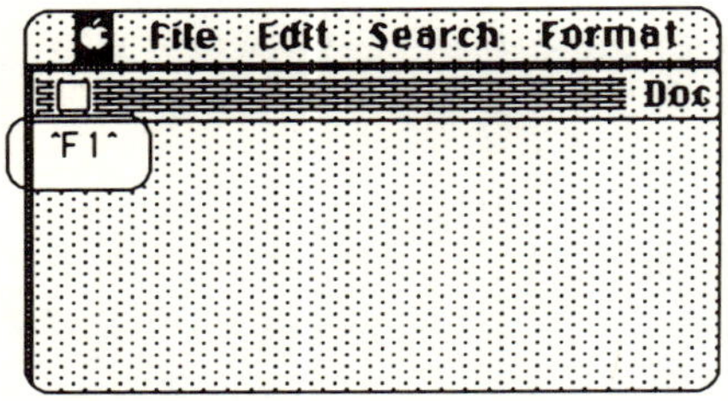

Figure 9-3. The screen with the first Retrieve Field command entered.

Step 5. Choose Retrieve Field from the Merge Codes submenu of the Special menu, or press Command-8 then *F* from the keyboard.
Step 6. Type 2 as the field to retrieve. This command will put the addressee's title at this location.
Step 7. Click on OK or hit Return.
Step 8. Press Return.
Step 9. Choose Retrieve Field from the Merge Codes submenu of the Special menu, or press Command-8 then *F* from the keyboard.
Step 10. Type 3 as the field to retrieve. This command will put the addressee's company or organization name at this location.
Step 11. Click on OK or hit Return.
Step 12. Press Return.
Step 13. Choose Retrieve Field from the Merge Codes submenu of the Special menu, or press Command-8 then *F* from the keyboard.
Step 14. Type 4 as the field to retrieve. This command will put the addressee's street or P.O. address at this location.
Step 15. Click on OK or hit Return.
Step 16. Press Return.
Step 17. Choose Retrieve Field from the Merge Codes submenu of the Special menu, or press Command-8 then *F* from the keyboard.
Step 18. Type 5 as the field to retrieve. This command will put the addressee's city at this location.
Step 19. Click on OK or hit Return.
Step 20. Type a comma followed by a space.
Step 21. Choose Retrieve Field from the Merge Codes submenu of the Special menu, or press Command-8 then *F* from the keyboard.

Step 22. Type 6 as the field to retrieve. This command will put the addressee's state (two-letter abbreviation) at this location.
Step 23. Click on OK or hit Return.
Step 24. Enter two spaces.
Step 25. Choose Retrieve Field from the Merge Codes submenu of the Special menu, or press Command-8 then *F* from the keyboard.
Step 26. Type 7 as the field to retrieve. This command will put the addressee's zip code at this location.
Step 27. Click on OK or hit Return.
Step 28. Press Return twice.
Step 29. Type *Dear* followed by a space.
Step 30. Choose Retrieve Field from the Merge Codes submenu of the Special menu, or press Command-8 then *F* from the keyboard.
Step 31. Type 8 as the field to retrieve. This command will put the proper salutation for the addressee including the first name, or title and last name at this location.
Step 32. Click on OK or hit Return.
Step 33. Type a colon.
Step 34. Press Return twice. This completes the address and salutation part of the letter. At this point, your screen should look like Figure 9-4.

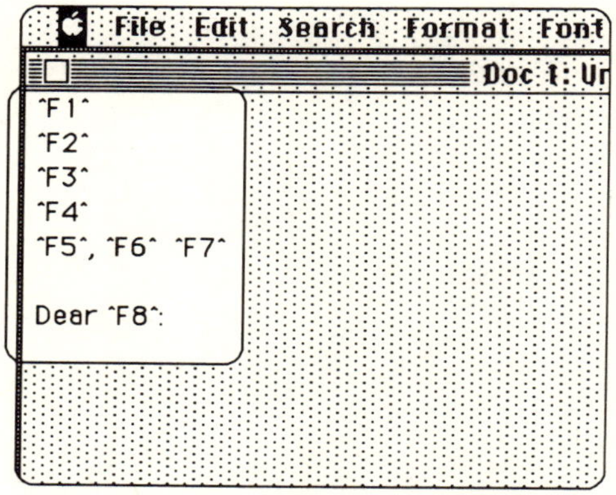

Figure 9-4. The screen after you enter the salutation code.

You may now retrieve the body of the letter by running the Paragraph 1, 2, and 3 macros:

Step 35. Choose Execute Macro . . . from the Macro submenu of the Special menu, or type Command-Shift-X.
Step 36. Select Paragraph 1 as the macro to execute.

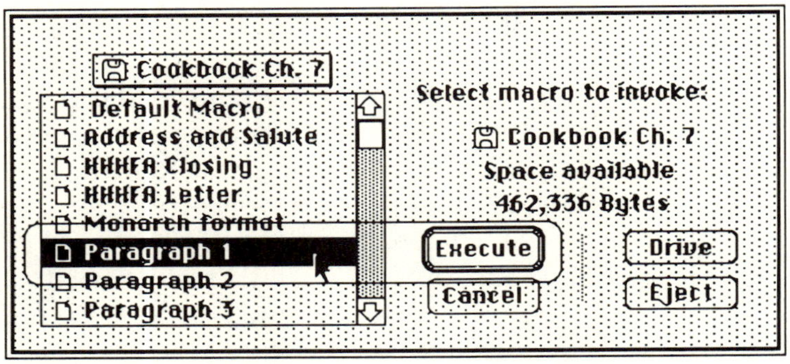

Figure 9-5. Select Paragraph 1 as the macro to execute.

Step 37. Click on Execute or hit Return.
Step 38. When the donation input dialog box appears, don't enter anything. Simply click on OK or hit Return.
Step 39. When the paragraph appears on your screen, position the cursor between the two spaces separating the words *of* and *will*. Use Show Codes to help you find the exact location.

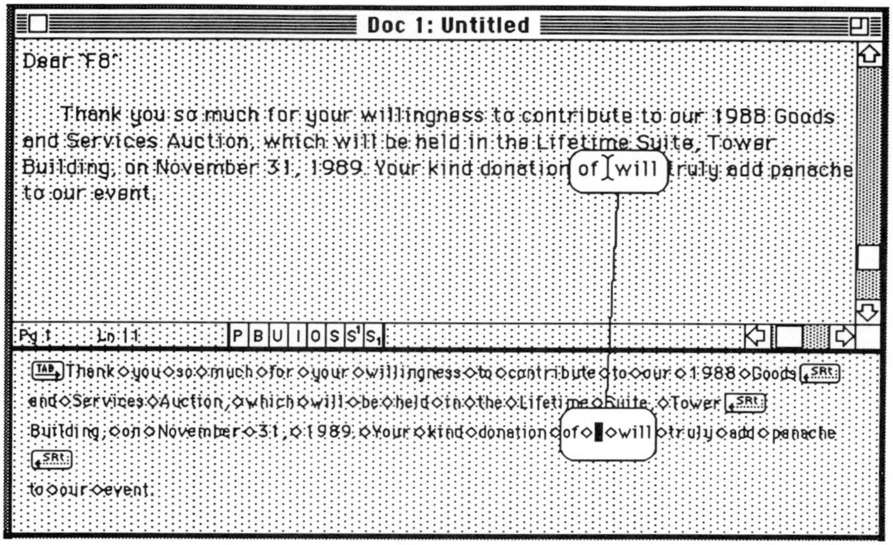

Figure 9-6. The cursor positioned where the Retrieve Field command will go for the donation field.

At this point in the primary file, instead of having an input box that prompts a response from the keyboard, you'll insert a Retrieve Field command that will retrieve the donation field from each record.

Step 40. Choose Retrieve Field from the Merge Codes submenu of the Special menu, or press Command-8 then *F* from the keyboard.

Step 41. Type 10 as the field to retrieve.

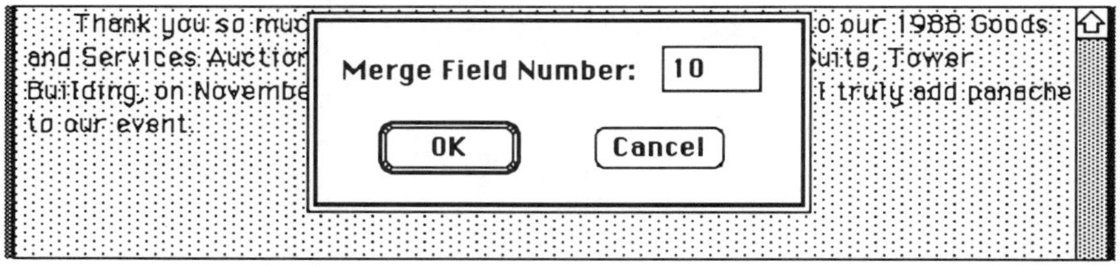

Figure 9-7. The Merge Field Number dialog box with 10 entered as the field to retrieve.

This command will retrieve the donation field from each record and place it at this point in the first paragraph.

Step 42. Click on OK or hit Return.

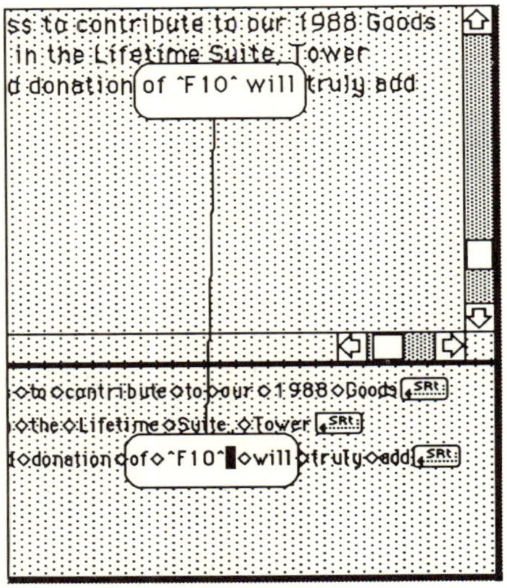

Figure 9-8. The Retrieve Field 10 code positioned in the first paragraph.

Step 43. Move the cursor to the end of the paragraph by pressing Enter, Enter, Down Arrow.
Step 44. Press Return twice.
Step 45. Choose Execute Macro . . . from the Macro submenu of the Special menu.
Step 46. Select Paragraph 2 as the macro to invoke.

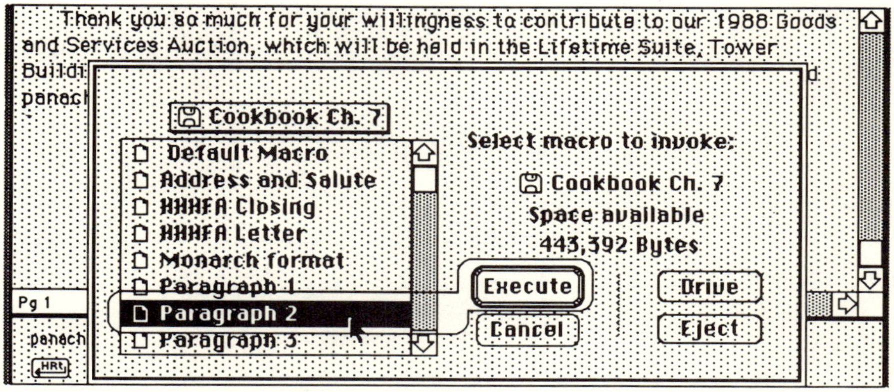

Figure 9-9. Selecting Paragraph 2 as the macro to invoke.

Step 47. Click on Execute or press Return. The contact person input dialog box will appear.

Step 48. Don't enter anything in the dialog box. Click on OK or hit Return. The second paragraph will appear on your screen, minus the name of the contact person who will follow the first word of the paragraph.

Step 49. Position the cursor between the two spaces separating the words *As* and *doubtless*. Use Show Codes to help you find the exact location.

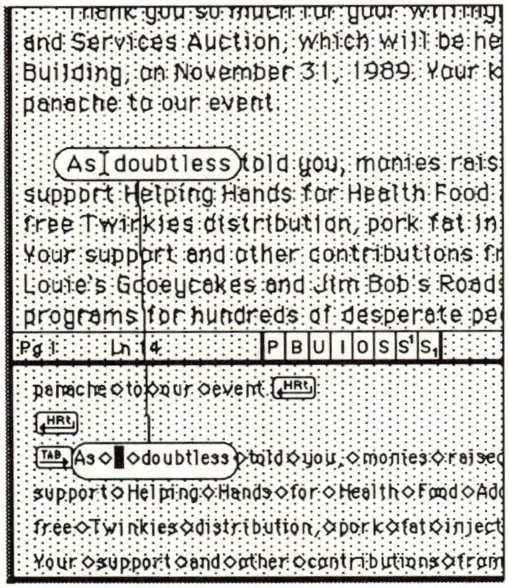

Figure 9-10. The cursor positioned where the Retrieve Field command will go for the contact person field.

Step 50. Choose Retrieve Field from the Merge Codes submenu of the Special menu, or press Command-8 then *F* from the keyboard.

Step 51. When the Merge Field Number dialog box appears, type 11 as the field to retrieve.

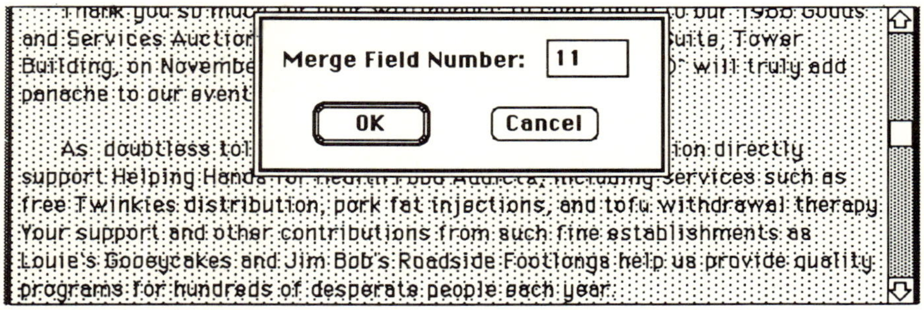

Figure 9-11. The Merge Field Number dialog box with 11 entered as the field to retrieve.

This command will retrieve the contact person field from each record and place it at this point in the second paragraph.

Step 52. Click on OK or hit Return.

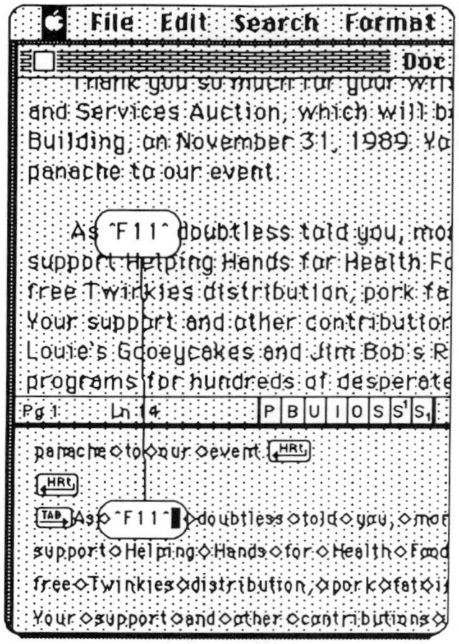

Figure 9-12. The Retrieve Field 11 code positioned in the second paragraph.

Step 53. Press Enter, Enter, Down Arrow to move the cursor to the end of the paragraph.
Step 54. Press Return twice.
Step 55. Choose Execute Macro . . . from the Macro submenu of the Special menu.
Step 56. Select Paragraph 3 as the macro to invoke.

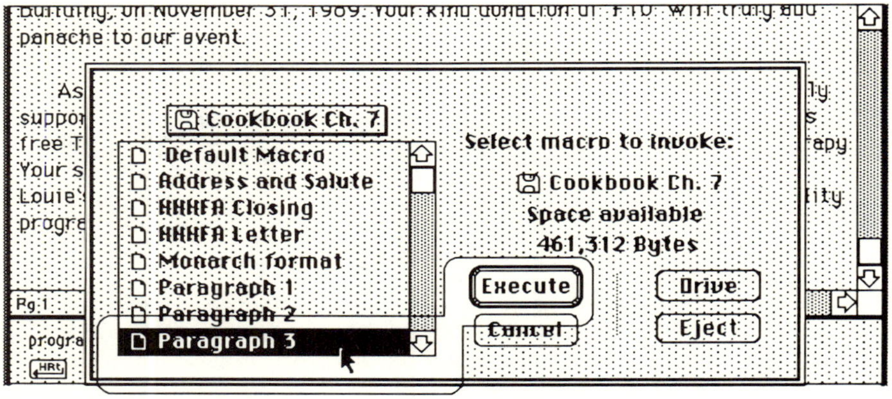

Figure 9-13. Selecting Paragraph 3 as the macro to invoke.

Step 57. Click on Execute or press Return. Since Paragraph 3 is pure boilerplate, no Retrieve Fields are necessary. This is also true of the closing.

Step 58. Press Return twice.

Step 59. Choose Execute Macro . . . from the Macro submenu of the Special menu.

Step 60. Select HHHFA Closing as the macro to invoke.

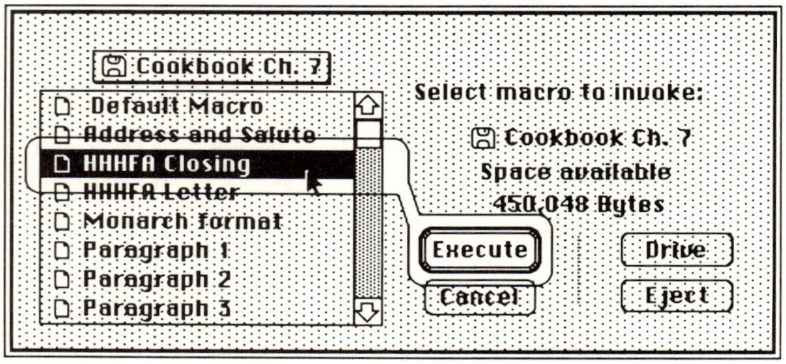

Figure 9-14. Selecting HHHFA Closing as the macro to invoke.

Step 61. Click on Execute or press Return. With this step you have entered the complete letter into your primary merge file.

^F1^
^F2^
^F3^
^F4^
^F5^, ^F6^ ^F7^

Dear ^F8^:

Thank you so much for your willingness to contribute to our 1988 Goods and Services Auction, which will be held in the Lifetime Suite, Tower Building, on November 31, 1989. Your kind donation of ^F10^ will truly add panache to our event.

As ^F11^ doubtless told you, monies raised through our Auction directly support Helping Hands for Health Food Addicts, including services such as free Twinkies distribution, pork fat injections, and tofu withdrawal therapy. Your support and other contributions from such fine establishments as Louie's Gooeycakes and Jim Bob's Roadside Footlongs help us provide quality programs for hundreds of desperate people each year.

I thank you on behalf of the Auction Committee and the many men and women who will benefit from your generosity.

Sincerely yours,

Priscilla T. J. Bonservice
Executive Director

Figure 9-15. The screen after completing the letter.

There is now one very important final step. You must add the merge codes at the bottom of the letter. Enter ^N, the control code that tells the Mac to go on to the next record, and ^P^P, which means to continue using the same primary file. (If you wanted the program to move on to a different primary file you would put the file name between the two ^Ps: ^P{filename}^P.)

The combined codes you'll want to use at the end of this primary file are ^N^P^P.

Step 62. Press Return twice.
Step 63. Choose Next Record from the Merge Codes submenu of the Special menu.

Step 64. Choose New Primary from the Merge Codes submenu of the Special menu.
Step 65. Again choose New Primary from the Merge Codes submenu of the Special menu.

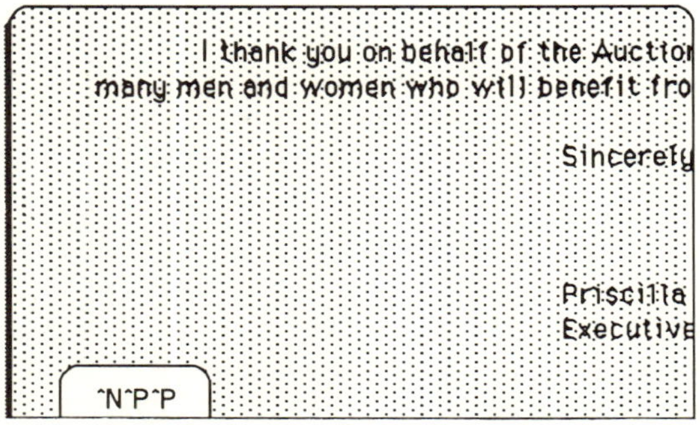

Figure 9-16. The end of the letter with the ^N^P^P codes, instructing the Mac to go on to a new record and to use the same primary file.

You could run the merge right now to test whether this program works, but instead, let's format the letter and put in the function that prints the current date.

Step 66. Move the cursor to the top of the file by typing Enter, Enter, Enter, Up Arrow.
Step 67. Choose Execute Macro . . . from the Macro submenu of the Special menu.
Step 68. Select Monarch format as the macro to invoke.

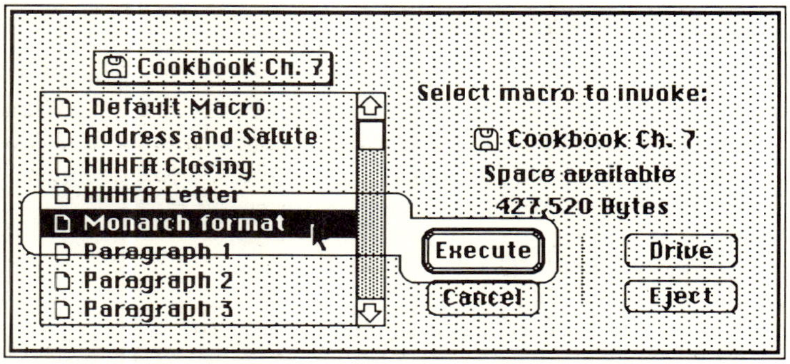

Figure 9-17. Selecting Monarch format as the macro to invoke.

Step 69. Click on Execute or press Return. The date now appears in the center of your screen near the top, and there is some blank space above it. It would appear, therefore, that the formatting commands have worked. However, you'll note that the date is in a different font than the rest of the letter.

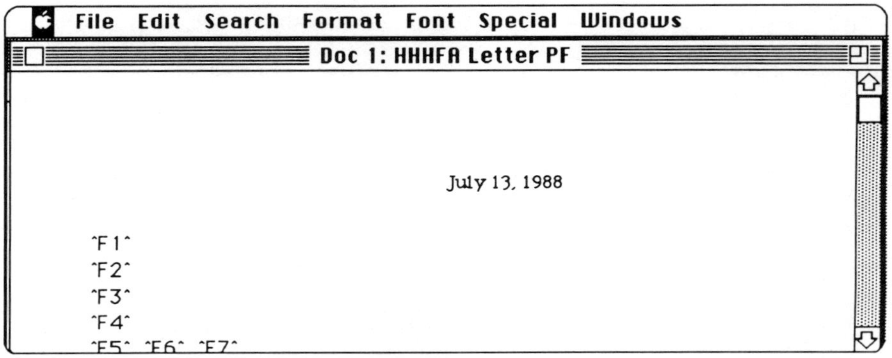

Figure 9-18. The screen after you execute the Monarch format macro. Note the difference between the typeface of the date and the typeface of the rest of the letter.

Step 70. Choose Show Codes from the Edit menu. Note the font type and size codes: 10-point New York Font.

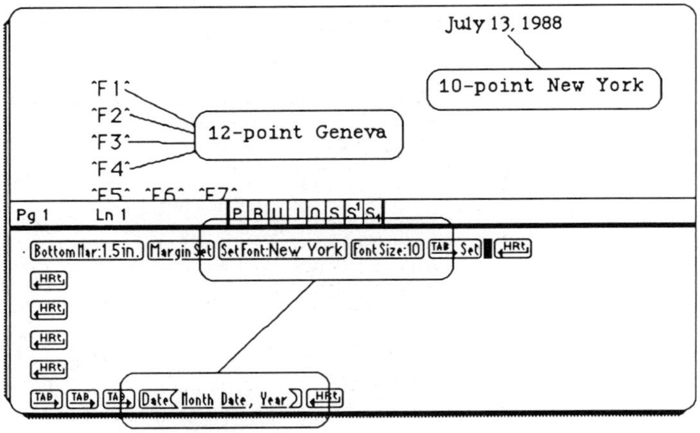

Figure 9-19. The font codes that control the date.

Step 71. Position the cursor in front of the ^F1^ code and you'll see the problem: those 12-point Geneva codes.

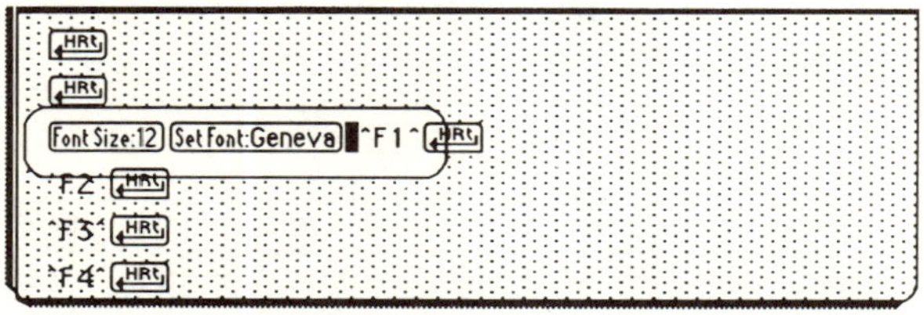

Figure 9-20. The font codes that control the rest of the letter.

Step 72. Use the cursor keys to move the cursor immediately to the right of the Geneva font code if it's not already there.

Step 73. Press Delete twice to erase the Geneva font code and the 12-point code. That solves the problem. Hide the codes again. You'll see that the font is now consistent throughout the letter.

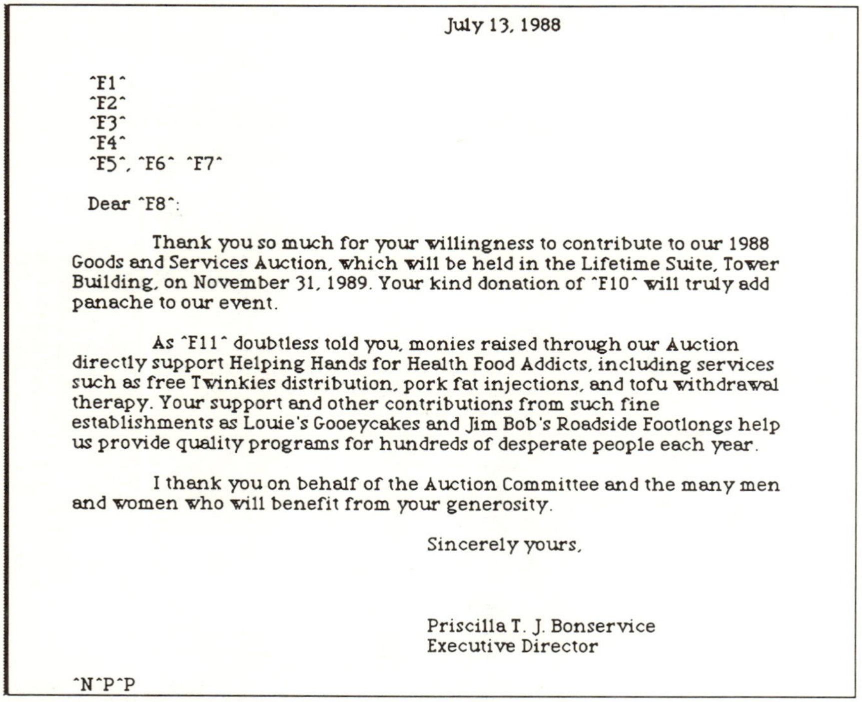

July 13, 1988

^F1^
^F2^
^F3^
^F4^
^F5^, ^F6^ ^F7^

Dear ^F8^:

Thank you so much for your willingness to contribute to our 1988 Goods and Services Auction, which will be held in the Lifetime Suite, Tower Building, on November 31, 1989. Your kind donation of ^F10^ will truly add panache to our event.

As ^F11^ doubtless told you, monies raised through our Auction directly support Helping Hands for Health Food Addicts, including services such as free Twinkies distribution, pork fat injections, and tofu withdrawal therapy. Your support and other contributions from such fine establishments as Louie's Gooeycakes and Jim Bob's Roadside Footlongs help us provide quality programs for hundreds of desperate people each year.

I thank you on behalf of the Auction Committee and the many men and women who will benefit from your generosity.

Sincerely yours,

Priscilla T. J. Bonservice
Executive Director

^N^P^P

Figure 9-21. The finished letter primary file.

Your primary file is now ready to be merged. Before you do anything else, save this primary file under the name HHHFA Letter PF.

Step 74. Choose Save As . . . from the File menu.
Step 75. Type *HHHFA Letter PF* in the Save Document As dialog box.
Step 76. Click on Save or press Return. The screen goes blank. You've done all the work. Will the files actually merge? Will primary and secondary files really get together? Will we address all the people by the proper names and thank them for the right donations?

Merging HHHFA Letter PF

Step 1. Open a new file by choosing New from the File menu.
Step 2. Choose Merge . . . from the Special menu.

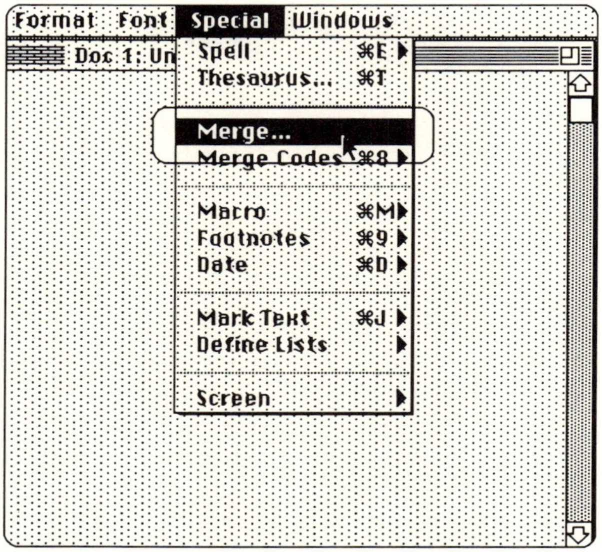

Figure 9-22. Choosing Merge . . . from the Special menu.

Step 3. When the dialog box appears, select HHHFA Letter PF as the primary file to be merged.

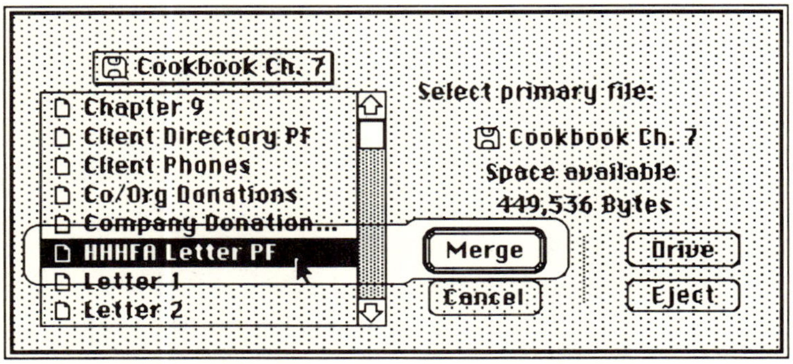

Figure 9-23. Selecting HHHFA Letter PF as the primary file to be merged.

Step 4. Click on Merge or press Return.
Step 5. When the dialog box appears, select Phone Book as the secondary file to be merged.

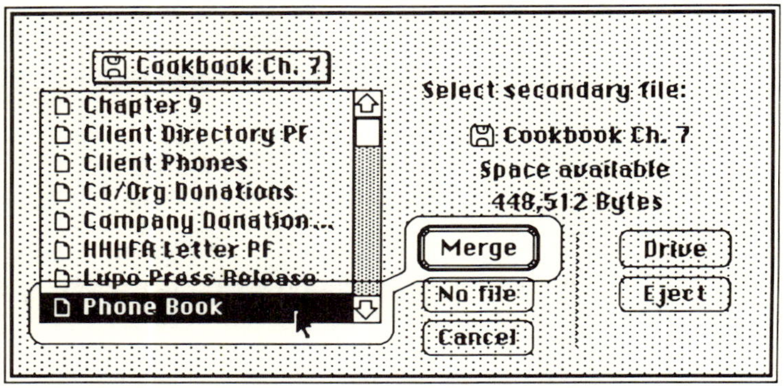

Figure 9-24. Selecting Phone Book as the secondary file to be merged.

Step 6. Click on Merge or press Return. In a moment, the end of a letter appears on your screen. If you scroll up, you'll discover that this is the HHHFA letter to Frank Lupo (who has turned out to be the mascot for this book), and just above it on the screen is the end of another letter: the Phyllis Phicklephoot letter. Sure enough, all five letters are on the screen. But how, you may wonder, do you print them out, especially when the page breaks seem to be in the wrong places?

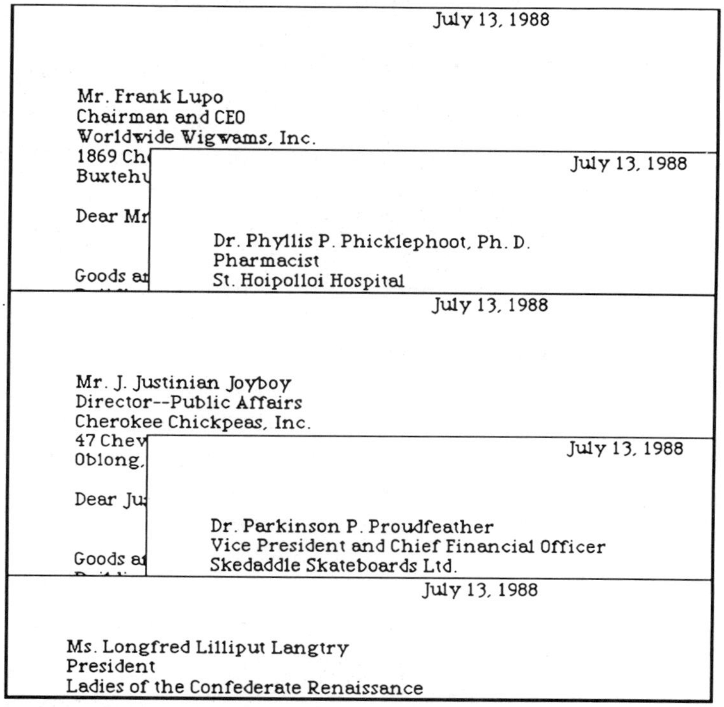

Figure 9-25. The five HHHFA letters.

Close this file and we'll perform the last quick bit of legerdemain that will send mail-merged letters streaming from your printer.

Step 1. Choose Open from the File menu.
Step 2. Select the HHHFA Letter PF.
Step 3. Click on Open or press Return.
Step 4. Hit Enter, Enter, Down Arrow to move the cursor to the bottom of the file.
Step 5. Hit Enter, Enter, Left Arrow to move the cursor to the left margin of the file, in front of the ^N^P^P codes.
Step 6. Choose To Printer from the Merge Codes submenu of the Special menu, or type Command-8 then *T* from the keyboard. When *WordPerfect* returns you to the letter, you'll discover that a new code, ^T, has been inserted in front of the ^N^P^P.

The ^T code sends the data to the printer. If you run the merge again, you'll discover that your printer turns out five separate letters, ignoring the onscreen location of the page breaks. That's it. You've produced your own mail-merge.

WordPerfect makes mail-merge virtually effortless, and you can use the technique to automate all sorts of repetitive jobs around the office.

For example, you might want to stop right now and do a test run on creating a primary file for the mailing labels to go with these letters. Here's another idea: If you regularly send memos to the same group of people, why not make a secondary file of their names, treat each new memo as a primary file, and insert a Retrieve Field code after the *To:* on the memo? Then, when you merge the files, your printer will print out individually addressed memos in one batch. The possibilities for increasing productivity are endless.

Chapter 10

How to Make the Most of Macintosh Graphics with *WordPerfect*

Chapter 10

How to Make the Most of Macintosh Graphics with *WordPerfect*

The Macintosh and graphics are virtually synonymous. The display on the Macintosh is a graphics-based display, created by mapping every single bit or pixel on the screen (hence the term *bitmapped*). For this reason, working with combinations of graphics or pictures and text is very rewarding.

WordPerfect makes it easy to take any sort of graphic—a drawing, a chart, a customized character, a digitized photograph—and insert it into *WordPerfect* text.

In this chapter you are going to take two graphics figures—a logo created with *MacDraw* and a bar chart created by *MacPaint*—and insert them into the document you created in Chapter 6: The Spectator newsletter. You will learn how to edit the graphics, adjust them for size, and move them in and out of the Scrapbook. When you've completed this chapter, you will have a printed page that combines text and graphics on a professional-looking page.

Begin by creating a logo for The Spectator.

Step 1. Open *MacDraw*. To do this quickly, use the Transfer feature of *WordPerfect*, which permits you to go to another program without going back to the Desktop. Choose Transfer . . . from the File menu.

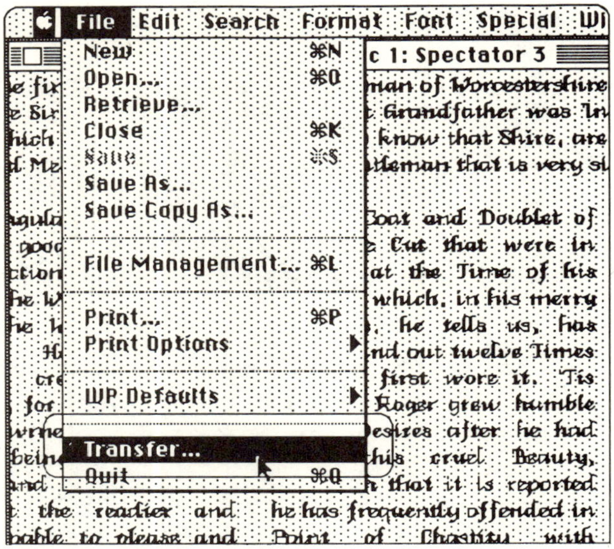

Figure 10-1. Choosing Transfer from the File menu.

Step 2. When the Transfer dialog box appears, select *MacDraw* and click on Transfer or press Return.

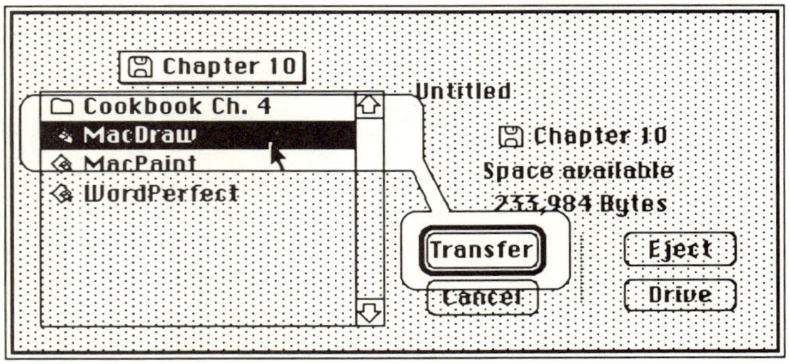

Figure 10-2. The Transfer dialog box.

Step 3. Create a logo for The Spectator. This design is up to you.

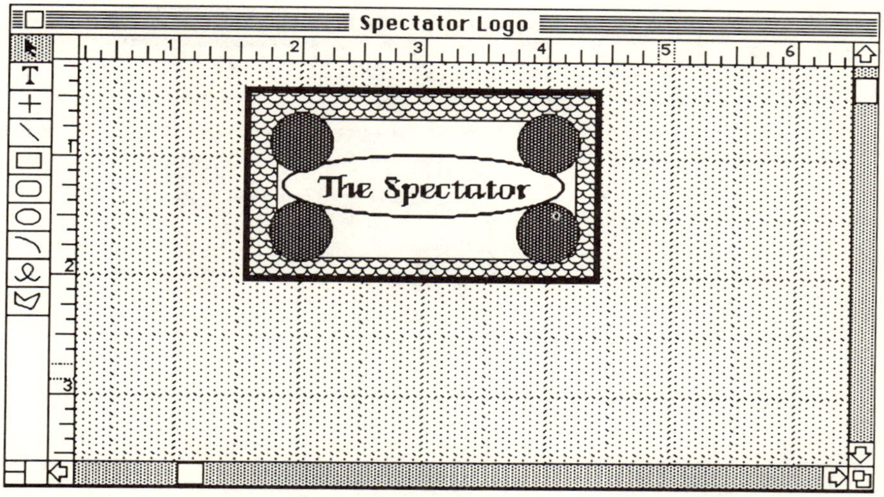

Figure 10-3. Possible design for the Spectator logo.

The design in Figure 10-3 was made using a square-cornered rectangle, a round-cornered rectangle inside that, an ellipse surrounding the name of the paper, four identical circles, and two fills. The idea was to achieve an 18th-century over-decorated rococo effect. The best thing that can be said for the design is that it was fast.

Step 4. Select the design by clicking on the pointer tool in the upper left-hand corner. Hold down the Mouse button while drawing a rectangle around the logo, then release. A whole gaggle of handles will appear on the various figures that make up the logo. When the handles are visible, the figure is selected.

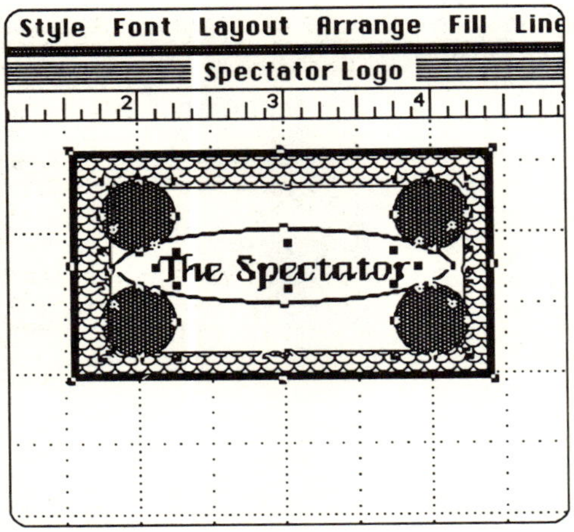

Figure 10-4. The logo selected, with all its handles showing.

Step 5. Copy the logo by choosing Copy from the Edit menu.

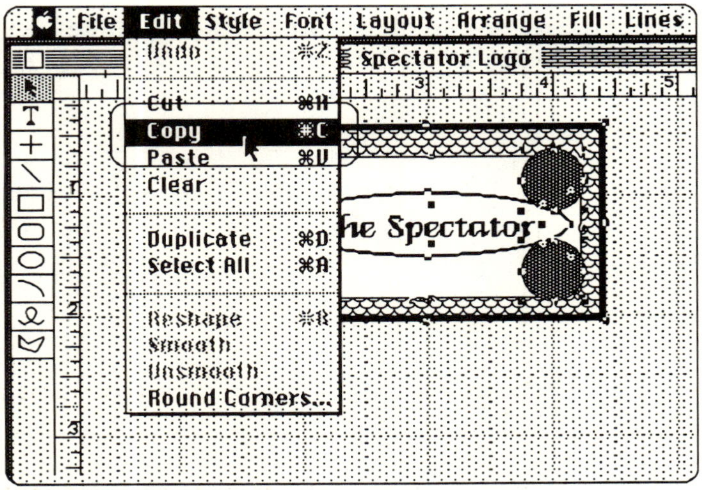

Figure 10-5. Choosing Copy from the File menu.

Pasting the Design into the Scrapbook

Step 6. Get out the Scrapbook by choosing Scrapbook from the Apple menu.

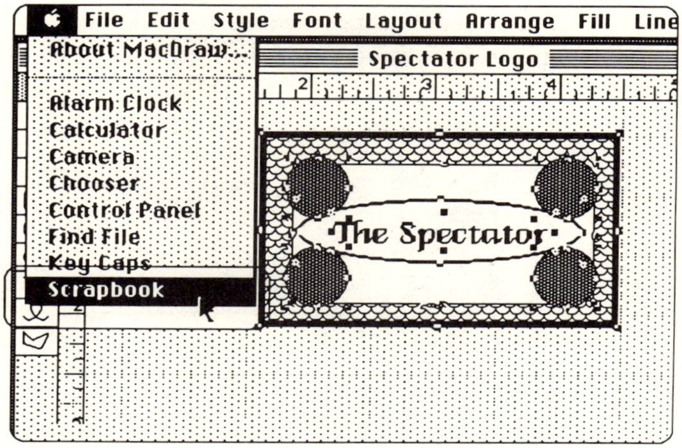

Figure 10-6. Choosing Scrapbook from the Apple menu.

If the Scrapbook is empty, it will appear as it does in Figure 10-7.

Figure 10-7. The Scrapbook showing empty.

Step 7. Paste the Spectator logo into the Scrapbook by choosing Paste from the Edit menu or pressing Command-V.

Figure 10-8. The Spectator logo pasted into the Scrapbook.

Step 8. Return to the Spectator 3 file in *WordPerfect* by closing the Scrapbook, quitting *MacDraw,* and opening the final Spectator 3 file.

Step 9. You want to put the logo near the very top of the file, so choose Show Codes from the Edit menu. The logo should be positioned so it's inside the margin settings that you installed for this document, but not inside the column settings. The graphic will be inserted into the file at the cursor location, so the cursor is probably best located just after the Margin Set code as in Figure 10-9.

Figure 10-9. The cursor located for insertion of the Spectator logo graphic.

Transferring a Design from the Scrapbook

The procedure for moving text or graphics from the Scrapbook to a document or other file: Open the Scrapbook, Copy the desired Scrapbook entry, close the Scrapbook, and Paste the Scrapbook item into the document. Let's run through it with the Spectator logo.

Step 10. Open the Scrapbook by choosing Scrapbook from the Apple menu.

If the Spectator logo is the only item you have pasted into your Scrapbook to date, it will appear on your screen with the numbers 1/1 in the lower left-hand corner. This means the Spectator logo is the first item in the Scrapbook, and there is only one item. If there were three items, the Spectator logo could be 1/3, 2/3, or 3/3, depending upon whether it came first, second, or third in the sequence.

Step 11. Copy the logo from the Scrapbook by choosing Copy from the Edit menu, or by pressing Command-C.

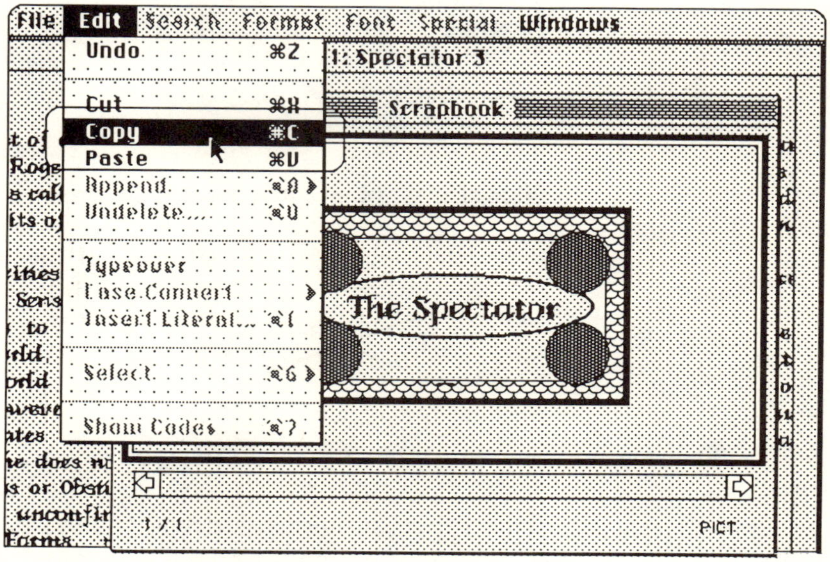

Figure 10-10. Choosing Copy to copy the Spectator logo from the Scrapbook.

Step 12. Close the Scrapbook.
Step 13. Prepare to center the logo by choosing Center from the Line submenu of the Format menu, or pressing Command-Shift-C.
Step 14. After checking to be sure the cursor is still located after Margin Set, but before Column, Paste the Spectator logo into the document by choosing Paste from the Edit menu.

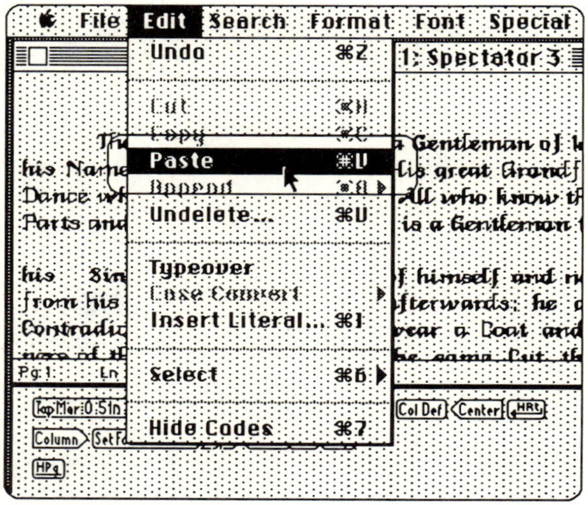

Figure 10-11. Choosing Paste to paste the Spectator logo into the document.

Step 15. Choose Hide Codes or press Command-7.

The logo is now positioned at the top of the document, but it's rather small, don't you think? You need to make it fit better. Maybe it should go all the way across the page. Can you do that with *WordPerfect?*

Sizing Figures

Sizing graphics in *WordPerfect*

WordPerfect provides you with handles on graphic figures that permit you to change the size by pushing and tugging the sides and corners. A new feature will allow you to scale a figure proportionally. Hold down the shift key when adjusting the size of a figure in *WordPerfect* versions 1.0.1 or later and the figure will automatically adjust horizontally as you adjust it vertically (or vice versa) to retain the original proportions of the figure.

Step 16. Click twice with the pointer anywhere inside the figure to turn on the handles.

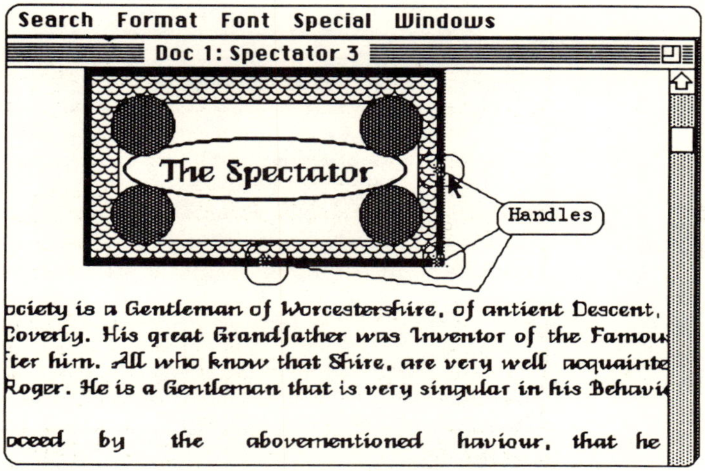

Figure 10-12. The logo with handles showing.

Change the vertical size (height) by dragging the bottom handle, the horizontal size (width) by dragging the side handle, and change both height and width at once by dragging the corner handle.

Step 17. Touch the pointer to the side handle and drag it to the right.

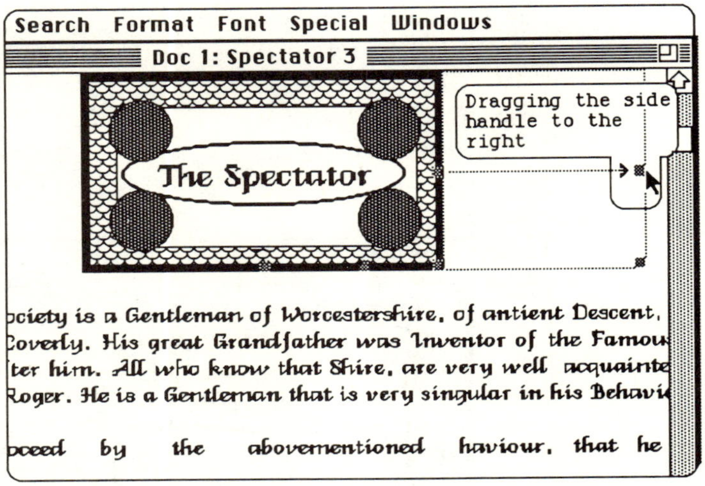

Figure 10-13. Increasing the width of the logo by dragging the side handle to the right.

Stretch it until the logo is the width you like. Note that *WordPerfect* keeps the figure centered, no matter how far you stretch it.

Step 18. Sideways stretching may introduce too much distortion, so click on the bottom handle and drag it downward until you find the proportions more to your liking.

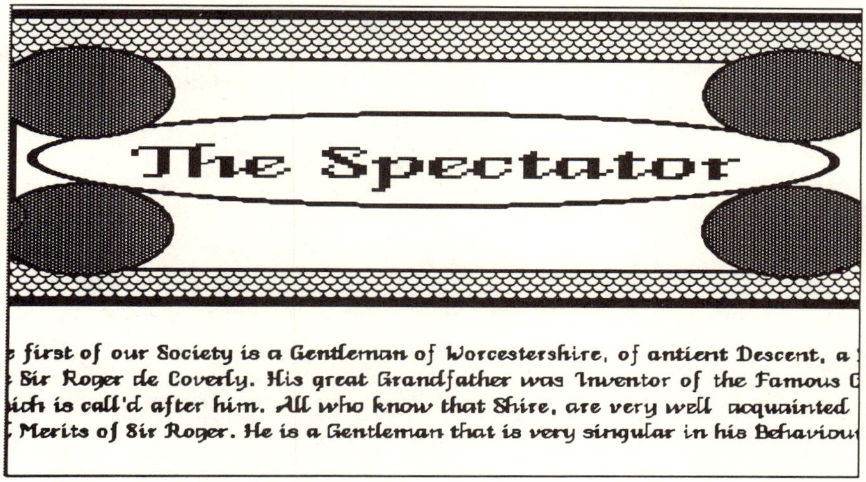

Figure 10-14. The logo expanded to fit the top of the page.

To get a sense of what the whole page looks like at this point, choose Print Preview from the Print Options submenu of the File menu.

Figure 10-15. The full page with the logo added as shown in Print Preview.

Now let's add a graph to one of the columns. Go into *MacPaint* or whatever paint software you have, and create a simple bar graph. Use the *WordPerfect* Transfer.

Step 1. Choose Transfer . . . from the File menu.

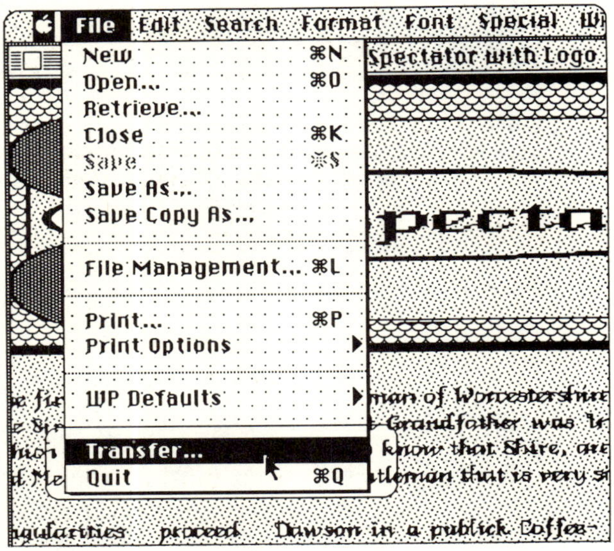

Figure 10-16. Choosing Transfer . . . from the File menu.

Step 2. When the Transfer dialog box appears, listing the programs you have on the current disk, select *MacPaint* as the program to which you want to Transfer.

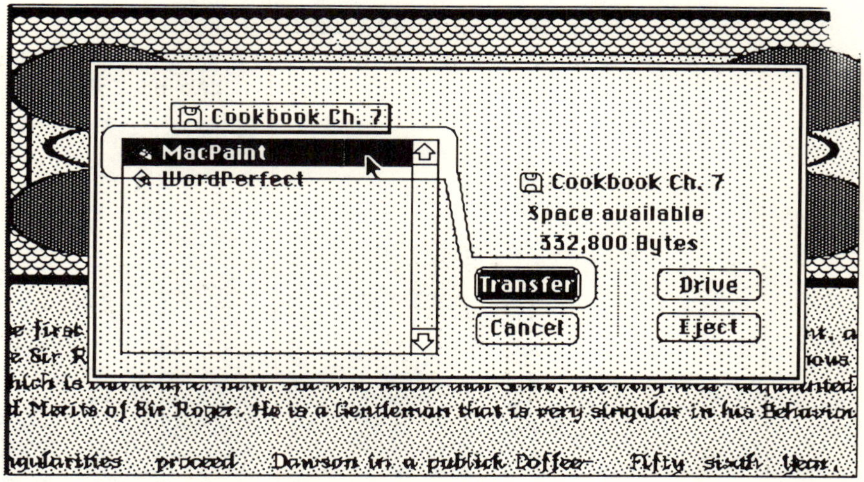

Figure 10-17. Selecting *MacPaint*.

Step 3. Click on Transfer or press Return.

Use *MacPaint's* straight lines, rectangles, and fill patterns to create a bar graph that might be appropriate for our Spectator excerpt. Figure 10-18 depicts a possible example.

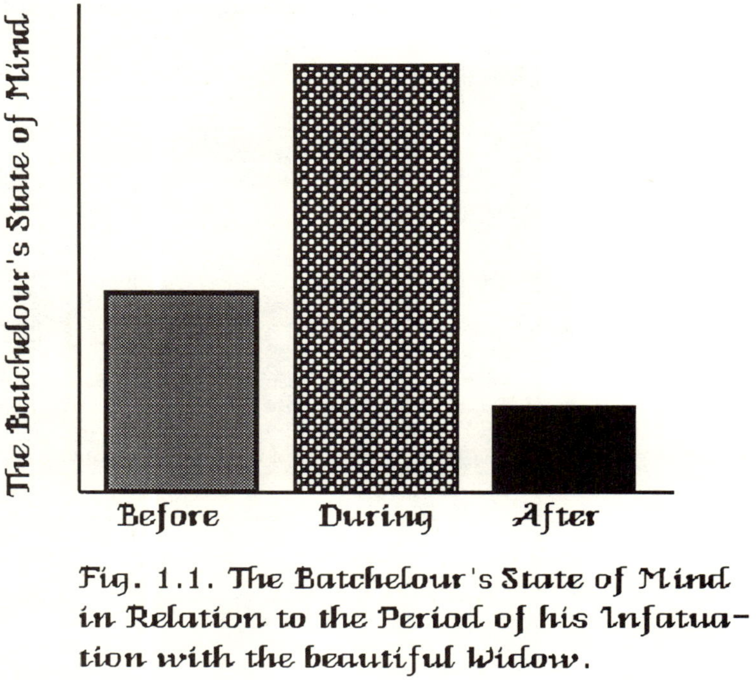

Figure 10-18. A bar graph for the Spectator.

Now let's put that *MacPaint* document into The Spectator. First, you'll copy it into the Scrapbook.

Step 1. Select the chart by clicking twice on Marquee tool from the *MacPaint* toolbox.

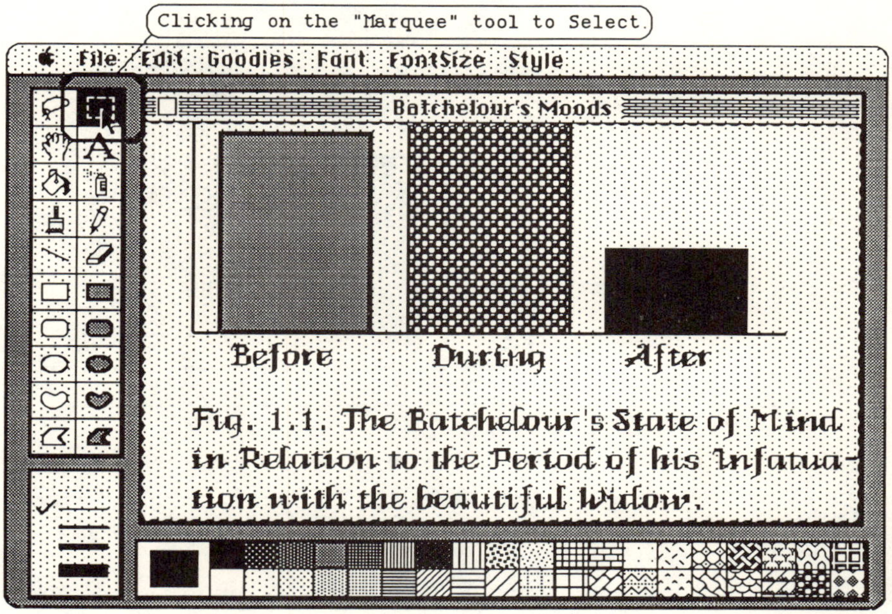

Figure 10-19. Choosing the Marquee tool from the *MacPaint* toolkit.

Step 2. Choose Copy from the Edit menu to copy the chart.
Step 3. Choose Scrapbook from the Apple File.
Step 4. Choose Paste from the Edit menu to paste the chart into the Scrapbook.

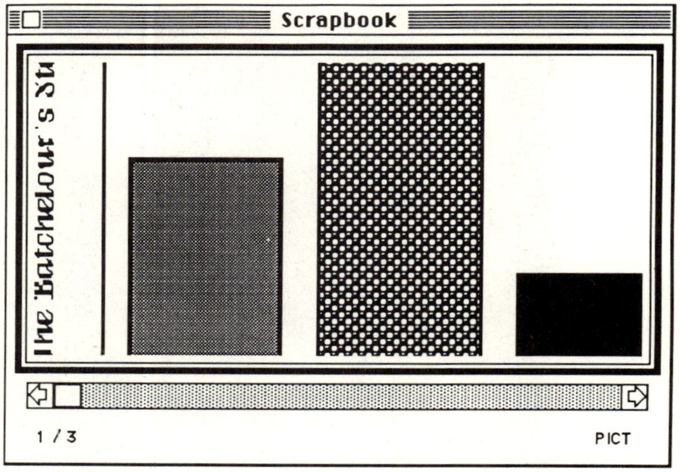

Figure 10-20. The bar chart pasted into the Scrapbook.

Step 5. Close the Scrapbook, and reopen the Spectator file in *WordPerfect*.

Step 6. Open the Scrapbook, and choose Copy from the Edit menu to copy the chart into *WordPerfect*.

Step 7. Position the cursor at the end of the sentence that ends, *. . . kick'd Bully Dawson in a publick Coffee-house for calling him Youngster*.

Step 8. Paste the chart into the document by choosing Paste from the Edit menu. You should now see a giant chart that takes up the rest of the page, so some sizing-down has to be done.

Figure 10-21. The oversized chart inserted into the middle of the Spectator document.

Step 9. Using the horizontal scroll bar at the right-hand end of the status line at the bottom of the screen, pull the chart to the center of the screen.

Step 10. Click anywhere in the graphic to turn on the handles. From this point, proceed to trim down the graphic to fit the column, much as you did with the Spectator logo. This process is a bit unwieldy, however, because of the small size of the screen (even on the Mac II) and the large size of the graphic compared to the size of the column. So here's an alternate suggestion: Bring the graphic first into an empty *WordPerfect* file, use the ruler to guide your crude alterations, then transfer the chart into the Spectator document and make the necessary fine adjustments. Let's see how that works: back up to Step 4 again.

You're in *MacPaint,* you have just finished the bar chart, and you have transferred it into the Scrapbook. Reopen the Spectator file as Step 5. From here, the moves are different.

You will size the graphic in a separate file before importing it into the Spectator file. First, you have to see how much room there actually is. Check the width of the Spectator columns by looking at the ruler.

Step 11. Locate the cursor anywhere in one of the columns, and then choose Show Ruler from the Format menu.

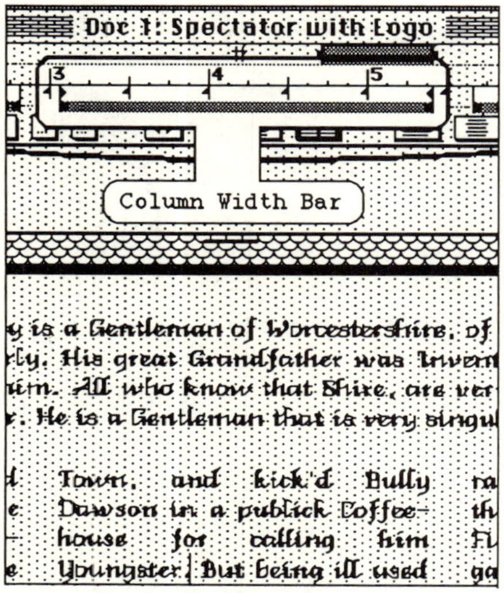

Figure 10-22. The ruler, showing that the center column extends from about 3 inches to about 5.3 inches. Thus, the column is about 2.3 inches wide.

Step 12. Open a new file by choosing New from the File menu.
Step 13. Open the Scrapbook by choosing Scrapbook from the Apple menu.
Step 14. Copy the chart from the Scrapbook by choosing Copy from the Edit menu.
Step 15. Close the Scrapbook by clicking on the Close box.
Step 16. Paste the chart into the empty file by choosing Paste from the Edit menu.

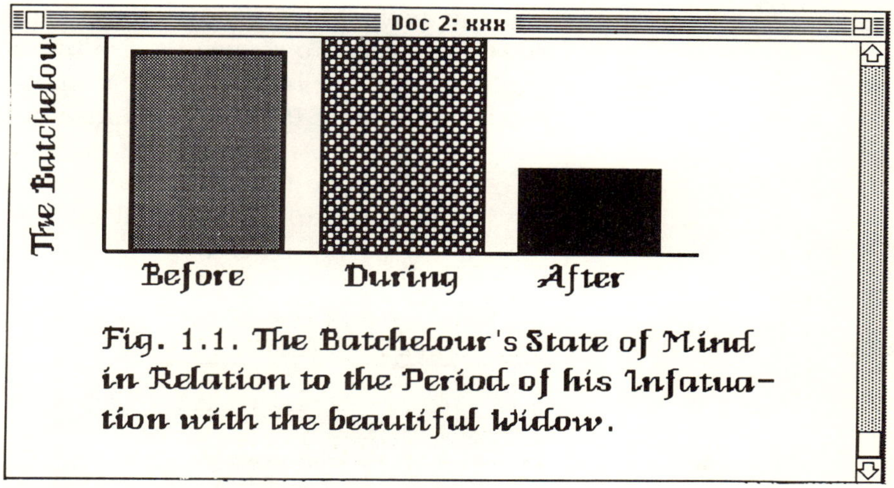

Figure 10-23. The bar chart pasted into a *WordPerfect* file.

Step 17. Turn on the ruler by choosing Show Ruler from the Format menu or pressing Command-R.

Step 18. Reveal the handles by clicking inside the figure.

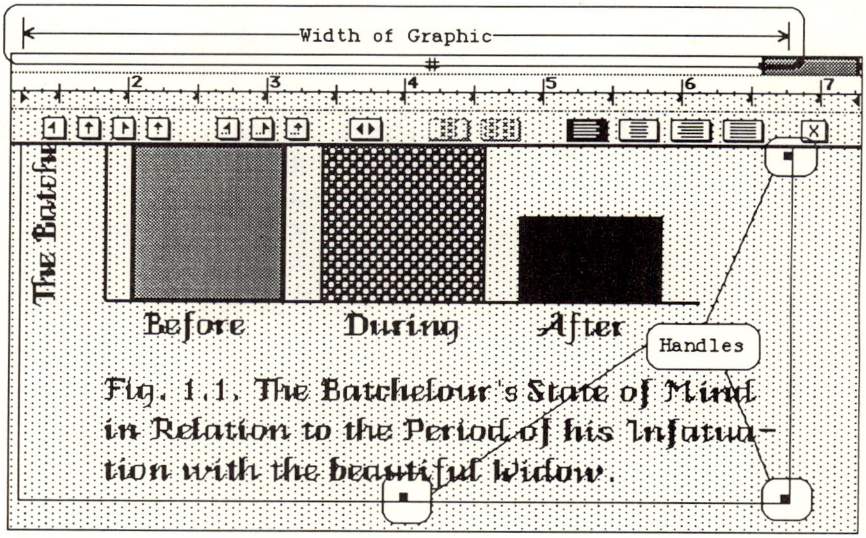

Figure 10-24. The chart with the ruler showing and the handles turned on. The approximate width of the figure is 5.5 inches.

The ruler shows the figure to be about 5.5″ wide, which means you have to reduce its size by roughly 50 percent to fit it into one of the columns in the Spectator document. This can be done by dragging the corner handles to the side handles.

Step 19. Move the pointer to the corner handle, press the Mouse button, and drag that handle to the bottom side handle.

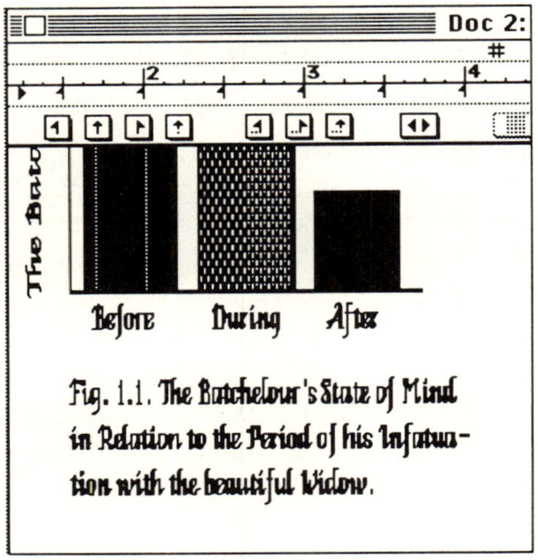

Figure 10-25. The figure reduced to half its original width.

Step 20. That reduces the width by about 50 percent. Now reduce the height by the same amount. Click in the figure to reveal the handles.

Step 21. Move the pointer to the corner handle, press the mouse button, and drag that handle to the right side handle.

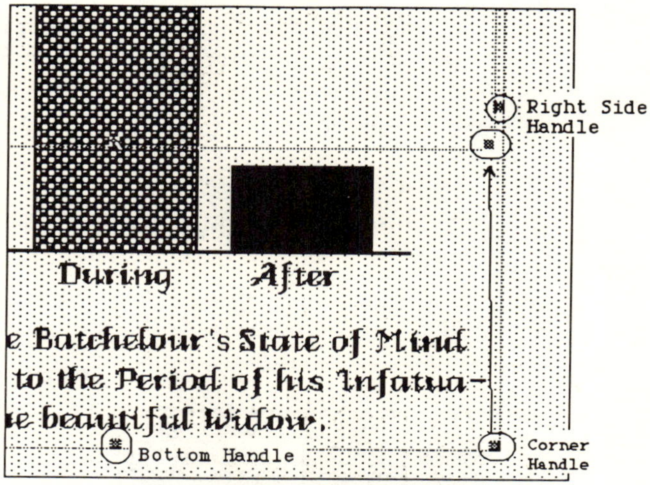

Figure 10-26. Dragging the corner handle up to the right side handle to reduce the height by 50 percent.

Step 22. Choose Show Ruler from the Format menu to check the current size of the figure.

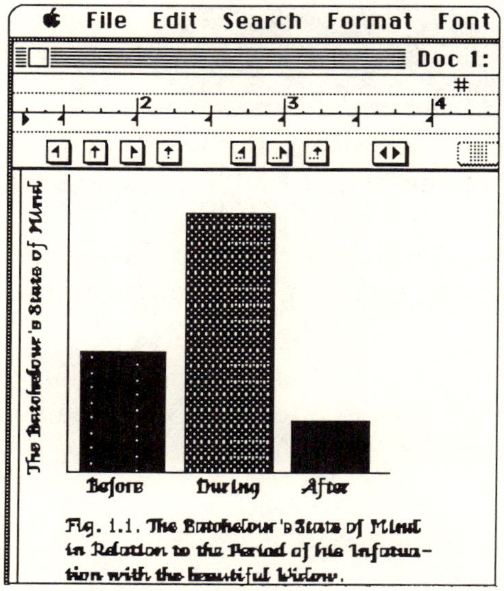

Figure 10-27. The chart in its new size, with the ruler showing the width of the reduced chart to be about 2.75 inches.

The width of the chart now appears to be about 2.75 inches. That may still be slightly large for your columns, but you can do the fine tuning after the graphic is inserted. You are now going to copy the graph, return to The Spectator, and insert it into a column.

Step 23. Hide the ruler by choosing Hide Ruler from the Format menu.
Step 24. Select the graphic for copying by choosing All from the Select submenu of the Edit menu.

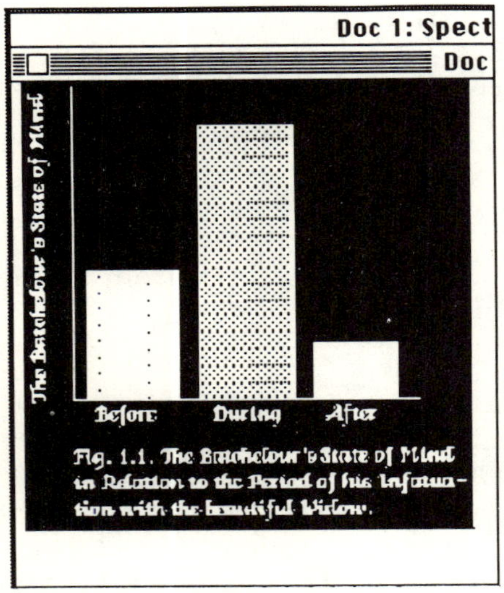

Figure 10-28. The graphic selected for copying.

Step 25. Copy the chart by choosing Copy from the Edit menu, or by pressing Command-C.
Step 26. Choose Cycle Windows from the Windows menu to bring up the Spectator 3 file. Be sure the cursor is located after the word *Youngster.*

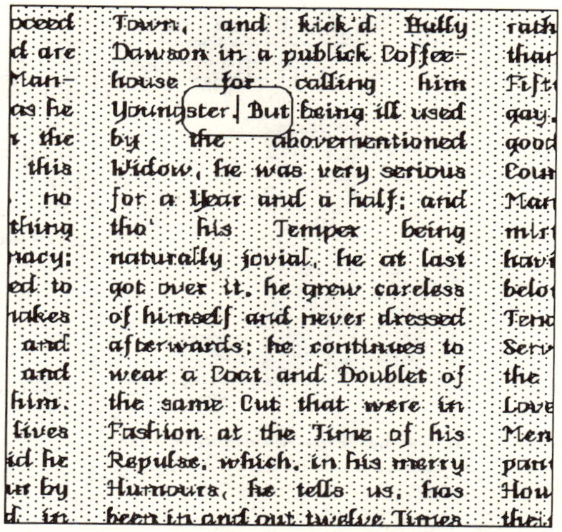

Figure 10-29. Positioning the cursor at the right point for insertion.

Step 27. Choose Paste from the Edit menu to paste the graphic in the center column.

Note that the chart is slightly large for the column. This isn't a problem. Just click in the chart to turn on the handles, and adjust the chart until it's right. There's a trick to it: When the imported graphic extends into the next column the first time you try to turn on the handles, they will cycle around once and then disappear. You have to have your pointer poised to click on the side handle. If you miss it, try clicking where you estimate it to be. Once you grab it, there's no problem in adjusting the size of the graphic.

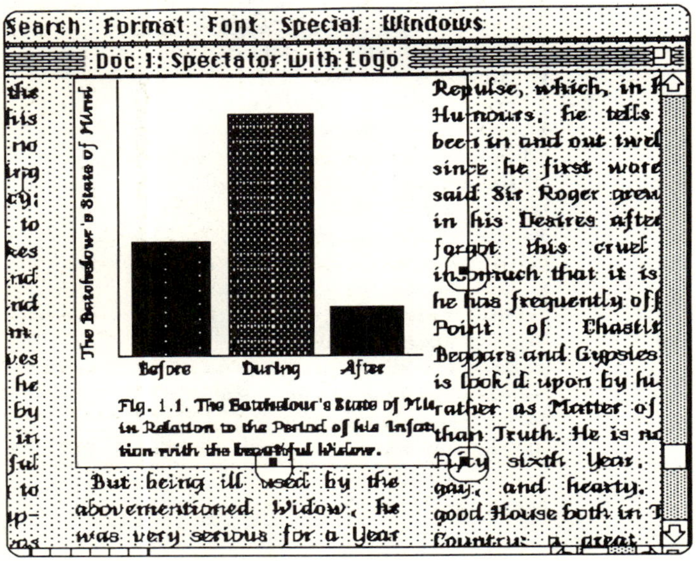

Figure 10-30. The graph with handles turned on.

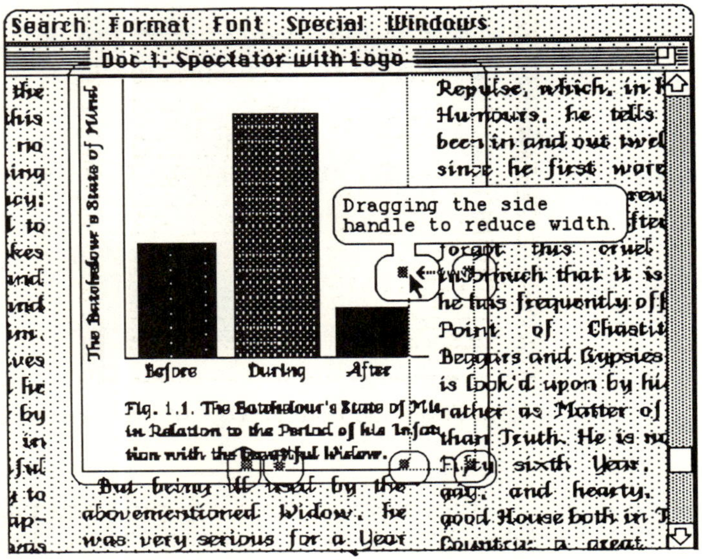

Figure 10-31. Dragging the side handle to fit the graph to the column.

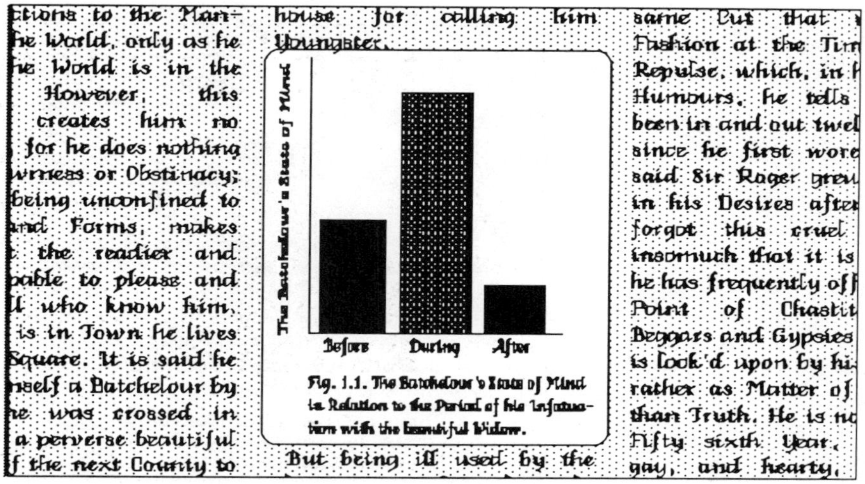

Figure 10-32. The final version of the graph.

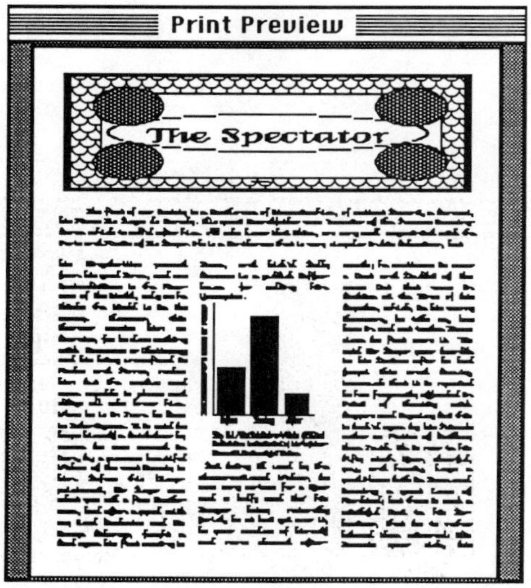

Figure 10-33. The Print Preview of the complete page, with logo and bar chart.

When you're finished, print the page just as you would any other *WordPerfect* document: Choose Print from the File menu, and click on OK or press Return in the dialog box.

The Spectator

The first of our Society is a Gentleman of Worcestershire, of antient Descent, a Baronet, his Name Sir Roger de Coverly. His great Grandfather was Inventor of the Famous Country-Dance which is call'd after him. All who know that Shire, are very well acquainted with the Parts and Merits of Sir Roger. He is a Gentleman that is very singular in his Behaviour, but his Singularities proceed from his good Sense, and are Contradictions to the Manners of the World, only as he thinks the World is in the wrong. However, this Humour creates him no Enemies, for he does nothing with Sowrness or Obstinacy; and his being unconfined to Modes and Forms, makes him but the readier and more capable to please and oblige all who know him. When he is in Town he lives in Soho-Square. It is said he keeps himself a Batchelour by reason he was crossed in Love, by a perverse beautiful Widow of the next County to him. Before this Disappointment, Sir Roger was what you call a fine Gentleman, had often supped with my Lord Rochester and Sir George Etherege, fought a Duel upon his first coming to Town, and kick'd Bully Dawson in a publick Coffee-house for calling him Youngster.

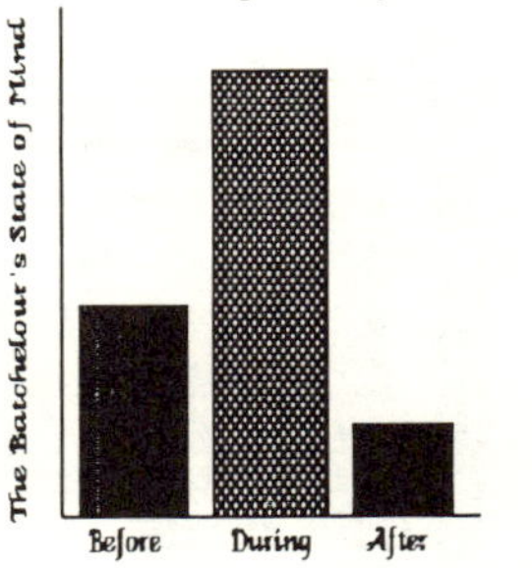

Fig. 1.1. The Batchelour's State of Mind in Relation to the Period of his Infatuation with the beautiful Widow.

But being ill used by the abovementioned Widow, he was very serious for a Year and a half; and tho' his Temper being naturally jovial, he at last got over it, he grew careless of himself and never dressed afterwards; he continues to wear a Coat and Doublet of the same Cut that were in Fashion at the Time of his Repulse, which, in his merry Humours, he tells us, has been in and out twelve Times since he first wore it. 'Tis said Sir Roger grew humble in his Desires after he had forgot this cruel Beauty, insomuch that it is reported he has frequently offended in Point of Chastity with Beggars and Gypsies; But this is look'd upon by his Friends rather as Matter of Raillery than Truth. He is now in his Fifty sixth Year, cheerful, gay, and hearty, keeps a good House both in Town and

Figure 10-34. The printed page.

The graphics possibilities of *WordPerfect* on the Macintosh are exciting. You can expect them to get more exciting as *WordPerfect* adds more sophistication to future releases, such as the Line Draw feature, which the PC versions of *WordPerfect* already have.

You have seen how to import a logo created by *MacDraw* and a bar graph created by *MacPaint*. Combined with *WordPerfect*, those programs provide you with a design and print shop right on your desk.

Index